THE MUSE THAT SINGS

THE *M*USE THAT SINGS

Composers Speak about the Creative Process

Ann McCutchan

New York   •   Oxford

Oxford University Press

1999

Oxford University Press

Oxford   New York
Athens   Auckland   Bangkok   Bogotá   Buenos Aires   Calcutta
Cape Town   Chennai   Dar es Salaam   Delhi   Florence   Hong Kong   Istanbul
Karachi   Kuala Lumpur   Madrid   Melbourne   Mexico City   Mumbai
Nairobi   Paris   São Paulo   Singapore   Taipei   Tokyo   Toronto   Warsaw

and associated companies in
Berlin   Ibadan

Published by Oxford University Press, Inc.
198 Madison Avenue, New York, New York 10016

Oxford is a registered trademark of Oxford University Press

Library of Congress Cataloging-in-Publication Data
McCutchan, Ann.
        The muse that sings : composers speak about
        the creative process / Ann McCutchan.
            p.   cm.
        Includes index.
        ISBN 0-19-512707-2
        1. Composition (Music)
    2. Creation (Literary, artistic, etc.)
    3. Inspiration.   I. Title.
        ML430.M33   1999
        781.3'092'273—dc21   98-47028

9 8 7 6 5 4 3 2 1

Printed in the United States of America
on acid-free paper

*A*rt is the path of the creator to his work.

Ralph Waldo Emerson

FOREWORD

It is hard not to feel sorry for composers. The very notion of waking up in the morning and feeling the obligation to create something of lasting value where nothing existed before seems arduous and exotic. Life seems easier for those of us engaged in the recreative process. The composer's desires and intentions are spelled out on the page, and conductors and musicians simply follow the instructions. Even for us, though, the creative muse intervenes. No sooner do we think we recognize most of the secrets of the score than we set about changing what exists. To that end, all artists are creators.

How does a composer create this something-out-of-nothing? Where does he or she begin? Is it structure, imagery, or a more elusive spark that lights the fire? How does a composer know if a piece is any good? Why write music in the first place?

Over the years, I have had the privilege of collaborating with most of the composers in this book. Though I have thought about it, I have never, even once, asked them these questions about the creative process. Yet it is fundamental to the understanding of composers and their works to know as much as possible about their creative and working ethos. After all, most interpreters spend a great deal of time reading and doing research about long-dead artists. It is only logical that we would want to know how composers who are still very much alive and productive think, imagine, and work.

In Ann McCutchan's provocative book, we have the opportunity to peer into this arcane world. Does the knowledge imparted here take away the mystery that is music? I don't think so. In fact, the answers to many of the questions she posed are so varied that they create even more of an enigma. There is, of course, no one way to write. The different methods that are employed by the different composers in this volume may astound some readers. Take something as simple as the best time of day to compose: there is no way, for instance, that I could even begin to write anything until late afternoon. One or two in the morning is just about perfect for my own creative juices. (This may explain why I am not a very good composer.) Yet some composers can work in a white heat as soon as the sun rises.

The insights of the composers here will undoubtedly prompt readers to explore some of the music described. The rich and various forms of expression are made quite clear in the text, and in some instances, it is not difficult to imagine the sounds emanating from these probing minds. Most schools of musical thought are represented, and some composers express candidly how they feel about peers and colleagues.

That this book can focus on American composers tells us much about how far music composition has come in the United States. It is hard to imagine a project like this coming into being even twenty-five years ago. How fascinating it would have been to have had the same dialogue with figures such as Copland, Schuman, Harris, Bernstein, et al. But we are an even more diverse musical nation now. Some decades ago, a composer whose background included popular music and jazz was considered a little shadowy. Now, as the profiles here illustrate, familiarity with these "suspect" areas is quite acceptable.

In the course of learning about the working methods of specific composers, we also come away with an intriguing picture of concert music in America at the end of the twentieth century. So much has changed since 1900, when American orchestras and other musical institutions were in their infancy, relying on European performers, training, and repertoire to build a tradition. This process has taken a number of turns, and the openness with which the creators in this book speak tells us much about our own times. This is not a crystal ball revealing the next century, but an honest discussion about where we have come from and how we got to this point. Even if the road has contained a few bumps, we learn in the end that each composer here is doing exactly what he or she wants and loves, and the rest of us don't have to feel sorry for them at all. In fact, we are jealous.

Leonard Slatkin
Music Director
National Symphony Orchestra

CONTENTS

INTRODUCTION

The Muse That Sings is a collection of soliloquies by twenty-five American composers who tell how they think in sound, work their ideas into written scores, and bring new pieces of concert music to life. They are the results of a series of interviews that I conducted in person from 1995 through 1998 and edited, with each composer's approval, to stand as informal monologues. In addition to the creative process itself, these free-wheeling excursions touch on related subjects: musical childhoods (where the first sparks come from), the professional life of a composer, composer-performer relationships, and more. Overall, they offer a rich picture of what it is like to be an American composer of serious concert music at the end of the twentieth century. They also serve as a nontechnical text on the art of music composition, illustrating in personal terms the notion that each composer's method of writing music is as individual as his or her fingerprint.

The impetus for this project came from my friend, the writer and editor Karen Kirtley, who one day asked me quite casually, "How does your husband compose? How do 'they' do it?" "Oh, *you* know," I said, brushing the question off. Karen persisted: "No, I don't have any idea. I'd like to know." When I understood that she was serious, I also realized that I knew a little about the subject—enough, anyway, to be able to ask some of the right questions. My husband is indeed a composer. Since 1982 I have watched him give birth to a dozen orchestra pieces, six wind ensemble pieces, an opera, and several hours' worth of chamber music. I have also collaborated with him on several works as writer or assembler of poetic texts. (He is included in this book.) But the authority by which I gathered the interviews for *The Muse That Sings* stems equally from my years as a clarinetist specializing in the performance of new music. In the 1970s and 1980s I worked closely with dozens of composers in bringing new pieces of music for ensemble or solo clarinet to the concert hall or warehouse stage. This activity was, before a wrist ailment curtailed it, unquestionably the most exciting part of my musical life. In a way, this book is a valentine to something that I miss very much.

That said, I would like to assure the reader that this is not a convention of old cronies but a mixed ensemble of nationally recognized voices, each one intriguing to me for different reasons. Some of the composers are favorites whose works I have performed or listened to frequently in concert and on recordings. Others I was drawn to by particular personal and artistic exigencies that I knew helped shape the composer's output: that is, my curiosity led to a deeper investigation and appreciation of the artist and the music. I wanted to represent a variety of musical styles, too. Some of the composers here write purely abstract music; others often base work on such extramusical sources as paintings, poetic texts, or historical figures. Some employ electronic tools for composing or write music that includes electronic voices. (Readers will find references to MIDI, or Musical Instrument Digital Interface, a method by which—in the simplest possible terms—computers and electronic keyboards interact with each other. Some composers use MIDI to realize an instrumental score electronically so they can hear a prototype before giving the score to live musicians. Others use MIDI to generate electronic music.) Some have been termed "minimalist" or "crossover," others have borne the label "New Romantic," although I believe that no one in this book can be so deftly categorized. Some have rejected the absolute serialism on which a significant percentage of a previous generation of composers built its house, while others have adapted or modified textbook serialism to suit their own expressive needs and intellectual tastes. There are independent composers here as well as composers who derive part of their income from conservatory and university teaching. A little more than half of them are based in and around New York City, while the others represent different parts of the country that also foster compositional activity. All of the composers here are members of the enormously eclectic generations born between 1930 and 1960, which means I have caught most of them midcareer. Only a few are in a position to take a long look back, and the senior composers included are among those who continue to ask big questions from work to work. Although this book is in a sense a document fished out from the middle of a particular stream (the 1990s), I hope that readers will find in it a wide variety of timeless musings about the nature of composing music and the creative challenges that composers face, regardless of their speculative places in history or level of notoriety in the current press.

What makes this composer interview book different from others is its focus. Most of its recent predecessors are concerned with biography or geared by interviewer, composer, or both for a specialized or "insider" audience.

With rare exceptions, such as Aaron Copland's classic *Music and Imagination* (The Charles Eliot Norton Lectures, 1951–52) and Ned Rorem's eloquent musings, generalists interested in the creative processes of composers must content themselves with the correspondence and biographies of long-deceased musicians. This material is fascinating but not immediate, and it does not necessarily lead to an exploration of creative musical work in progress *now*.

In fact, the current public conversation on creativity often avoids the world of fine art in favor of science. This isn't to say that living artists are ignored; however, the individuals usually addressed are poets or novelists, perhaps because they are assumed to be most able to describe verbally the indescribable. Composers, who are considered especially mystical, perhaps because they work in a language Americans are not consistently taught, are often viewed in the context of larger psychological, scientific, or spiritual inquiries, such as Jungian psychologist Anthony Storr's *The Dynamics of Creation* (which includes anecdotes from the long-gone lives of Mozart and Wagner), multiple intelligence theorist Howard Gardner's *Creating Minds* (highlighting Stravinsky), and Kay Redfield Jamison's book on manic-depressive illness *Touched with Fire* (citing the very late Robert Schumann and others). None of these books, nor the composer interview books alluded to previously, addresses the creative process in music with the clarity and energy that might attract both the music specialist and the general reader. *The Muse That Sings* is intended to help fill that gap.

The format I employ here might invite speculation about the raw interviews, and I would like to explain that although I approached each composer with a set of basic questions, each conversation took a unique route, as any interesting foray will. My first question in all cases was simply "Why do you compose?" which led first to either a childhood story or philosophical reflection. The other subject I made certain to cover in each meeting was a description of how the composer conceives and executes a work. A few composers addressed this question in general terms, but because the process is sometimes different from piece to piece, many seized on a recent composition whose creation they clearly recalled. Other topics of discussion included the ongoing genesis of ideas, the influence of the commissioning organization and performers on a new piece, the process of revision, the role of doubt in the creative process, the importance of environment to good work, and the challenge of living a creative life amid teaching commitments and the business of getting music commissioned, played, recorded, and tucked inside the public ear.

In the context of these talks, several notable points emerged. As I mentioned above, many of the composers I spoke to rejected the teachings of High Serialists in order to strike out on a more forgiving—but no less rigorous—path toward a personal voice. They are still interested in "systems" of composition, but ones that they feel more comfortably serve emotional as well as intellectual content. Departing from received teachings is a typical rite of passage for any student, but as a group these composers unquestionably reflect a generational impulse to abandon what they saw as a politically charged, cloistered approach for modes of communication that are more inviting, yet not condescending, to sophisticated audiences. Without my urging, many of the men and women in this book named as models (in addition to masters like Beethoven, Stravinsky, Mahler, and Debussy) several distinctively "American" composers such as Aaron Copland, Leonard Bernstein, and Charles Ives, and it was no surprise to learn that many of them had played jazz, folk, pop, or rock music in addition to their classical training.

These interviews demonstrate, I think, that the art of music composition in America is alive and well, at the turn of the millenium. The composers here are just the tip of a creative iceberg. They have plenty of outstanding colleagues throughout the country working not just in the world of concert music but also in film, theater, and other media. Many serious composers work in related professions to earn a living, just as novelists take day jobs in public relations and write in the evenings. In other words, serious compositional activity runs deeper than most people suspect, and because it is a part of our artistic culture that is seldom recognized or publicly rewarded, it is continually in danger of death by neglect. I fear, too, that the music education academy may be among the killjoys. I recently chatted with a university music education researcher who asked me if I planned in this book to draw "measurable conclusions" about composers' "cognitive skills." I was dismayed by those buzzwords, which negate meaning instead of enlighten; her question illustrated for me the remove at which many "experts" in arts education operate. I wish she had asked, instead, how a composer's mind works, to which I would have answered, "Let's dump your database and ask one of the five composers on your faculty, or go listen to a child fool around on a piano." The composers in this book are extraordinary people with exceptional careers, but most of them began under the tutelage of a school orchestra or band director or a neighborhood piano teacher who did not measure progress with a bar graph. They are individuals with a special talent, perhaps a particular vein of intelligence that in many cases did not truly flower until their formal education was completed. As with any creative project—a piece of music or a whole life—the outcome is not clear until long after the seeds have been sown.

Along with advocacy, a word of warning: these interviews are not puff pieces about success. I have purposely kept the introductory biographies extremely brief—in full regalia, each one sparkles with important commissions, performances, prizes, and other accomplishments. These chapters instead focus on hard work and growth, brick walls and breakthroughs. They are about a seldom publicized athletic event, the wrestling match with the self and with materials of one's own making. They are also about the composer's relationships to other people: the performers who bring written scores into full, sonic existence, and the listeners who greet and react to new sounds. More than half of the composers interviewed here have held a residency with an orchestra, opera company, concert series, or music festival and have been directly involved with audiences of all ages as well as the business of presenting concerts. They are artists who by inclination and necessity are working, outwardly and inwardly, to continue a tradition of American concert music that stretches back to the pre-Ives symphonists and has grown as marvelously varied as a frontier crazy quilt or a full-body tattoo.

Just as this book represents twenty-five musical voices, so does it reflect twenty-five human personalities. I wanted to hear this book more than write it, and to that end I have edited the composers' statements for clarity only, keeping the casual asides and exclamations that in an oral text lend freshness. It is my hope that the voices of these individuals will lead readers to their music, some of which is available on selected recordings listed at the end of each chapter. Performers will find lists of selected works and the addresses of the composers' publishers, as well. I should add that the works lists are slim representations of total output and will be out of date as soon as a composer's newest piece is premiered.

Recordings of contemporary music often go out of print after a few short years; although the records listed here were available at the time I assembled the text, it is possible that some have since disappeared and new ones have taken their places.

A number of people have helped me with this project, including Theodore Wiprud, former program director of Meet The Composer, and my assistant Paul Richards, who is also a composer. Composers Elliott Schwartz and Dan Beaty offered valuable suggestions and recommended "readings toward writing." Violist Joan Kalisch, one of my oldest new music performance compatriots, and my friend Emily Fox Gordon, the essayist, read parts of the manuscript, caught my oversights, and assured me other readers would enjoy it. I am most grateful for the reflections of Maestro Leonard Slatkin, music director of the National Symphony Orchestra, conductor laureate of the St. Louis Symphony Orchestra, and champion of American composers and their music. I wish to acknowledge the Rockefeller Foundation for its kind and generous support of my work and to offer warm thanks to Maribeth Anderson Payne of Oxford University Press for her editorial expertise and her confidence in this book's value.

The Muse That Sings is dedicated with admiration and affection to composer John Duffy, founder and former director (1974–95) of Meet The Composer, the organization dedicated to the creation, performance, and recording of music by American composers.

Ann McCutchan
Austin, Texas
September 1998

THE MUSE THAT SINGS

ERIC STOKES

(1930–1999)

*E*ric Stokes was born and raised in Haddon Heights, New Jersey, and educated at Lawrence College, the New England Conservatory, and the University of Minnesota. From 1961 to 1988 he taught at the University of Minnesota, where he founded the university's electronic music program and First Minnesota Moving and Storage Warehouse Band, a new music performance group. He was an active proponent of new music in the Twin Cities for more than thirty-five years.

Stokes's early tonal voice expanded to include collage, theater, and mixed media elements reflecting the influence of Charles Ives in the use of stylistic juxtapositions and Henry Brant in the spatial deployment of forces. American subjects and vernacular music (folk song, hymns, jazz) comprised his home territory, which was almost always infused with playfulness. His first opera, *Horspfal*, concerns the misadventures of the American Indian since the coming of the Europeans. *The Continental Harp and Band Report*, commissioned by the Minnesota Orchestra, is a miscellany of nine contrasting pieces that can be played in any order. Later on Stokes employed "found sounds" in such compositions as *Rock and Roll*, a piece for five performers playing river stones and pouring gravel down a wooden chute.

Eric Stokes was commissioned by the Minnesota Opera, the St. Paul Chamber Orchestra, the London Sinfonietta, the San Francisco Symphony, and others. He lived in Minneapolis for many years with his wife Cynthia Stokes, flutist in the St. Paul Chamber Orchestra. This interview took place in Minneapolis in May 1996. Eric Stokes died in an automobile accident March 16, 1999.

As a kid, I loved music. I could hardly ever have enough of it, especially the classics, and I wanted to be part of that, you know? I said, "I want to do that, too!"

I think I was first called to a life in music by the Sunday radio broadcasts of concerts and opera that my mother and sister sang along with. The gramophone and radio also introduced me to ragtime, jazz, swing bands, country and western, and popular song. I first participated in music-making at the age of six, as a boy soprano in the church choir. When my voice changed I switched to the bass section.

But composing . . . I remember one day when I was at the piano in the back bedroom, and I was supposed to be practicing for my weekly piano lesson. Well, I was bored with my assignment and drifted into endless improvisations. My younger sister opened the door and said, "You're just making that up as you go along!" She was right, and that's what I've been doing ever since: making it up. After years and years, composing seems like the only thing to do—it's the one thing that keeps presenting interesting challenges. Every piece is new and different.

When you're very young you tend to accept given forms, the way music is made in that time of your life. The symphony orchestra was the model when I was a boy. Then in my late twenties I discovered Ives and learned from his example how to *live* music. After that I became acquainted with the thought and music of John Cage and Henry Brant. I also admired Copland's music for its marvelous clarity and succinctness.

The work of John Cage changed my way of thinking about what is musical and what is not. The first time I heard him lecture was like being thrown into the first melt of the lakes in springtime! Later I had a chance to see him in action with Merce Cunningham, when I assisted backstage at one of their performances. The experience freed my ear, the way I listened. One of Cage's main accomplishments is an attitude shift about listening and feeling, and all the attendant questions that go with that: What *is* music? What is *musical*?

Those encounters with the ideas and music of Brant, Cage, Ives, and many others like them, mostly Americans, served me well. They restored me to a kind of childlike innocence about sound. They rescued me from conservatory attitudes as to what is musical and what is not. They opened my ears—which had been stuffed to near deafness with academic givens and prescriptions— to the wonders of sound. Later on, fate allowed me a further broadening of my sonic perceptions and ways of thinking about my music, through my work in electronically generated and processed sound.

Many of my pieces start out as panoramas, sonic landscapes that constantly change as features of the landscape are forgotten, replaced, expanded, brought into the foreground, or placed in the background. So my initial concept of a new piece isn't rigid. It has to give, it has to lose, it has to be lopped off or painted over, and it may or may not be the actual core or the essence of the piece when I'm done. Sometimes I have to let the music take me by the hand. The music speaks. It says, "I need more of this, right here," or "I'm too short. You're squelching me." I have to listen to that. I have to listen *for* it.

Yet the process always comes down to finding the substance, the real nugget of the piece, you know? Music is momentary. It has to have very specific gestures, which is where I depart from John Cage. I do use his ideas of happenstance or accident. I set up accidents to happen, and I don't know exactly how they're going to work out. On the other hand, I know about how fast each collision is going to occur.

Composing means dealing with a fleeting succession of instances, one after the next, after the next. It's the way I imagine a choreographer thinks of steps. Every "now" that's in a dance has a before and an after, and becomes a before and an after. So the dance must be created organically, because everything is related to everything else. There are no parts that aren't acted upon by all the other moments.

Sometimes composing is like chasing butterflies. You try to capture moments and articulate them as clearly as possible. You help them become inevitable.

Martin Bresnick [the composer] said that there comes a time in the composing of almost every piece when you pass the center of gravity, and the piece starts pulling you toward the end. It's as if you get to the top of the hill and can finally see the other side. Reaching that point isn't so much a relief as a satisfaction. The piece is making itself clear, and you know what to do to fulfill it.

In the end, there's what Mozart called "the scribbling," which is particularizing all these thoughts with the notational language we have. Debussy said, "I have these magnificent dreams, and then I have to think about quarter notes!" It's true, you *do* have to think about quarter notes. You have to ask yourself, is it a quarter note? What kind of a quarter note is it? Is it *staccato*? Is it *martelatto*? What is it, and where does it go?

Some composers take a constructivist attitude to writing, and although there's merit in that kind of thinking, I feel it can be a trap. As a student I rebelled against it, and I still do. I resented the twelve-tone concept of music-making, which is the epitome of constructivism. The total control of serialism was the worst. I understand abstract notions — they can be very seductive. But they lead composers into a cul-de-sac where they end up as helpless prisoners of those mechanics. I don't think that serves the spirit of music.

Another trap is being too programmatic. I've fallen into it a few times, I admit. If you have a very extensive program in mind — a narrative, something concrete you're trying to illustrate — it can tie you all up.

I think it was Haydn who said that the melody is what counts, and everything else is secondary. That's my way of looking at it.

Deadlines used to be almost overwhelming to me, but I don't feel that way anymore because I've been through the process so many times. I say, "OK, I know I can do it, I just have to get going." But if I have a whole year to write a piece, I'll procrastinate awhile.

It's easy to underestimate how much time it's going to take to finish a piece. I repeatedly say, "Oh, I think I'll finish it today." Well, I won't. I can't know when a piece will end, really, not until I'm writing it out. I'm just slogging through, putting it on paper. On the other hand, writing it out slows me way down. I can't write a piece as quickly as I hear it. Nobody can.

Once you write a piece down, changing it can be difficult. Let's say you have a hundred-page score—a *lot* of donkey work has gone into it. Well then, what if the music says, "You really have to delete this," or "You need to add something here"? You can be seduced by all that paper into talking back: "But I've already done so much work. It'll be OK as it is." Nevertheless, you'll keep hearing the piece whisper to you: "I'm not right yet. You haven't put me together right." Eventually you'll have to be willing to use the eraser or a larger instrument—the hatchet!

I've never allowed any unfinished work out to performers, but I have discovered oversights—for instance, a tempo change that I failed to notate in the rush to put the music down on paper. I don't have a problem making changes if I think they improve a piece, even if they're suggested by someone else. David Zinman [the conductor] has been a wonderful collaborator. Sometimes he's suggested changes that are so right I've thought, "Yeah, gee, why didn't I think of that?"

I leave old pieces—ten, twenty years old—alone, because I really can't go back and become the person that I was, enter the work in the same spirit. I don't do a lot of rewriting after the book is closed on a piece. Sometimes, if a piece is just not good, I destroy it. It's true that an old or unsuccessful piece can be used like a body shop—you can recycle or mine parts of it to good advantage, even though the piece didn't work as an integrated whole.

I don't keep a lot of notebooks. I sometimes regret that I haven't. But I sure have developed a memory notebook—I have lots of ideas for pieces that I haven't done yet. One piece I've had in mind for fifteen or twenty years is a setting of Walt Whitman's "Out of the Cradle Endlessly Rocking," a landmark American poem. I have so many notes for this potential piece interleaved in my copy of *Leaves of Grass* that the book looks like a cabbage in bloom. So in a sense I do have notebooks—collections of ideas partially worked out, here and there.

Words can be a wonderful partner to the musical imagination. I'll fall in love with the words of a particular text and the ideas those words carry with them. The sounds of words can be wonderful stimuli to my melodic and rhythmic interests, and to a lesser extent harmonic or instrumental ones. However, I do believe that some texts are inherently so musical that marrying them to musical settings takes away from them. I've been fascinated for years with Dylan Thomas's "On Fern Hill." It's so musical that it seems to say to me, "Leave me alone, I've got it already." So I've never done it and I probably won't, although I've made a lot of notes on it. Every time I look at it, the poem itself tells me, "Don't."

But Whitman has a kind of cadence and language that seems to say, "Yes, do it." It's hard to analyze why that is. "Out of the Cradle" has gorgeous metaphors, images that could be set to music beautifully. I know how it has to be done. I won't use the entire text. Anyone who's worked with Whitman knows he can go on and on. He has reasons for that as a poet, but in a musical setting it might string out the central section of the piece too much, sacrificing musical integrity and compactness.

The circumstances of a commission often define what kind of piece it is going to be, how it will turn out. Very often a commission fits something I was already dying to do. The first important one was my opera *Horspfal*. I had dreamed for years of having a chance to work in opera—few composers get to do it because of the sheer cost and the forces required, as well as the general conservativeness of the people who are involved in it. But I was very fortunate to work with a young company that wanted to make a mark. In the process I found a lifelong collaborator, a librettist (Alvin Greenberg) who has been wonderful to work with. We made a piece that was noticed all over the country, with a repeat performance in New York a couple of years later. But since then, no one has breathed a word about producing it again. Getting a second production is about as difficult as getting it done the first time.

A different kind of commissioning circumstance came about when Cynthia and I and the children lived in Vienna for a year. One of the musicians we met, the virtuoso recorder player Hans Kneiss, asked me if I would compose a work for him. I said sure.

I was thinking about writing this recorder piece for him when I returned to the University of Minnesota in the fall of 1970, and at that time the School of Music said, "Eric, you have to start up an electronic music program for us." Well, I hardly knew how to turn on a tape recorder at that time! I had to teach myself everything, which was great—it was like an adventure. I learned all kinds of things. I met up with wonderful people who knew more than I did and wanted to help. I discovered for myself the notion of quadraphonic sound, and I decided to make a piece for Hans and three self-recorded channels. The piece is called *Eldey Island*.

In that case I was charmed by the idea of quadraphonic sound, with the live player onstage and three loudspeakers, one on either side and another behind the audience. The persona of the solo flute or recorder became a fourfold presence.

I created *Center Harbor Holiday* for the New Hampshire Music Festival in 1963. It was my first large orchestra commission, and on top of that, I knew that Roger Bobo, the incredible virtuoso tuba player, would be participating in the festival. I didn't have to compose for Roger, but I did—I turned the piece into a kind of rhapsody with a prominent solo tuba part. In that case, the circumstances presented a welcome opportunity.

I wish I had a daily routine like Hindemith said he had, but I don't. I'll procrastinate sometimes—take a walk, read a magazine, do some gardening. The best thing for me is to go up to my studio in the attic of my house, sit down at the desk, and start. The procrastination opportunities may be close by, but I'm in my place. I wish my studio were bigger so I could have more toys to play around with—drums and stuff. I have a little piano up there.

The hardest part is writing that first note, drawing that first line on the paper. The next one is less difficult—and then the phone rings! Saved by the bell! Oh boy. Then you have to start all over again.

I can listen to the radio when I'm working, if it's talk. I like *Talk of the Nation*. I don't pay a lot of attention to it, but I'll phase it in and out. When they play their musical leads it drives me nuts and I turn it off. I don't think I can work well traveling in a car. I can think about a piece sometimes, but there's always stuff whizzing by and noises and the confinement. I've tried working on an airplane, but it doesn't seem to come off. The person sitting next to me always gets curious and starts talking.

But even though I need privacy to work, composers are called to serve people, not themselves—that's central to my credo. And music is for the people, for all of us: the dumb, the deaf, dogs and jays, the crazy, weak, hurt, the weed keepers, the strays. The land of music is everyone's nation—her tune, his beat, your drum. One song, one vote.

Eric Stokes, Selected Works

SMALL ENSEMBLE

Brazen Cartographies (1988)
brass quintet

Caccia (1980)
two singers, cello, two sound
    assistants
text: E. Stokes

Inland Missing the Sea (1976)
soprano, tenor, baritone, oboe,
horn, cello, harp, piano,
    percussion
text: Keith Gunderson

Rock and Roll (1980)
theater piece for five performers
    with rocks

Song Circle (1993)
soprano, flute, harp
texts: Robert Samarotto, Keith
    Gunderson, Eric Stokes

Stages (Homage to Kurt Weill,
    1988)

flute, clarinet, trumpet, trombone,
two violins, bass, Cimbalom
solo

LARGE ENSEMBLE

*The Continental Harp and Band
Report* (1974–75)
symphonic wind ensemble

Prairie Drum (1981)
chamber orchestra

Prophet Bird (1992)
chamber orchestra

Smoke and Steel (1989)
men's chorus, tenor solo, orchestra
text: Carl Sandburg

Symphony no. 4: *The Ghost
Bus to El Dorado* (1991)
orchestra

STAGE

Apollonia's Circus (1994)
opera in three acts
libretto: Alvin Greenberg

Publisher: Horspfal Music
Concern, 1611 West 32nd Street,
Minneapolis, MN 55408.
Tel. 612-825-2922.

Eric Stokes, Selected
Recordings

*The Continental Harp and Band
Report*
Louisville Orchestra/
Davies
Louisville First Edition Records,
LS 760

Eldey Island for flute/piccolo
and tape
Cynthia Stokes, flute: CRI 415
Carol Wincenc, flute: Advance
FGR 285

On the Badlands: Parables
St. Paul Chamber Orchestra/
Davies
CRI 415

Song Circle
Jubal Trio
CRI CD 738

Tag for alto saxophone and tape
Richard Dirlam, saxophone
Innova, MN 109

STEVE REICH

$(\text{B. } 1936)$

Steve Reich received his formal music training at Juilliard with William Bergsma and Vincent Persichetti, and at Mills College with Luciano Berio and Darius Milhaud, then went on to study non-Western music, particularly African drumming, Indonesian gamelan, and Hebrew cantillation. In 1966 he founded an ensemble to perform his music; Steve Reich and Musicians has since toured and recorded extensively for a broad audience. In 1997 Nonesuch released a ten-disc retrospective box set of Reich's work, a rare event for a living composer still breaking new ground.

Often defined as a minimalist composer, Reich has long been fascinated with the strongly articulated "subtactile pulse" that lies beneath the surface of most musics (to greater or lesser degrees), as well as the transformative possibilities of technology that gave birth to his early "phase" pieces. His music, which is rooted in diatonic and tonal harmonies, continues to marry live performers with technological tools and/or the precise, complex rhythmic processes technology invites. His newest work at this writing is a collaborative effort with his wife, the video artist Beryl Korot. *Hindenburg* is the first act of a documentary "video opera" with five singers and instrumental ensemble.

Steve Reich lives in New York. This interview took place in New York in May 1998.

.   .   .

Composing is really the only thing I want to do.

When I was a kid I took piano lessons but I was not terribly enthusiastic. I liked the music that I was exposed to—middle-class favorites like Beethoven's Fifth, Schubert's Unfinished, Overture to *Die Meistersinger*, Broadway shows, some Caruso records—but it didn't make me want to become a composer. None of it.

Then at the age of fourteen, it was as if someone said, "Well, you've lived here for *x* number of years, and now we're going to show you this *other* room." And just by chance or maybe not by chance (I'm not sure I believe in chance—I don't agree with John Cage on most things, and that's definitely one of them) a friend of mine said, "Hey, you've got to come over and listen to this," and he played me a recording of *The Rite of Spring*. A few weeks or months later, I heard the Fifth Brandenburg concerto of Johann Sebastian Bach, and my first recordings of Miles Davis and Charlie Parker and the drummer Kenny Clark, at which point I stopped keyboard lessons and started to study drums. I was lucky, because the local good drummer in Mamaroneck, New York, where I was going to high school, was Roland Kohloff, who is now the timpanist with the New York Philharmonic. In those days he used to play Gene Krupa drum solos in the local movie theater with glow-in-the-dark sticks. I just did rudimentary studies with him, but I applied myself with a seriousness of purpose I had not had with the keyboard. I had a friend who was a much better piano player than I was and who played some jazz, and I said, "We've got to start a band." The light was lit at that point. The combination of Stravinsky, Bach, and jazz, or more generally, Western music before 1750 and contemporary music, particularly Stravinsky and Bartók, and jazz (meaning bebop and later John Coltrane) drew me so powerfully nothing else could hold a candle to it. I wanted to stop doing everything else and just listen, or create *that*!

A little later, when I was in college at Cornell, I wanted to be a composer, but at sixteen I thought I was too old, since Mozart was five when he started and Bartók was six, and so on. But luckily William Austin, one of my teachers there, said, "You know, it's OK, you can start at sixteen." At that point I was studying philosophy and could have gone on to graduate school. I was accepted at Harvard, but academic life just didn't attract me. My parents were divorced, and my mother, who was a singer and a lyricist, was very encouraging about a musical life, but I hadn't spent much time with her as a child. I really grew up with my father, which was unusual in those days. I think my father, who was a lawyer, wanted me to work in industrial labor relations. I just had no interest in that. He was completely negative about music. I think, he felt that (a) I hadn't studied harmony or counterpoint as a child (and was thus unprepared), and (b) I was being like my mother. That was upsetting. I'm sure a lot of people in the arts have had run-ins with parents of a mindset who would never involve a child with the arts unless they are prodigies at the age of three. So it wasn't easy for me, but there wasn't any alternative.

Again, I had trepidation about the fact that I might be starting composition too late, that I didn't have enough technique. But then one of my first teachers, Hall Overton in New York City (who I studied with before I went to Juilliard) asked me to do an assignment, and I said, "Oh, I don't think I have enough technique." And he looked me right in the eye and said, "You'll *never* have enough technique. *Do* it." At first I thought he meant that *I* would never have enough technique. But he was saying that one should always be honing one's skills and learning, and that is true. Hall Overton also brought me back to the keyboard with the easy Bartók *Mikrokosmos* pieces, which were fantastic models of composition. That's where I was introduced to the modes and canonic technique, which formed the backbone of almost everything I've ever done.

In 1965 I discovered the area that I've been working in through experimenting with a couple of tape recorders, making tape loops of a black Pentecostal preacher saying, "It's gonna rain . . ." I thought that I would make a relationship between two loops: "Rain, rain, rain, rain" simultaneously with "It's gonna, it's gonna, it's gonna, it's gonna." I had a pair of stereo headphones and those cheap little Wollensak tape recorders, and I plugged one "ears" plug into one tape recorder and one into the other tape recorder, and put the headphones on, and by pure chance the two tape recorders happened to be lined up in unison. But it had that funny quality of two things that are more or less together but not *exactly* together. And as I sat there, sort of struck with this, it seemed that the sound moved from the center of my head over to the left side of my head, and down my left arm, and down my left leg, and across the room. What was really happening was the machine feeding my left ear was slightly faster than the other machine (or the loop might have been cut infinitesimally smaller), so that it was working its way ahead of the second loop. As a result, I heard first the unison, then a change of directionality, then a kind of reverberation, a larger reverberation, then a kind of echo, and finally, about five minutes later, I heard, "It's gonna, it's gonna, it's gonna, it's gonna, rain, rain, rain, rain." And I thought to myself, "Well, that's nice, but what's really interesting is this whole process of starting in unison and dragging these voices apart until eventually they come back together again."

A lot of people would have said, "Well, that's an accident. Now let's see if we can get these things lined up again!" But for me, the light bulb went on and I said, "Now, wait a minute. This is a whole seamless process of making music that changes extremely gradually." A couple of days later, I thought, "Am I on Planet Zork, or does this really have something to do with what's been done musically in the past?" And I began thinking, Well, this is like a two-voice canon, or a round, like "Row, Row Your Boat," but it's as if two people started in unison and the second person slowly got faster than the first person. In the canon, the second person begins to sing "Row" when the first one is singing "Merrily." Here, they were both in unison and then the second one gradually speeded up, so eventually it got to that point [of strict canonic relationship]. I used to call this the "change of phase relationship," but that's a tech-word. If you want to speak in musical English, you say it's a unison canon, and the rhythmic distance between the first voice and the second voice is variable. That was a new wrinkle. If you like, the whole thing was a kind of footnote to canonic technique as we've known it in the past. The piece *It's Gonna Rain* resulted from that kind of thinking.

After some time [and another tape loop piece, *Come Out*, 1966] passed, I began thinking, this technique's fantastic, but it has nothing to do with live music. This is for machines, or windshield wipers on a bus. *People* can't do it. I went back and forth on this for a good six months, and finally said, "That's it, I'm going to be the second tape recorder." I made a recording of a twelve-note pattern, spliced both ends of the tape together to make a tape loop, put it on the tape recorder, sat down to the piano, and said, "OK, here goes." I shut my eyes because I had memorized the twelve-note pattern. I knew I had to start in unison with the tape, and then gradually accelerate until I got one sixteenth note ahead of the tape, as slowly as possible. And I started doing it, and Wow! I *could* do it! I didn't have the perfection of the machine, but doing it was musically interesting—an interesting way to perform. I wasn't improvising, I wasn't reading, I was performing, if you like, a musical task. And the doing of that was a whole new experience. It's a little bit like a musical meditation, because your mind is very focused. Your ear has to be exactly fixed on what's happening on the tape so that you won't go too fast and move a sixteenth or a whole quarter note past the arrival point, or slow down and drift backward the other way. When you're trying to slide ahead, it's as if a vacuum cleaner is pulling you up to the rational relationship—it's hard to stay in the irrational netherland where you're shaking between the two. So the artistry, the control, is in moving smoothly from one point to the other, so that the listener hears this sort of magical blur-r-r-r in the process.

Then the question was, Can anybody else do this? Can we forget about the tape? And in those days, being young and without many financial resources, it was hard to find two pianos. Fortunately, a sculptor friend of mine asked me to do a concert at Fairleigh-Dickinson University, and I asked my friend Arthur Murphy to try this with me, and that was the beginning of my ensemble. So Arthur and I got together and—Look, Ma! No tape! It worked, just two guys playing piano! He stayed put, which is probably the harder part, and I moved ahead, being a nervous, fast-talking-type person. And once that happened, in a sense, the piece was written. It begins with a twelve-beat pattern, followed by an eight-beat pattern, and finally a four-beat pattern. In each of those three sections we would start in unison and then go completely around 360 degrees and come back together again.

Now, notating the piece [*Piano Phase*, 1967] took half an hour. It was only two pages of music. But the piece lasted twenty minutes. The process of composing it was first getting that pattern, which I fooled around with over a period of a few weeks, improvising at the piano. Then playing against it on tape to see what the different relationships were, and whether the whole thing really worked. (Since it was a twelve-beat pattern, there were six different positions, and the second six are really retrograde versions of the first six.) Put another way, I quickly came up with something intuitively, jotted it down, recorded it, played against it, and fleshed it out, in a sense, in rehearsal, with myself, and then with another player.

That's one extreme. Now let's go to *Proverb*, which is the most recent fully completed piece I've done [1995]. Paul Hillier (who's well known as a conductor and performer of early music and also of the very beautiful music of Arvo Pärt) and I had been corresponding for years, and he was very interested in my music. And while we were working together on *The Cave* [an opera in three acts], he said, "You know, you've got to write me a piece just for voices. You ought to set The Song of Songs." He knew I was interested in the Hebrew Bible.

Now, I don't really accept commissions, normally. What I do is figure out what I want to write next and try to find someone who's going to pay for that. I'm very fortunate to be able to do that. Then I can do the best job for the people concerned, because I've got my head of steam up, and I know what I have to do next to keep that head of steam going.

But Paul was a musician who knew my work intimately, and when he asked me for a piece, I knew that it would be done by his early music singers, who are just the kind of people I like to work with. When he brought this up I was already at work on *City Life*, which was the third large work that involves sampling. [The others were *Different Trains*, which involved prerecorded voices played with string quartet, and *The Cave*, also with prerecorded voices. *City Life* had both prerecorded voices and city noises played live on sampling keyboards.] After *City Life* was over, I was just sampled out. Enough of this stuff—I didn't want to see anything electronic, I just wanted to write a piece of *music* with a short, easy text. So Paul made his suggestion when it was right to do something simple and direct. It was perfect.

For a text I went first to The Song of Songs, a long and enormously complex and rich text, and I felt it was beyond me to set it, and it wasn't a text that lent itself to excerpting. I needed something more emblematic and brief, like a flag, if you will. So I went to the Book of Proverbs and found a couple of things, but I wasn't 100 percent sure. Then I bought one of those encyclopedias of world proverbs, and I must have found sixty things that I thought were fantastic. And I thought to myself, "Wait a minute. I wanted to write a short piece and this is turning into a symphony of proverbs—forget about it." At the time I also happened to be rereading Ludwig Wittgenstein, the philosopher who I read at Cornell. It was a book about life, religion, and the arts, and one sentence [translated from the German] read, "How small a thought it takes to fill a whole life." And I thought to myself, "That's it." I knew that I wanted to write a canonic piece—nothing to do with tape—just a canon, a round, that would become an augmentation canon, where the subject, the tune, would slowly get longer: "How—small; Howww—smalll; Howwwww smallllllll." It would lengthen irregularly in groups of twos and threes. The small thought would fill the whole piece.

When I began work on *Proverb*, I had the text in front of me. My first job was to look at the words and have some tune begin to suggest itself in my mind, write it down at the piano, play it and sing it. It's very important when you're writing a vocal piece to sing it, because that will keep you attuned to the idiom of the voice. That is one of the most important things you can do, because if musicians don't enjoy performing your piece, then no matter what the music critics say, your piece will not live. And if the musicians do enjoy playing it, and the audience enjoys listening, it doesn't matter what the music critics say, your piece will be played and enjoyed. That's an important lesson for everybody to learn.

So I sang and eventually ascertained what the basic musical material was. I knew it was going to be in B minor, that it was going to be a descending line. It starts out on a D, an octave and a step above middle C, and then works its way more or less straight down. It has a certain character.

The piece is for three sopranos and two tenors, who have rather different roles to fulfill. We wanted to keep the piece small, so it could be traveled with, and so others who wanted to do it wouldn't have to harness a whole lot of hardware. The only instruments are two vibraphones that play quietly in the background, and two double manual electric keyboards that are filled with a sample, a digital recording of a baroque organ. (You could do it on a real organ, but it's a lot easier to have sampling keyboards, which are easily rentable in any city on earth.) You use this little disc that the publisher supplies, and voila, you turn the keyboards into baroque organs.

The organ basically doubles the women's voices. Every choral composer is aware of the importance of doubling voices, to give them a kind of security. I'm fond of making what friends of mine call the "voicestrument," where the timbre of the electronic organ, which is slightly reedy, sort of becomes part of the vocal sound. It gives the voice a kind of buzz, a kind of electricity. You find this effect in the tromba, a brass-reed instrument that Bach used in the Fourth Cantata. Anyway, doubling the voice is a great trick—it worked 500 years ago, and it works now, because the singer feels they've got those pitches. They have a security that's transmitted in performance. So you get a timbral effect, you get an acoustical difference, and you get a human emotional quality, all of which are plusses.

The vibraphones keep the time moving in an audible way, because there are a lot of changing meters. The voices are heard at first without the vibraphones, as if they are singing without barlines, just with an unpredictable lilt, and then the vibraphones come in and you perceive the rhythms more clearly.

I feel most comfortable working at the keyboard—I ask myself what are the chords I'm using, how are they voiced. The piano has certain advantages over any electric keyboard. Being an acoustic instrument, it doesn't lie. It's a very accurate picture of acoustical reality, more so than more portable electric keyboards. Electronic instruments don't give you the balance of a chord as accurately as the piano does.

After I've worked at the piano, I'll go to the computer and enter the things that I've decided to use. I use a program called Sample Cell, which is a group of prerecorded musical instruments. They're loaded into the memory of the computer, and when you play back what you've notated in a program called Finale (which is widely used), you hear a mock-up of your piece, similar to an architect's model of a building that allows his clients to see what this thing will look like when it's built.

I don't have an aural imagination perfect enough to hear all the details of my pieces. Many composers have this; I simply don't. So this system has been useful, pretty much all my composing life. Before Finale I used multitrack tape recorders. I have a tape of *Desert Music* [scored for large orchestra and chorus] with me playing every single note, either on the piano, percussion, or electric keyboard, and singing the men's parts and also the women's parts, which I sang down an octave and speeded up. We call it the chipmunk tape.

Right now my composing involves getting the intuitive ideas, the real raw material, at the piano, working it over in my head, entering it into the computer, playing it back, and then just continuing that process until the piece is done. There was a large stretch between 1966 and 1976 where I would write just so much of the piece, then have my ensemble rehearse it, and make orchestrational changes during rehearsals. (Not so much note changes, but: do I want a piccolo or an E-flat clarinet? The answer is I *never* want to have an E-flat clarinet!) But then my ensemble got older and wiser, and needed to be paid for rehearsals, and these computer tools came in. Now we rehearse when the piece is finished.

Up to 1978 I wrote without commissions. I don't teach for a living. I had an instinct to avoid that. For awhile I did all kinds of jobs. But even then I was a practical composer, on the model of baroque composers like Handel, who arranged his own concerts or tried to get them arranged by friends. There would always be a deadline: "We can get you Town Hall around this time—can you be ready?" Then in the early '70s, when my ensemble was beginning to go to Europe, I found there was enough money over there to pay for concerts. A lot of people in America don't understand that the BBC and Radio France and other European radio and television stations are hollow buildings—i.e., they actually contain concert halls for presenting jazz, Balinese music, Stockhausen, me, John Cage, whatever. That's played a very large role in my work and the work of a lot of American artists since World War II. So I started earning my living mostly in Europe in the late 1970s.

I need a deadline. The idea of the artist waiting in his studio for inspiration to strike is a romantic unreality, and it would mean being cut off from the rest of the world. I want to feel that someone out there cares about what I'm doing. I want performances, which hopefully will lead to other performances, so that my piece will have a life, and the months and sometimes the years that I've put in will not have been spent in vain.

Now that I've said that, I do remember I was late with *Proverb*. I'd only gotten seven or eight minutes of *Proverb* done when it was due to the BBC for the Proms, and I let them do an in-progress version of the piece. I was not happy with what I'd done, and after that, I threw it out—kept only one minute and wrote the other thirteen minutes of the fourteen-minute piece between that September Proms performance and the following February, when the real world premiere took place at Alice Tully Hall with Paul Hillier. I think *Proverb* is one of the best pieces I've ever done, and I'm very glad that I consigned so much of the earlier version to the trash. I have thrown out hours of music. I think it's very important for composers to be self-critical, to not be afraid to just rip something up or slide your file over to the garbage can on your computer screen and start all over again.

For some reason, both *Desert Music* and *Different Trains*, which are rather large pieces, were—I don't know what else to say—inspired from beginning to end. I mean they took their time because they were long, but they went very rapidly for me. God knows why. All I know is it felt like the energy never stopped and it was always intuitively clear how to move on.

I revise a lot while I'm composing. What happens in 95 percent of the pieces is that I work a lot, I trash a lot, I revise a lot. I'm alone in this room, or in our place in Vermont. Occasionally I'll play something for my wife, Beryl, whose feedback I value, but ultimately it's me. Because I can play back the MIDI, or the tapes I've made, I listen to what I'm doing a lot. If there's some part that gives me a little twinge in my stomach, I know that in two or three days that twinge is going to be insufferable, and I'll have to do something to make it sit right. In *Proverb* there was a lot of that, and after awhile I began to think, "You're just tweaking this thing to death—you're poking it, picking it, and what are you doing?" Because very often, your first instincts are the best—but not always! So I poked and picked, and you know, eventually it was great. It's a really good piece, it just floats, and it's effortless, but it was far from effortless to make it.

Once a piece is out, I will make some slight changes, almost always in orchestration. And then the idea of even thinking about that piece compositionally again is anathema. When people make a new edition of a piece and want me to proofread it, I say, "Look, I'd rather get a root canal. Find somebody else who can proofread it—I *don't want* to see that again."

If you're working with a piece with words, then those words will be the essence of what that piece is. They will determine in many ways the rhythm of the piece and the feeling of the piece. You have to set the words in a way that makes sense of them. If you work as I have with prerecorded people speaking, that's all been decided. They speak a certain way, they say a certain thing. You're not setting a text, you're including a human being, so all the emotional overtones of that person's voice are part of the piece. In an instrumental piece, the instrumentation will determine what's happening. For example, in a piece like *Six Pianos* (1973) there are no long tones. It's a busy, churning piece. In *Four Organs* (1970)—sure enough, huge long tones. So instrumentation really lets you know what you can do, and what you can't do. As Stravinsky said, "I don't want complete freedom—it's terrifying. I want to have some friction, something I can push against."

There have been lessons to learn in all of this. After *Music for Eighteen Musicians* (1976), a very successful piece, came out, there was so much touring that I didn't write anything for almost a year. When I came back, the faucet was dry, and it was terrifying. What I learned from that experience is that it's very important to make sure that you put in your hours. There *is* something called inspiration, and it comes as a result of sitting yourself down in front of blank music paper and just working away until something begins to catch fire. If I don't put in those hours—and I'm a slow worker—then there ain't no inspiration. You've literally got to clock in the hours. For me, there are quite a few of them.

There are ups and downs. Morty Feldman used to say, "I think the most important thing is I gotta find the right chair." Even if you get yourself located and put in the time, there is no guarantee. It's absolutely clear in my contract that if I don't put in the hours then I won't get anything. But it's not so clear in my contract if I *do* put in the hours I *will* get something.

The hardest part is the blank page, which Sondheim has written a song about. Therefore, what I try to do (and again, this is following Stravinsky's advice) is ask myself, OK, what's my instrumentation, what's the length of this thing, how many movements am I going to work with, what's the approximate length of the movements, how am I going to treat the various instruments, what key am I in, what tempo am I in . . . The more of those questions I can answer, the less difficult it will be. Am I going to use a repeating pattern, and if so, what's the pattern? Is the piece going to be harmonically structured, and if so, what is the cycle of harmonies? Will there be an arch form so that the first movement and the fifth movement are similar and the second movement and fourth similar and the third unique? Or am I going to work with a simple three-movement fast-slow-fast form? All of these things have to become clear, and the sooner they are, the sooner I'm going to hit something real.

The piece I have to pay attention to now is a commission from the Kronos Quartet for their twentieth anniversary. It is a piece I wanted to do before *Different Trains*, which I want to call *Triple Quartet*. It could be played by twelve musicians—three first violins, three second violins, three violas, three cellos —but for Kronos it will be for two prerecorded string quartets and a live quartet. So there will be two forms of the piece. Those facts immediately get a bunch of things going in my mind. What are the roles of the quartets? Are we dealing with all the fiddles together, and then all the violas together, or are we dealing with all the quartets together? Those are two basic way of looking at the piece, and I suspect it'll be the second way, all the quartets together. Then, how will they be seated? Seating makes you think of how the lines are relating to one another, musically. In performance it's very good to seat people together whose parts are rhythmically interrelated. And the more tightly interrelated they are, the closer they should sit.

These are the kinds of questions that will help me get started on this piece, and they have already been popping in my head, even as I've been finishing *Hindenburg*. I feel a tug on the line. I think I've got a good fish here, and I've got to treat it right and get it reeled in.

Steve Reich, Selected Works

SMALL ENSEMBLE

Different Trains (1988)
string quartet and tape

Music for Eighteen Musicians
   (1974–76)
Four female voices, two clarinets,
   four pianos, three marimbas,
   two xylophone/vibraphone,
   violin, cello, conductor

Nagoya Marimbas (1994)
two marimbas

New York Counterpoint (1985)
clarinet and tape or nine
   clarinets (one doubling bass)
   and two bass clarinets

Proverb (1995)
three lyric sopranos, two tenors,
   and small ensemble
text: Ludwig Wittgenstein

Vermont Counterpoint (1982)
flute (including piccolo, alto)
   and tape or eight flutes (five
   doubling) and three alto
   flutes

LARGE ENSEMBLE

City Life (1995)
for large ensemble

The Desert Music (1982–84)
twenty-seven amplified voices/
   orchestra or ten amplified
   voices/chamber orchestra
text: William Carlos Williams

Tehillim (1981)
four female voices/chamber
   orchestra or four female
   voices/ensemble
text: Psalms 19, 34, 18, 150 (Hebrew)

Three Movements for Orchestra
   (1986)

STAGE

The Cave (1990–93)
documentary video opera in
   three acts
video: Beryl Korot
text: Torah, rabbinical commentary, documentary material
forces: two lyric sopranos, tenor,
   baritone; two woodwinds
   (doublers), four percussion,
   three keyboards, four strings

Publisher: Boosey & Hawkes,
   24 East 24th Street, New York,
   NY 10010-7200. Tel. 212-228-
   3300; fax 212-979-7057.

Steve Reich, Selected
Recordings

The Cave
Steve Reich and Musicians
Nonesuch 79327

City Life; *Proverb*; *Nagoya
   Marimbas*
Steve Reich and Musicians
Nonesuch 79430

Different Trains; *Electric Counter-
   point*
Kronos Quartet; Pat Metheny
Nonesuch 79176

Drumming
Steve Reich and Musicians
Nonesuch 79170

Early Works: *Come Out*; *Piano
   Phase*; *It's Gonna Rain*;
   Clapping Music
Nonesuch 79169

Music for Eighteen Musicians
Steve Reich and Musicians
ECM 1-1129

Music for a Large Ensemble;
   Octet; *Violin Phase*
Steve Reich and Musicians

Sextet; *Six Marimbas*
Steve Reich and Musicians,
   with members of Nexus and
   the Manhattan Marimba
   Quartet
Nonesuch 79138

Tehillim; *Three Movements*
Shönberg Ensemble with
   Percussion Group The Hague/
   de Leeuw

London Symphony
   Orchestra/Thomas
Nonesuch 79295

"Works, 1965–1995"
ten-disc box set; previously
   released material and new
   recordings
Nonesuch 79451

WILLIAM BOLCOM

(B. 1938)

William Bolcom has always been attracted to, as he puts it, "picking up a thread from our American musical history, and taking it to the next step."

Born in Seattle, Bolcom began his musical training as a pianist and entered the University of Washington at age eleven to study composition with John Verrall. He later studied with Darius Milhaud in California and Paris and earned a master's degree from Mills College and a doctor of music degree from Stanford University. Among his many honors is the 1988 Pulitzer Prize in music. He has been commissioned by the New York Philharmonic, the Philadelphia Orchestra, the Saint Louis Symphony, the Chamber Music Society of Lincoln Center, and many others. Bolcom's 1992 opera *McTeague* was the Lyric Opera of Chicago's first commission by an American composer. His gigantic score *Songs of Innocence and of Experience,* a three-hour "entertainment" from the William Blake poems, took twenty-five years to write and has been performed in both Europe and the United States.

As a solo pianist and concert artist with his wife, mezzo-soprano Joan Morris, Bolcom has recorded and performed widely the American popular song repertoire. His huge catalogue holds everything from ragtime and theater scores to chamber and symphonic works. William Bolcom teaches at the University of Michigan and lives in Ann Arbor.

This interview took place in Ann Arbor in January 1997.

•   •   •

I don't know how I compose—I just *do* it. It's like the old joke about the centipede: somebody asked him how he could walk with all those feet, and when he thought about it, he fell over.

I can't help doing it. If I ever stopped feeling that way, of course it would be a great relief to stop. Composing is very labor-intensive, and the reward is getting a piece played, I guess. I mean, it doesn't make any money, it doesn't necessarily get you girls. We all seem to have rather nice wives, but I think the reason they stay with us is they know where we are most of the time. You know, we're available for taking out the garbage.

In a mercantile society people look at us as if we're crazy to do this. If you try to measure composers by the standards for success in the United States, we're fools! When writers win the Pulitzer Prize it makes a little bit of an impact on their careers. But composers? You have to explain to most people what a composer is.

I can't understand the hundreds of students who want to study composition every year. It's possible that they have this kind of mind, that they just have to do it. That's wonderful. But if someone *doesn't* have to do it, heavens, they shouldn't! There are so many other things you can do and have a lot more fun, besides. Composing is drudgery, compared to most everything else. And when you're finished, where *is* it? There's no tangible thing. If you make a painting, there it is! My friend Daniel Milhaud made a wonderful sculpture —it's *there*. But when a composer writes a piece, there is no physical object in the end. Everything is against it—it can't be seen, and it takes other people, performers, to prove that it exists.

Every piece comes differently. Some pieces go page by page, some pieces go in spurts, some pieces take a long time. Every piece has got its own little agenda. It's not going to come any other way except the way it's gonna come, and that's that.

Sometimes it happens that I have an idea I've marinated for a long time. When it's ready, I sit down to write, and it works itself out. Other pieces are a struggle every single minute. I'm finding that it gets harder as I get older because I have gotten very, very picky. I want things just so, more than I ever used to, although I always was careful. I think you get more careful over time, but you have to try also not to let the work become pinched by all that care. You can kill your own piece by giving it too much balance, moving it around too much, worrying yourself silly over tiny details. There comes a point where you have to say, OK, enough, let's go on.

It's all decisions: decisions followed by decisions followed by decisions. A work has a kind of logicality, but this logic reveals itself as you're working. That doesn't mean I try to make my pieces logical for other people. I try to make them logical for me, under the assumption that if my work makes sense to me, it will make sense to somebody else. It doesn't always, at first. Maybe sometimes it never does! Some things make sense to me that won't make sense to anybody else, ever.

I've been interested in clarity a great deal recently, because I feel it is necessary to be clear, particularly at a time when so much in art is fuzzy. But I also realize that you can't clarify past the point of kicking the stuffing out of the idea. Some people go for clarity as a kind of virtue or simplicity of its own. Now you can make your idea as clear as you can, but you shouldn't go for clearness, period. You want to make something as simple as you can, but the reductive process, taken far enough, can kill the thing.

Some pieces will be more immediately comprehensible than others because that's the way the idea went, not because you tried to be audience-friendly or impress someone. I've written pieces that are very much out there for an audience to pick up, and they have a lot to do with the person I wrote them for. James Galway and I hung out when we were in Paris back in the early '60s; he was studying with Rampal, and my roommate was also studying flute. Jimmy was always kind of a leprechaun and still is—he's very much an audience person. I don't know how much people see of his introspective side, because it's kind of covered with a lot of public stance. So I wrote a flute concerto for him in which there are only one or two sections that emerge from an interior feeling. And the Irish tune I used—that was definitely close to the artist, from the world James Galway was born into.

You can try to write a one-size-fits-all piece, but really, a piece has to be a particular size to start with. Otherwise, it would be generic, and people sense a generic thing. You want to give a piece the feeling that you've written it just for the person who's playing it at the moment, even though it might have been written for somebody else. Some pieces stick to a certain kind of player, but most of the time it's the particularity in a piece that makes different kinds of people want to play it or listen to it.

I've certainly gone through different periods in my life, but it's also apparent to me that underneath it all, there's a sound that's mine. I never went out after a "stamp." Some people crawl into a style and pull the door shut, and I think if you do that, in the end you kind of dry up. There are people who are known for a particular kind of thing, and sometimes they are lucky enough to die early. There are many cases of strong composing personalities who happened to die before taking the next step, but they did what they did perfectly.

David Schiff [the composer] remarked that Boulez might be like a lot of mathematicians who do most of their real path-finding work before their middle thirties, after which it's a kind of a rehash. What Boulez does is go back to his old pieces, and chop them up, mix them up, revise them. He doesn't do much new work. George Crumb is a case of somebody who has made his niche, maybe painted himself into it, to a certain extent. I am not criticizing the music itself, which is beautiful! It's just that there's a question of where that style would go.

The art gallery people have laid it on their painters not to change style, especially in the 1950s New York School. I can tell a Morris Louis from three hundred feet away, but I never know whether he did anything else at all. The point is that I know it's a Morris Louis, and to a lot of people, that's more important than whether it's an interesting painting. A persona gives you immediacy, makes you identifiable. Some people want to jump on me for avoiding this; others like me for having done so many different things. I'd really be bored if I hadn't taken the routes I did. The people who want me to stay in one place, and behave? Well, too bad for them.

There was a very understandable trauma during the world wars that hit Europe directly. It hit Americans, too, although we don't often realize it. It comes out in the need to repudiate the influences that brought about the big holocausts of our time. We're rather scared of ourselves! So the idea has been to start over from scratch. When I was a student we were all starting over from zero: tonality was dead, because in composers' minds it helped bring on the ugliness of the whole Fascist era. Someone was responsible for millions of people getting gassed, and part of the blame was pinned on the hubristic, romantic feeling of music and the whole history of harmony, which excites those kinds of feelings. We thought we needed something completely free of what brought us to that ugly point. It's perfectly understandable. This reaction was immediate with Europeans. I think Americans, looking up to Europe, thought they had to jump on the bandwagon, too.

I remember a composer who was teaching at the University of Washington who had studied with Hindemith. He wrote in a very emotional style, which I thought was quite moving when I was a student. (Today I might find it rather corny.) Well, he went off to Europe and studied with some German, and when he came back he was writing this acid, arid, ugly, clunky, twelve-tone music. He said, "You know, the world has changed—I gotta get with it!"

One reason I'm involved with American popular song is that it exists close to the real choices that make us who we are. I always reject the American Composer with the flag in his piece. That's not my way, but I do realize one has to be what one is. In order to be universal, you have to be particular. Maybe there's a little nationalism in that.

I think some American composers have tried to internationalize themselves out of existence. The Babbitt folks were certainly not interested in any sort of national identity, although Milton's got jazzy stuff in a lot of his best pieces, and he's not ashamed of it. There's an irrepressible humor there, when he lets it out. A lot of his students are worse. That's the way it happens. The acolytes are always more purist than the original practitioners.

Sure, I've been tempted to quit. Oh my Lord, yes. Many, many times. And one day I might even do it. I always think of Rossini's terrific courage, how he said, "Well, I'm not sure whether to go along with what these guys are doing right now, so I'm just going to write when I feel like it and get out of the rat race." Which is what he did, and he supposedly had a wonderful time after that. To me, that's better than scribbling away after you've stopped having anything to say, writing little pieces that dilute the better ones. You do your own work a disservice if you keep writing past the point of having to do it. If it turns out that you don't write up to the end of your life, that's OK. You have to be true to your own space, and your history, and your own way of operating, and try to find out what that is, and try to work in some kind of harmony with it. You are who you are, not somebody else you might admire.

I'd rather hang out with writers and painters than composers, as a rule— they're more fun to talk to. Composers are such drudges. They get so snippy, and they're socially not much fun, often. I don't know why that is. Painters are a lot of fun; they don't think life's a dirty joke, they're straightforward and concrete. Writers are complex and funny. In fact, my other love is writing. From the very earliest I was interested in literature, and I was lucky enough to work in Seattle at college with the poet Theodore Roethke, for example.

Text-setting varies with every poet, with every lyricist, but that's the fun part. You try to go for the subtext, you try to clarify through the music what the poem is about. Most people don't know how to read poems out loud (this includes poets!) or understand them when they read them. Poets themselves are a little bit distrustful of the lyrical ear; again, they had their own kind of drying-up period, just as we composers did. The whole idea of the grand bardic style, standing up and intoning—no poet dares read like that today. Now poets read as if they are giving you the minutes for the latest Rotary meeting, and it destroys their work half the time because they're sort of saying, "Gee whiz, aw shucks, I don't really mean to be that lyrical, not really." That "aw shucks" attitude does a disservice to their own good ear. A composer can find the buried, lyrical parts in a poem and help bring them out.

I compose whenever I can. I did some work recently on a three-day trip to Ottawa. I had a whole morning to work on my sixth symphony, which was good because I've been struggling over parts of it. It's still presenting itself to me, bit by bit, and it's going to be a toughie. That has nothing to do with how good or how bad it is. Like I said, some pieces just get written out—you sit down and start and suddenly it's over. Others take a lot more work.

But most of my work's done here at home. The best time is before the phone starts ringing, which means I'm up at 6 A.M. I'll have an espresso and get toast and put jam on it and drink a glass of juice. I don't even clean up. I've got these skivvies I wear around the house, and I put those on, and do my work at the desk and put in sometimes three and four hours before things get crazy. If I'm on a deadline, I'll work all day, and even at night. I'm so glad that Joan and I do run-out concerts, because sometimes I need to get away from the work. You have to give yourself a little time to think about something, put it on the back burner and let it simmer for awhile.

I don't work at the piano. Sometimes I find students who work at the piano who shouldn't, and others who don't and should. It might have something to do with their piano chops; if their chops aren't strong enough, their heads can be limited by what their fingers can do. Sometimes the opposite happens—your virtuosity can run away with you. It was a problem for Beethoven and Stravinsky. That's why Beethoven stopped writing at the piano; Stravinsky had such a set of chops that he was afraid his fingers would run away with him, and he muted the piano so he wouldn't let that happen.

For a big piece, I pull together a big morgue of sketches—little notations, jottings that will remind me of how a particular passage might go. When there are enough of these things, I'm ready to write. That's exactly what happened with the *Songs of Innocence and of Experience*. Suddenly I realized that I was ready to start, I was ready to get the thing done, after sketching, working on bits and pieces, for quite a number of years.

My biggest problem with that piece was how to do it with the many disparate styles I found myself using in the settings. (Blake did that, too—there are different styles all over that particular set of poems.) This led me to a juxtaposition of modes and styles, tonality and atonality, which dominated my work for twenty, twenty-five years. Now I'm finding that my work is less like that. I still love to deal with juxtapositions, but they're smoother—more amalgam than juxtaposition.

Once I have my materials, I start at the beginning of the piece and go to the end; otherwise I don't have a sense of the shape of it. It's very important to me to get the proportions right, and the timing. Keeping the line going was especially important in *McTeague* [his first opera] because McTeague is not an articulate character. He rants and raves at the end of his life when he's gone mad; he can't stop talking because he can't help it. The rest of the time, though, he can't tell you what he feels; he doesn't know how. So it was important to keep everything moving around him rather quickly. When I understood that, I realized the whole opera had to be a flashback, a dream, as he remembered it. It needed that funny, fragmentary reviewing quality, so I went after a kind of dreamlike atmosphere.

As a teacher I try to help everybody find out who they are—what he or she is going to do, what their interest is going to be. Then I try to give them the chops they'll need. I'm getting back to believing in strict disciplines. I think the kids are beginning to realize they need them, and why. For years we practiced a brand of musical analysis that was kind of political. [Heinrich] Schenker [Austrian music theorist whose reductionist approach to harmonic structure has been popular for the past fifty years] was useful in showing how to play the first movement of a Beethoven trio, but it was not meant to cover all music. It already doesn't work with harmonies like Chopin's. The kids nowadays are trying to write some kind of tonal music, but they don't really feel the same tonal impulses I grew up with, so what are theirs going to be? Is there a sense of any kind of functionality, or inevitability? They need to find out how to bring it about. If they don't, they'll realize at some point that they're hamstrung, and they'll have to learn. That's not much fun if you're twenty-five years old, or thirty. A lot of kids are buffaloed even as late as their graduate degrees because they can't do the simple things—make an effective tonal cadence or write a tune.

The way to teach tonality is to teach the literature. The Chopin mazurkas are full of wonderful lessons in tonality. You can explore, for example, why you got a little visceral twinge when this passage here turned into something else—that's the kind of contextualizing that's interesting to students.

A composer has no idea which of his pieces are going to be played a lot. Even if you tried to plan it, decide "this is going to be a big potboiler," you would have no reason to know it's going to actually boil. Something else you just wrote off the cuff might turn out to be the most commonly done piece, instead. You have no way of predicting. You can't plan to have a child who has certain characteristics, you can't just feed the information into the system—it doesn't work that way! The kid will come out the way the kid is going to come out, and that's that. You just have to be as kind as possible to the work, as nurturing as you would be with a child.

I've never destroyed any of my pieces, but I've kept them from being played, which is not very hard to do! I've taken a couple of pieces out of circulation, but I have not actually done a ritual fire. My teacher, John Verrall at the University of Washington, told me that I should never throw anything out because he himself *had* done a ritual fire and regretted it all his life. That's why I have never done it. But there's such a thing as not putting something in the catalogue in the first place.

The most exhausting part of being a composer, I think, is the social life having to do with getting a piece performed. I mean, I love all these people, but I get so tired of chitchat and socializing and running around and having to make nice. You need to do this, because the people who've paid the freight have a right to some of your time. But that's the part that wears you out in this business. Joan and I have a fairly good career as performers, but we aren't superstars. And that's good enough for me, because if we had any more of it, we'd have no time to ourselves. We'd have no life of our own.

William Bolcom, Selected
Works

SOLO, SMALL ENSEMBLE

Briefly It Enters (1996)
soprano and piano
text: Jane Kenyon

Cabaret Songs (1963–96)
medium voice and piano
text: Arnold Weinstein

I Will Breathe a Mountain (1990)
medium voice and piano
texts: Elizabeth Bishop, Louise
    Bogan, Gwendolyn Brooks,
    Emily Dickinson, H.D., Alice
    Fulton, Denise Levertov, Edna
    St. Vincent Millay, Marianne
    Moore, Anne Sexton, May
    Swenson

Second Piano Quartet (1996)
clarinet, violin, cello, piano

Twelve New Etudes (1977–86)
piano

Violin Sonata no. 2 (1978), no. 3
    (1992); no. 4 (1995)
violin and piano

LARGE ENSEMBLE

Concerto in D (1984)
violin and orchestra

Fantasia Concertante (1985)
viola, violoncello, and orchestra

Lyric Concerto (1993)
flute and orchestra

The Mask (1990)
SATB chorus and piano
text: T. J. Anderson III, Gwendolyn
    B. Bennett, Richard Bruce, Paul
    Lawrence Dunbar, Charles
    Cyrus Thomas

*Songs of Innocence and of
    Experience* (1956–81)
vocal soloists, choruses, and
    orchestra
text: William Blake

Symphony no. 3 (1979), no. 4
    (1986, w/medium voice), no. 5
    (1989), no. 6 (1997)
orchestra

STAGE

McTeague (1991–92)
opera in two acts
libretto: Arnold Weinstein and
    Robert Altman, after Frank
    Norris

Publisher: Edward B. Marks Music
    Company, 126 East 38th Street,
    New York, NY 10016. Tel. 212-
    779-7977; fax 212-779-7920.

William Bolcom, Selected
Recordings

Casino Paradise (theater piece)
Joan Morris, mezzo-soprano;
    Timothy Nolen, baritone
Koch International Classics KIC 7047

Concerto for Piano and
    Orchestra
Bolcom, piano; Rochester Phil-
    harmonic Orchestra/Hodkinson
Vox Classics VOX 7509

Ghost Rags for piano
Paul Jacobs, piano
Nonesuch 79006-2

"Let's Do It: Bolcom and Morris at
    Aspen"
Joan Morris, mezzo-soprano;
    William Bolcom, piano
Omega Classics OCD 3004

Quartet no. 10 for Strings
Stanford String Quartet
Laurel LR 847 CD

Quintet for Brass
American Brass Quintet
New World NW 80377-2

Sonata no. 2 for Violin and Piano
Maria Bachmann, violin;
    Jon Kilbonoff, piano
Catalyst 09026-62668-2

Symphony no. 1; Symphony no. 3;
    Seattle Slew Orchestral Suite
Louisville Orchestra/Smith
Louisville LCD 007

Symphony no. 4
Joan Morris, mezzo-soprano;
    St. Louis Symphony
    Orchestra/Slatkin
New World NW 80356-2

Twelve New Etudes
Marc-Andre Hamelin, piano
New World NW 80354-2

JOHN CORIGLIANO

(B. 1938)

*J*ohn Corigliano comes from a musical family. His father was concert-master of the New York Philharmonic, and his mother was a pianist. Corigliano played the piano and composed from an early age and studied at Columbia College with Otto Luening and at the Manhattan School of Music with Vittorio Giannini. He worked as a composer, arranger, and producer in radio and television for a number of years, and his score for Ken Russell's film *Altered States* received an Academy Award nomination in 1981.

Corigliano has gained a wide audience through live and recorded performances of his Symphony no. 1: *Of Rage and Remembrance*, an impassioned response to the AIDS crisis. The work was written for the Chicago Symphony, where Corigliano was composer-in-residence for three seasons. The Chicago Symphony's recording of the work received Grammy Awards for best contemporary classical composition and best orchestral performance, and a second recording with Leonard Slatkin and the National Symphony won the Grammy for best classical album in 1997. In the same year, Corigliano's string quartet won the Grammy for best contemporary classical composition.

John Corigliano's commissions have come from the Metropolitan Opera, the New York Philharmonic, the Chamber Music Society of Lincoln Center, flutist James Galway, the Boston Symphony Orchestra, and more. Among his many professional honors is the 1991 Grawemeyer Award. Corigliano teaches at Lehman College, City University of New York, and the Juilliard School. He lives in New York City. This interview took place in New York in August 1996.

•   •   •

I first started composing because of an incredible curiosity: can *I* make these sounds that I want to hear? Can I write something down that will do what I want done? Now, what is more important to me is the idea that I have, out of nothing, made something solid. That I've made something real out of totally amorphous things: pitches, rhythms, and sonorities. From them I have built an architecture, a structure that stands. That, to me is very, very satisfying. It's like building a building—I have something that is there, even when it's not played. It's not that I think that music should exist for no one. It should be played, it should speak to people. But there is an architectural solidity about a symphony or a concerto that I feel very comfortable with, knowing what those notes can be made to do when necessary. The piece is real to me, even when it's just on the page.

I started writing in a world that I loved, that I had experienced by listening: the world of Americana, the Copland, Piston, kind of Barber-Bernstein combo of sounds that is clean and American, and not angst-filled, and has the kind of rhythmic profile American music has. But I wasn't interested in classical music until high school, and that was mainly because of the advent of the LP record, and my getting a hi-fi set with a fifteen-inch speaker, and listening to *Billy the Kid* (with Copland conducting) mainly for the bass drum of the gunfight scene, and being fascinated by all the things Copland did before and after that bass drum—the way he spaced a triad so it sounded totally fresh, or juxtaposed irregular meters that I was not acquainted with. I played those things on the piano then and found them very exciting, and from there grew in love with that kind of music and wanted to write in that language.

So in the beginning I accepted a language, a vocabulary, a set of techniques, because I didn't know them well and I wanted to master them. That lasted until the 1970s, because I needed to learn. Even when you're working through things that other people have done, there's a certain freshness in discovering them for yourself. I'm not sure it would have stayed fresh if I'd continued writing that way for the rest of my life. I eventually needed to move on, and that's what I did.

One of my biggest problems then was wanting to write faster. The actual notational act for me is cumbersome. I know from having taught in conservatories that students are made to write a tremendous amount of music, but at Columbia, where I went to school, I could slough off and not write a lot. So the act of writing slowed me down enormously, and the fact that I am super-, hypercritical also slowed me down, so that I accepted almost nothing of my own ideas. That combination meant it would take me a year to write a piece, and that hasn't changed! I'm much slower than just about any composer I know, and therefore my frustration is not with moving on to other kinds of music, but just in finishing the very piece I am working on.

What *has* changed is my musical vocabulary. In the 1960s, I knew the world I wanted to write in, and I could start right out producing music. You know, Mozart basically had a vocabulary, a set of accompaniment figures, a form—a lot of things he could drop his music into, very beautifully, whereas

Beethoven was figuring out new ways to go. He wrote less music, but he thought a lot more about where to take it. I'm more the Beethoven type, now, than the Mozart type. If you wanted me to write a melody, I would have to ask, "What kind of melody?" There are many melodies I could write that would reflect me, but they would come out of many different worlds. The more divergent the sources, the harder it is to get an immediate idea, until I start to build the piece. (I should add that it's not degrading to say that someone can write like Mozart. It just means that you don't challenge the world around you, but fit into it. If you're Mozart, of course, you do it like a genius.)

I just hate having to confront my inadequacies. When I start a piece and I haven't made decisions yet, everything I'm trying to do looks so bad—I strain so hard to get so little. My limitations are so clear to me. My friends know that this is a sincere thing, it is not artifice. I really feel this staggering sense of having to drag myself up, heaving, past my limits, to write a decent piece, you know? That's what it feels like when I write. So I don't want to do it! I want to say to people, "Look at my *other* pieces! Listen to *this* piece! How 'bout *this* piece?" I don't want to have to go through the process again. I really hate composing. I love having composed. When a piece is nearly over, I feel good, because I've built this thing, and I can see it. But until I see it, I don't know if I'll ever be able to build anything again.

The art of composing can start very early in the process of making a piece, or it can start very late, depending on what you accept. I tend to start as early as I can, because I think the earliest decisions are the biggest ones. I don't even want to accept a commission until I sort of know where I want to go with the piece. The decisions in music are so staggering, so arbitrary—music is so arbitrary in itself, that to make the decision less arbitrary, you have to make some arbitrary decisions! Now, you can be like Mozart and can say, "My decision is to accept sonata-allegro form, the tonal system of my time, the instrumental ranges, the accompaniment patterns of my time, and now I will search for my theme." But if you're like Beethoven, you say, "Well, I don't accept the form of my time, I'm interested in a single movement that spans forty minutes, does X, Y, and Z, and goes in a new direction rhythmically— now, how do I do this?"

Also, what are you going to write, a concerto or a symphony? That's a pretty big decision, compared to F-sharp and G. How many movements will it have? What is your orchestration? What is this piece about? *Why* are you writing it?

Just deciding on an oboe concerto is a decision of structure. Then I'll say, "All right, but the problem with every oboe concerto I've heard up till now is that you could play it on any other instrument and it would sound fine. Why not write an oboe concerto that can only be played on the oboe?" And I'll sit down and ask an oboist, "What's oboistic?" We talk about everything that makes an oboe oboistic: the long line that it can sing because of the small amount of air coming out; the fact that it has a reverse arch in dynamics—

the lower you go, the louder and coarser it gets, and the higher you go, the thinner it gets. The oboe tunes the orchestra, it has an Arabic heritage, it can do multiphonics as well as other sounds—from all those things, then, I can make a very specifically oboe concerto.

The inspirations for pieces are always different. For the clarinet concerto for New York Philharmonic, the inspirations were a clarinetist who was a supreme virtuoso, the conductor Leonard Bernstein, a theatrical man, and my father, who died two years before the commission and had been concert-master of that orchestra. For the *Pied Piper Fantasy*, the inspirations were James Galway, imagining his personality as a pied piper, and fashioning a seven-movement piece that was theatrical.

Once I have those kinds of reasons for writing a piece, I begin to impose limits based upon technique, time, and personal taste. Small matters gel after the big elements are decided. Very often I type out descriptions of these larger elements, and I also draw pictures of them.

For example, when I was writing *The Ghosts of Versailles* for the Met and I wanted ghost music, I typed out in words the kind of sound I wanted as a background to the world of ghosts. I also drew it in colored crayon because I couldn't figure out how to do it musically. I wanted the color of the sound to change as a single line moved. And so I drew a single line with colored pencils, going from oranges to reds to greens, to blues to purples. I ended up making a timbral fugue, in which the timbres play against each other, and I used a twelve-tone row, just because it was curvaceous and chromatic. Eight or nine instruments were given the same notes in the same amount of time but were not to play them, only to finger them or bow them silently, while making crescendos and diminuendos from *niente* to piano and back, ad libitum. That way the sound would appear and disappear, and combine in various colors, but unpredictably. It would be like cigarette smoke, which was one of my verbal images.

Then I made pointillistic fields of light. I wrote, for example, "When does a chord become a cluster? In adding notes, can you add pitches to a cluster or a chord and then dissolve certain pitches to leave a new chord?" That became a technique I used. "Pointillistic halo of light" is what I wrote.

If there's a text, it's a whole different matter. I carry it around with me, typed triple-spaced, and I draw relationships between the text and musical ideas: "Theme returns here," "crescendo tutti here," "orchestral interlude," whatever occurs to me.

If I write a theme, I want to know it's the best possible theme. I want to etch it out and make it the best. The theme from Beethoven's Fifth Symphony is a real thing. Once Beethoven devised it, he locked himself out of a tremendous amount of possibilities by limiting himself that way. Decisions like that early in the game fascinate me, because there is the opportunity to go in so many different directions. Each of my five concertos is an excursion into a completely different world of music. The *Pied Piper* deals with sonority in the flute and pictorial representation, the clarinet concerto deals with the virtuoso clarinetist and my feelings about the New York Philharmonic, the oboe concerto is about the properties of the oboe, the guitar concerto is about the loss of innocence (as the guitar is an instrument of innocence), and the piano concerto is a red-blooded piano concerto. Put them all together and you will find that although the same person wrote them, they portray very different worlds.

Anyone's personal style is usually not apparent to them, because style is made up of the unconscious choices you make, not the conscious ones. When I say style I mean the individual voice, which people confuse with technique. When you write a twelve-tone piece, you're using a technique, not a style. If I use classical techniques in *The Ghosts of Versailles*, they're not a style. But the reason any piece has my voice is because I make certain choices, whether I'm using classical techniques or the twelve-tone system, or whatever. I will make certain choices of sonorities, pacing, rhythms, that are common threads throughout my work, like my handwriting. When I sign my name, I do not consciously sign my name, and if I think about it, I can't write it. It's a series of gestures that depict me, and it's different from anyone else's attempt to sign my name. The same thing applies in music.

Leonardo Balada, a composer and colleague, pointed this out to me. Years ago I said to him, "Oh, I don't have any style," and he said, "Oh, yes you do." And he pulled out two piano pieces of mine. One was called *Etude Fantasy* [1976], which was actually five etudes in the form of a fantasy, starting with a left-hand etude. (Actually, the mechanics of the left hand built the etude, which became the generating force of the materials for the other four etudes.) It's a twenty-minute virtuoso piece. The other one is called *Fantasia on an Ostinato* [1985], based on the second movement of Beethoven's *Seventh Symphony* and the major-minor descent of harmony in that, et cetera.

So Leonardo turned to a page in the left-hand etude, and a page at the end of the *Fantasia*, and he showed me exactly the same music. Now it was really interesting to me, because both of these things were written with the same pitches—it was the same music, one derived from Beethoven, one derived from the left-hand etude. In both pieces, I had come up with the same thing! Leonardo said, "You see, that's your style!" I had no idea I had done that. So style is unconscious. It comes from decisions I don't even know I'm making, and those are the ones that bind everything together and unify a composer's work. It's not anything one has control over.

I was looking at Beethoven's sketches of the funeral march of the *Eroica* Symphony. There are millions of them, and he begins with something so dumb it's hard to believe any human being could have written it, let alone Beethoven. Then he revises it, and it's still dumb, then he tries something else, and finally, down the line, at the end, he makes something fabulous. But you can really see this man struggling.

I go through the same struggle when I write. I get something that's interesting, but I don't feel it's right, and it takes me *so* long to make it right, or to discard it and find the right thing, and . . . I *hate* that! I really, really hate that. Once I have the right thing, I feel a lot better, because I know I can manipulate it. I have something to work with. I don't feel like I'm at sea.

As an eclectic composer I don't come out with a million different themes the same way a composer who is very tonal and lyrical might. I'm more likely to find themes I can etch out for a specific purpose. But there won't be a whole barrage of them. I don't have a trunk full of tunes and sketches that I can apply to any piece. For me, the theme has to grow out of the need of the piece I'm writing.

Most people think that music is generated from melody, but I think that melody is actually very difficult to remember. What's most important in a piece is shape and direction. What people remember best is sonority, because it's vertical, not horizontal. Sometimes, if I want something to be memorable in the sense that I want people to understand that I'm recapitulating something, I will try and find a unique sonority that I can recapitulate.

It's the smaller decisions that have to do with pitches, not the bigger ones. The big decision is why you are writing this piece, and that question you have to answer at the start. Then, from your reasons, you find out what the piece should be like. If you don't even ask the question, and you just start composing, you'll compose in a very limited way, to my mind. In a sense, you will have given up the most important part of the process.

I don't take commissions and line them up. I don't want to line up pieces and then not want to do them when I get to them. I want to do a piece because I think it's the right thing for me to do at the time. I just turned down a commission for a horn concerto for the Chicago Symphony, because I didn't want to do it. I don't want to face writing for orchestra right now, because I don't think that's where I want to go. I want to go in another direction.

The reason I wrote the string quartet is that I wanted to do a string quartet. Word got sent around that I'd like to do it, and the Cleveland Quartet said they'd be interested, and that's how that happened. I'm in a luxurious position, but I can't do *everything* I want—for instance, I can't say I want to write another opera and suddenly there's a commission. But I like to be able to figure out what I want to write, so that I can grow and explore something that I haven't done before. I don't want to write the same piece over again. I tend to write one of each—you know, a string quartet, a symphony.

I've been really curious lately about dealing with amplification and the human voice—the idea of adding the twentieth century's innovations to the nineteenth-century orchestra. Basically, I have been composing with a nineteenth-century orchestra and vocal palette, even though I've used twentieth-century techniques. The orchestra itself is the same as it was in 1900, with a few percussion additions. And yet in this century we have developed something called amplification that makes it possible to sing in a completely different manner, make different sounds, make every word audible, and change the entire perspective—which is why musicals, which are really like operas now, have mass audiences. These pieces are in English and they're amplified. The same audiences do not want to go to the Met. But if an opera at the Met, say *La Traviata*, were done in English, with mikes, on Broadway, it would sell! It's so bizarre.

Oh, yes, I abandoned a piece once. I was supposed to write a marimba piece for Leigh Stevens, and I just feel terrible that I never finished it. I tried so hard, and, well, if only the marimba sustained, I would have a piece. But I just couldn't take the dropout of sound, the constant tremolo. It's not that it can't be done—there are some wonderful marimba pieces out there. But I couldn't make it work for me. I finally just gave up and gave back the money. I heard a marimba piece Jacob Druckman wrote for the same commissioning series and I said, "God, that's a fabulous piece!" But I couldn't have written it. A solo marimba piece seems to be a vision I can't cope with.

There are a few friends I talk to about my work when I'm in the middle of a piece, and for different reasons. For example, I call people like Bill Hoffman [the playwright], my closest friend, just to cry and scream and say, "Will you still love me if I don't write anymore?" There are other friends I have called on for musical buoying up. When my friend Sheldon Skrolnik was alive, he was really wonderful to talk to because he had a very similar mindset. Talking to him was really clarifying.

There are a few other people—Steve Mercurio, and John Adkins. Mark Adamo is really terrific to talk to, because he has very good sensibilities and is a real ally. Dan Welcher's been great over the years, because I can send him something and we can talk about it over the phone. It's very psychiatric. Sometimes I end up doing all the talking and he doesn't even say anything. I just talk and solve the problem. Sometimes all I need is someone to say, "It'll be OK, you know."

But only a trained professional with similar sensibilities can look at a piece, understand what I'm getting at, and say, "Yes, properly played, this will work." Those people are almost impossible to find, but they certainly have been important to me. As a teacher, it's easy for me to see what's wrong with what someone else does. But when I'm doing it myself, I sometimes need to talk it out. Composers generally don't do that very much, but I think it's a very good thing. It gives them objectivity.

I've been thinking that we live in a noncommittal age. There are a lot of non-committal pieces. Some people finish writing a piece and start the next piece two days later, and finish that, and start the next one two days later, and never ask why they are doing this in the first place, why something is important to write, for themselves or for anyone else.

There's a lot of music now that avoids human contact, and it avoids it in very interesting ways. For example, it avoids human expectations having to do with the balance of opposites. Minimalism in its strict form does that, the same way serialism does. Both are repetitious organizational forms, and both avoid the need for contrast in art. So they're both kind of noncommittal, in a sense. Anything the composer may have to say personally is not part of the statement. It's a type of avoidance.

There's also the whole idea that music is something to accompany medi-tation, thought, or doing the dishes—that music should exist so that you don't have to listen to it. You can leave, come back two minutes later, and not have missed anything! It's socially motivated. Music has moved out of the concert hall and into living rooms, dining rooms, elevators, supermarkets. People seem to want music that doesn't drop out, leave a void, or, conversely, deafen people or interrupt a conversation. This music stays around the same volume and is attractive. I've seen movies where the background music plays all the time, as if someone left the radio on. Not a moment of silence.

This sort of music is functioning differently. There's nothing wrong with that. The problem comes when that type of music is given the same care and attention in the concert hall as music that has been built by a composer to say something terribly important. You can't place this noncommittal music in a serious listening situation and expect it to provide the same thing that Beethoven does. Yet people are doing it.

In the 1970s and before, I often wrote at the piano, but after my vocabulary became more eclectic, I started to conceive and write a good deal away from the instrument. It's still important for me to test out harmonic subtleties. Copland did it, Stravinsky did it, and I'm not ashamed to say that I do it. However, if you're working with a textural language, the piano can be very de-ceiving, because it's a percussion instrument and it only plays halftones. If you want to deal outside those twelve tones in a kind of textural manner, you've got to get away from the piano.

When I compose, I have to have everything around me very neatly in order. If the bed isn't made and the house is messy, I can't compose. It's because I'm going into this chaos inside my brain, and I want to be able to look around and see order. I want my things around [posters from world premieres, his published scores, etc.]. I like to look at my things and say to myself, "You did this in the past, so maybe you can do what you're about to do now."

I know some people can write anyplace, but I can't do that. I couldn't just take a trip for a weekend and bring music and write. It also takes me time to get into writing. I can't write on command; I have to work up to it. In the summer I have the time to do that. Then, the best method for me is to work in the morning, have lunch, go to sleep, wake up at 3:30 or 4, work till 9:30 at night, make dinner, and go to bed. That gives me the equivalent of two mornings, two work periods, in a day of high output. I used to try to work through the day, and I found I got tired. So the best periods for writing, for me, are late in the day and early in the day. Not in the middle at all, especially after eating.

When I'm working this way, I just keep writing until I can't write anymore. Then I worry and think about the next part. I do it kind of by leaps, in groups, writing two or three pages of music at a time. After a group is done, I put my subconscious to work on the details of what's coming up. I go to sleep and hope that sleeping helps, and then go on solidifying the next few pages of music, writing them down. It's like leaping over hurdles—every time you leap over a hurdle, there's another one there.

See, my entire life is a roller coaster. I am at this moment in the guilt phase. The guilt comes from not writing. I haven't been writing lately, and I'm very guilty about it! I still haven't committed to a new project, but as soon as I do, fear will take over from guilt. And that will continue during a good part of the creative process, until joy comes near the end, when I really have the piece, and then, when it's over, I'll feel exultation. Then the piece will be played, and I will feel wonderful for awhile, and then guilt will set in again. So at this point I'm getting to the low end of my roller coaster ride. I will climb upward again, if I write another piece. At this point I don't know what I'm going to write next, so it's really a little scary. And I feel very at odds with myself—I'm doing all sorts of chores, getting cabinets built for my studio, doing everything but writing music. What can I say? It's frustrating!

John Corigliano, Selected Works

SOLO, SMALL ENSEMBLE

Etude Fantasy (1976)
piano solo

Fantasia on an Ostinato (1985)
piano solo

Quartet for Strings (1995)

Sonata for Violin and Piano (1963)

Three Irish Folk Song Settings
   (1988)
voice and flute

LARGE ENSEMBLE

A Dylan Thomas Trilogy (1960–76)
"Fern Hill," "Poem in October,"
   "Poem on His Birthday"
chorus, soloists, and orchestra

Pied Piper Fantasy (1982)
concerto for flute and
   orchestra

Symphony no. 1 (1988–89)
orchestra

Three Hallucinations (1981)
orchestra (based on the film score
   Altered States)

Troubadours (1993)
variations for guitar and chamber orchestra

STAGE

The Ghosts of Versailles (1991)
grand opera buffa in two acts
libretto: William M. Hoffman

Publisher: G. Schirmer, 257 Park Avenue South, 20th floor, New York, NY 10010. Tel. 212-254-2100; fax 212-254-2013.

John Corigliano, Selected Recordings

Concerto for Clarinet and Orchestra
Stanley Drucker, clarinet; New York Philharmonic/Mehta
New World Records NW-309-2

Concerto for Oboe and Orchestra
Bert Lucarelli, oboe; American Symphony Orchestra/Akiyama
RCA (Gold Seal) 60395-2-RG

Concerto for Piano and Orchestra; *Elegy for Orchestra*; *Fantasia on an Ostinato* (for orchestra); *Tournaments Overture*
Barry Douglas, piano; St. Louis Symphony/Slatkin
RCA 09026-68100-2

Gazebo Dances; *Promenade Overture*

Louisville Orchestra/Smith
First Edition LCD 008

The Ghosts of Versailles (video)
Teresa Stratas, Marilyn Horne, Håken Hagegård, Gino Quilco, vocalists
Metropolitan Opera Orchestra, chorus, and ballet/Levine
Deutsche Grammophon Laser Disc and Video VHS
072-430-1/-3 (PAL) 072-530-1/-3 (NTSC)

Pied Piper Fantasy
James Galway, flute
Eastman Philharmonic/Effron
RCA 6602-2-RC

Poem in October
Robert White, tenor; Thomas Nyfenger, flute; Bert Lucarelli, oboe; Joseph Rabbai, clarinet; American String Quartet; Maurice Peress, harpsichord and conductor
RCA (Gold Seal) 60395-2-RG

Quartet for Strings
Cleveland String Quartet
Telarc CD 80415

Symphony no. 1: *Of Rage and Remembrance*
Chicago Symphony Orchestra/Barenboim
Erato 2292-45601-2

Troubadours (Variations for guitar and chamber orchestra)
Sharon Isbin, guitar; Saint Paul Chamber Orchestra/Wolff
Virgin Classics CDC 55083

JOHN HARBISON

(B. 1938)

*J*ohn Harbison grew up in Princeton, New Jersey. He began improvising on the piano at five years of age, started a jazz band at age twelve, and as a teenager received guidance from Roger Sessions, his Princeton neighbor. Harbison studied at Harvard University, the Berlin Hochschule für Musik, and Princeton University, where his teachers were Walter Piston, Boris Blacher, and Earl Kim, respectively.

Harbison's catalogue contains a great deal of sacred music, the outcome of his long association with Emmanuel Church in Boston, and numerous settings of American poetry, one of his great passions. His orchestral works have been commissioned by the Boston Symphony, the San Francisco Symphony, and the Baltimore Symphony, among others, and his chamber music has been championed by ensembles such as the Emerson Quartet and the Chamber Music Society of Lincoln Center. Much of his violin music has been written for his wife, the violinist Rose Mary Harbison.

John Harbison has been composer-in-residence with the Pittsburgh Symphony, the Los Angeles Philharmonic, and the Tanglewood, Marlboro, Aspen, and Santa Fe Chamber Music Festivals. He was creative chair with the St. Paul Chamber Orchestra for two seasons, and as a conductor he has led a number of orchestras and chamber groups. He has been honored with a MacArthur Fellowship and the 1987 Pulitzer Prize. Harbison teaches at the Massachusetts Institute of Technology.

This interview took place in Austin, Texas, in February 1997.

•   •   •

I think I can say something about how I got into composing, which is that I played the piano, and I wanted to hear new things. I remember being quite capable of finding these new things for myself, so it didn't seem like a big jump to start emulating the composers who must have written the pieces I played for piano lessons. Although I never really had the knack for practicing other people's music, I always wanted to make pieces of my own.

My reason for composing has been different things at different times. When I started to imagine music as a profession, the "reason" was very far from my thoughts. When I was a graduate student in 1963, Elliott Carter came to give a talk at Princeton, and the discussions were about practical issues like your relationship with your publisher, how to get more performances, and so forth. We students were all rather shocked because that was not the orientation of composers and future musicians at the time. It was more of an idealistic thing with us.

Today we have the Briefcase Composers, the ones with an automatic c.v. update, but certainly the reason for composing that I developed as a very young kid seemed like a pretty good one — that is, it was a natural activity, something that I did, part of how I was occupied. I was very fortunate to be part of a community that encouraged that sort of attitude. The vocation of "composer" didn't seem to be begging for validation. I had a choral conductor in high school who would make copies of my pieces and pass them out so we would sing them. I had a sort of charmed existence there, because the choral conductor made composing seem not a peculiar thing to do. It was so integrated that sometimes I misjudged my environment slightly. One time the school principal asked me to play something in a big high school assembly. I played the piano pieces that I was playing at the time, the Schoenberg opus 19. Socially, it didn't go so smoothly — I gradually rebuilt my reputation by being a jazz player, but it took a long time.

My piano teacher was a composer and a very perceptive teacher, because she had me studying the pieces that were then new — the Sixth Bartók Quartet, Stravinsky's *Agon*. These pieces were just a few years old, so there was no sense that music was something of the past. That's why I'm always surprised to have waked up in a culture in which music is historical.

There was also in my town Roger Sessions, who was regarded as an important composer. Not many people felt they understood his music, but the sense in the community was that his presence was valuable. In the summer of 1954, I traveled to Europe for the first time to play with a jazz group, and my parents suggested I go over with Sessions, who was traveling there with his family. It was important for me to begin the trip with Sessions, to find out just how a composer lived. Of course in the case of Sessions it was not opaque because he put his profession right on his passport: "Composer." When he reentered the States, the customs guy said, "I've never heard any of your tunes." I think he sort of liked that.

It's only been gradually, as I've gone along, that issues of a composer's social value have come up. Over time, concert music has been marginalized, in terms of the intelligent people who read books and look at paintings. I've had the same kinds of worries that almost anyone in music has: if this is important, why don't we get more general confirmation?

I think the public assumes that whoever is put in front of them as the most important *is*, and of course that's wrong. In fact there are probably rock bands who play much better or as well as the ones we hear, just as I know that there are composers who are not household words but who, due to personal setbacks or other quirks, didn't see their careers work out too neatly. It's much easier to persist at the career level than at the making level. You can always get the energy for busy work, but to make the next piece is very fatiguing.

There have been a few times in my life when I've been somewhat directed toward other kinds of activity—for instance, going down to Mississippi in the summer of 1964 with the Freedom Summer people. We were doing some music there, but our primary purpose was obviously not about music. I did a good deal of thinking about whether there might be something more important for me to do with my life. Of course there could be, I suppose, but my abilities seemed to lie in a certain direction. I've never felt like I had another calling, just waiting to be answered.

I went through all the anxieties that most musicians go through early on about how to make a living. I was a conductor for awhile, and I turned out not to be very good at switching back and forth between conducting-thinking and composing-thinking. The music I conducted was very preoccupying. I used to marvel at Gunther Schuller, who seemed to be able to completely switch over without losing a second. And I began to feel that in order to do a substantial amount of both it would be necessary to have that capacity. I didn't, so I gradually scaled back.

The composing experience for me is remarkably different from project to project, because I never developed anything like a good methodology, although I always imagine that I will. I think that my process is one of recognizing what I'm doing without bringing direct pressure on it. It is very much unresponsive to direct concentration. I recognize, without putting out a stern call, that something has been accumulating. And very often I find that the way I write a piece is to not notice that I'm writing it while I'm at the same time [more consciously] writing down another one. In other words, if I finish a piece and another one hasn't started off on the side, I know I'm in real big trouble.

Usually I finish a project with much more done on the next one than I thought. That's why I've developed this procedure for having a bunch of colored notebooks around, so that I can keep my projects straight. Once some music gets started in my head, it's usually very clear which piece it is. I'll take a break from what I'm [consciously] doing at the moment and write something down in the right notebook.

I also write few pieces in sequence. I think it has to do with wanting each piece to be different from the others. I think I put a lot of stake in that. The result is that I say to myself, "I won't really get into this piece until I recognize that it has a profile of its own." So I tend to throw up quite a few roadblocks. Lately, in fact—maybe this is partly philosophical—I've been thinking that there's enough music in the world. I tend to want to resist a piece quite a bit, and not write it unless it really bothers me. I think the procrastinating and the defeating of the purpose is all to the idea that if a piece is tough enough, it'll come out, but if it isn't, it shouldn't. Maybe it's a sort of a ripening process, a waiting until I'm sure that the thing is really ready.

I don't care for real deadlines, so I usually invent primary deadlines which are before the real ones. I construe my own deadlines as important so that I don't have to work in relationship to the actual deadline. I have plenty of colleagues who are best off facing the *real* catastrophe, but I'd just freeze up at the actual deadline, become quite useless. I don't usually run very close to the real deadlines at all, which means that these pieces that are working off on the sides with their own time scales can be brought to full attention at a time when they're not under a death sentence.

I'm not sure why I work like that, but I must say I've never, as a composer or performer, particularly relished getting everything right at the last minute. I remember once when a composer gave Collage [new music ensemble] two-thirds of a new piece in the dress rehearsal, which we sight-read and then performed about three hours later. I think some people found it fun, but I felt like I had aged about a year. Maybe it's a matter of temperament.

I certainly enjoy projects that are directed by outside circumstances, but I've also had the experience, very often, of receiving a commission—either by design or good luck—for something I was already doing, anyway. Sometimes it's just synchronicity, other times it's because I'm in a good relationship with a commissioner, and I can say, "Here's the piece that is coming along; how would you like to take that?" Also, I still do pieces that are not commissioned. No one can imagine that I volunteered to write my wind quintet, because most composers don't like wind quintet. But when I got a commission for one, I was already writing it.

Some of my biggest pieces have been completely volunteer. *Motetti di Montale*, for voice and piano, which is an hour long—that would be an unlikely volunteer piece! But there have been a lot of these, and there always will be. That piece started out to be a rather modest little group of songs, and it just kind of went out of control.

I don't have orderly work habits at all, as to time of day or how much time I spend at it. And in truth, when a piece has moved into the center, I sometimes get some surprising discoveries. For instance, my piano sonata—I brought it into the center, and I said, "Now I will work with this material." I was thinking it was going to be a big piece, a little over thirty minutes long, but suddenly I realized that this piece was already finished! It's only fifteen minutes long.

I have never been a great polisher of detail. I've had students bring in scores with wonderful polish in every sound, and I say, "What have you been doing?" They say, "Oh, I've been studying Jacob Druckman's scores." I say, "Gee, I'm going to do that someday." But I don't have the knack at this point, for that kind of polish and detail. That's in the offing.

Sometimes polishing can become a trap. A kid at Cal Arts brought a piece in to me and said, "You saw this last week, when this chord was a *mezzo-forte* crescendo to *sforzando*. Now, I've taken out the *sforzando* and made it an accent." And that was all he had to show for an hour lesson.

Lately I have been giving more care to the issue of projecting details, practically speaking. In two recent pieces, I forbade myself the middle dynamic levels, *mezzo-piano* and *mezzo-forte*. I thought the projection of the piece might be enhanced by disallowing those. I was also thinking about the fact that they don't appear in Beethoven and Mozart, or Haydn, either. I like the way those two pieces of mine are marked—that was my way of burrowing in on the issue of how to make detail more telling, how to exaggerate a bit more the profile, even if it means going against the grain sometimes. I think I had the sense that I was depending too much on the performers' lived-in comprehension of the music, not the realities of the orchestral situation, and had to acknowledge the fact that 90 percent of the time the music *won't* be lived in.

I've had this ongoing dialogue with my friend Chris Rouse, who is always looking at my scores and saying, "My God, your extremes are two *f*s and two *p*s!" He says an orchestra will just go to sleep looking at that. He says five *f*s is the only thing that will wake up the players, and two *p*s is equal to what *mezzo-forte* used to be.

Well, he has a point, but I wanted to go at it in a different way, so that was the genesis of the idea of getting rid of the middles. For me, it's another approach to the problem that orchestral performances are more like sketches than full renderings. Chamber music performances can be much more particular, because small ensembles like string quartets work with each other all the time. With chamber groups, composers do have the experience of what our music might be played like if it were around awhile, but we don't get that in large ensemble situations, for the most part. So we really are challenged to try to figure out how we can help an orchestra move more quickly to a satisfying result.

It's a serious problem, and not one that I feel I have any handle on, because ultimately you do believe that performers will need to live with the music to be able to get it right. That's one of the reasons that I've come to feel that certain kinds of chamber music are what I'd be most glad to do, because there we can look for and expect and actually experience a situation where the music can become internal. We won't have to mark every little thing, because the players will hear it eventually.

We know that's true in the music that we've inherited from the past. So much is straightened out the first time in a Brahms symphony, dynamically and expressively, because we know the pieces. The most important aspects of the music are very likely to be the things that are hardest to communicate. Do you write in the tempo inflection that seems to originate in the phraseology of the music, or do you hope that people will get it, in the five or six or twenty times it will suggest itself? Those are very difficult decisions, and they have to do with the way the music is conceived.

What makes concert music so fascinating is that it is a *collaborative* venture. It's so different from the commercial world, where more and more people go to concerts of popular music expecting and demanding that it sound like it did on the records. There, much technical expertise is put at the service not of a performance that will illuminate the qualities of the music, but of one that will sound exactly as the CD did. In concert music I think we've always believed that what we want from a performance is a series of insights that may be entirely different from the ones that occurred the last time it was played.

In fact, we try to build into the piece the opportunities for this, as much as we can, such that learning a piece confirms that the performer's invention is valid; this is what all composers, over and over, hope for. Fighting always against that are commercial and practical issues that we can't just give in to. I believe that we should write pieces for orchestra that are still idealistic. If we wrote for the number of hours of rehearsal that we know we're going to get, we wouldn't be able to do very much.

I tend to need to be by myself more. I don't know why that is, but it's true, and I tend to feel that even though I may not have a methodology, there is a solitude that is helpful to me to reinforce an inspiration. I can function, for instance, with a very small library, one that I choose, of music and books. Usually a physical environment is very helpful if there is some place to get out and walk, and if it is not horribly ugly.

I don't have much need to discuss anything. I don't have a great colony aptitude, much as I find people in colonies very interesting. I also find that more and more I tend not to focus on what's happening out in the world. One of the things that almost all composers discover as they go along is that their musical world becomes more private and more peculiar. There's less willingness to take in the rest of the world, but at the same time the increasing ability to absorb solitude ensures that one's train of thought holds firmer.

One reads accounts of composers like Mahler who went to a different mountain place in the summer—I understand that better now than I did. I also understand why we insist we are inspired much by our inner state, and there are physical settings where the inner state pushes itself up into the right place more easily.

Working in Wisconsin [at a farm he and Rose Mary Harbison own and go to in the summers] has been more difficult since we have a summer festival there [the Token Creek Chamber Music Festival]. It's now a very professional situation, so it's changed the way we relate to our surroundings. For that reason I've stayed away from composing there in recent years.

Britten used to talk about his confidence going up and down. I think it is true that some projects just won't go well if you're telling yourself what crap you are every day. Perhaps some type of insulation is good. Stravinsky, in his seventies, living in Hollywood, had Vera screening every bit of information that came in, including the reviews. Every once in awhile one would get through and he would be thrown off his game for a week or two. The most incredible one of all is Verdi, who got so upset about what some jerk wrote about *Aïda* in a small paper in provincial Italy that for close to a year he did nothing but pursue a kind of polemics against this critic. Now, that's a loss! It would have been better if Giussepina had grabbed that review before it landed on his table. Nobody, no matter how immune they claim to be, is immune to what is said about them.

You're not working for the audience who doesn't have enough time to really learn the piece, and you're not working for the critics, for God's sake. You're working for yourself and whichever members of your community will live with your music at a substantial level, give you some degree of support. Support is a very multicolored thing. It includes the people who will actually tell you, in one way or another, if you're on the track or off the track. But only when you know the source well should you listen to it, at all.

When I was a student I asked Maxwell Davies, who had already done quite a lot as a composer, if he worried about whether what he was writing was any good. "Good?" he said. "I don't have time for that." I like the flavor of that very much, because he was simply making his best effort. More and more I'm choosing what to do on the basis of whether it's something I *want* to do, not on the basis of whether I think it's a *better* thing to do.

There's a level of revising in which you're just trying to get a clearer rendering, and then there's the much more painful matter of real surgery. In revising you want to feel that even if what you take out is *good*, it's just not right for this situation. It seems to me our critical faculties are best put into play in the interstices, when we've made the large-scale decisions about the kind of thing we want.

The revision work after the performance I don't have much stomach for. I have friend, Nick Maw, who is a really wonderful composer. For him the performance is the preliminary stage, and afterward, he'll really get down, work this thing out. He'll chop out half of a movement. I try to do that beforehand, if it's necessary. I can't imagine what it would be like to be him, cutting almost half of the last movement of his violin concerto. That he did it in a public arena, with everyone having heard the first version, strikes me as quite amazing. That kind of "cut your heart out" revision is more often done in the theater. I like to just send my piece on, do something else.

Tchaikovsky's letter about his Fifth Symphony always interested me tremendously, because he had a tough time with that piece. Many things were sort of hung together, and he thought it sounded terrible. But the listener doesn't care how jerrybuilt and uninspired some of the music seemed to him. He was too good a composer not to convince us that we were hearing pure inspiration.

With Mozart, if a movement wasn't running right he would often just start over again. That turned out to be a good strategy for him. The decision to do that never feels good—kind of sad, actually. But eventually you have to come to a more level point of view. Just having been very good and worked very hard doesn't amount to anything. Only the result matters.

The whole idea of being paid to write music doesn't justify itself in terms of any given piece. Some cost you a lot, some you get for free. In the end, I think you're being paid for your ability rather than for your work. We're never going to have a glut of truly serious artists, because the price is too high.

Writing for specific performers can make composing easier. I can sometimes reduce the possibilities of a composition in the most productive way by focusing on the people that it's for. Reducing possibilities is very important, because that gives the piece its character, its profile.

Another thing that's sometimes easy about composing is getting an idea for a project that is very global, which makes an otherwise kind of intractable task fall together very simply. For instance, I was asked to write a saxophone sonata. Now sax and piano is not a combination I would go looking for. But I had an idea to base the piece on a rather momentary experience of hearing a Latino group play in San Antonio. It's a kind of touristic piece, in the sense that I have absolutely no claim on knowing what that music really is—only what sort of stayed in my head. Once that premise was established, writing the sonata for the alto sax and piano suddenly became no problem.

I tend to not choose the texts I set too consciously—I'd rather they be things that I've been concerned about for a very long time. Very often the composing of the piece is an effort to put that text to rest. Sometimes I succeed in that, and sometimes I remain interested in the writer involved, but I don't care to set him anymore. I work with a poet and maybe set a good deal of text by him, hoping in some way to sort of solve my relationship to this poet.

I can't imagine spending an entire life with Lorca, like George Crumb has, or just staying with Alice [in Wonderland], like David Del Tredici has. If you're a musician, you're very glad that music isn't explicit. The text that you set is as confessional as you wish to get, I think. But the texts do add up, and with the composers that I know, they certainly are very indicative. In cases like Schubert's, they're as close to a reliable character study as we have.

Working with a librettist has never appealed to me at all. To have that relationship become a daily discussion would drive me nuts. What happens when you set words to music is that you displace the words, quite violently, and turn them into something else. Only the most musically sophisticated or dense poets can stand that. All of those in the middle, which is about 85 percent, are going to be very uncomfortable. I understand that, given their profession, but as a working relationship, it's not good.

There's an argument to make for setting poems that are mediocre, poems that might not stand so well on their own. And certainly there have been plenty of examples in history. But I would also argue that a really terrific setting of a great poem can go much further. (Although maybe I'm wrong about that—you can't go any further than *Winterreise*, and those aren't great poems.) The difficulty of setting any kind of great literature is that it's already realized and complete. There are certain Emily Dickinson poems where she seems to have not quite got it worked out. It always struck me that those are the perfect ones to set to music.

The church I write for is my community, but I also think of it as a great arena with a rather little filter. That is, people are listening differently—the critic's not part of the mix. It's a completely different environment where it's possible to reach out to an audience and form a bond with it. Those are advantages that I can't find anywhere else. The relationship between the provider of the music and the receptor is totally altered by the occasion and by the simplicity of response, and that to me has been very nourishing. The choir that I write for is extraordinary—that makes a big difference. I do think the condition of a less critical response is one of the reasons that both Stravinsky and Schoenberg wrote their best pieces as sacred music.

If you were to look at the music of this century as a whole, the percentage of the best of it that is sacred in a supposedly secular century is a bit shocking. Poulenc found a whole new dimension there. A third of Dallapiccola takes advantage of a kind of dialogue with the divine. Steve Reich's big pieces fall into that category. *Tehellim* is totally in the tradition of the ritualistic side of sacred music. The performance arena for almost all of this has not been in the church, but that doesn't change the psychic realm of the composer.

I've been through phases in my life where I was very down on everything I was doing, also phases where I was quite confident. Obviously, it's better to work from confidence, in terms of the experience. Maybe the work is better, too, although it's not altogether clear in my case if that's true. I am more and more trying to deemphasize the doubt that I once thought might be productive, because I don't really believe it functions positively or even particularly negatively. All the hours that I used to spend, trying to pull myself off the floor of depression to do some work, were to some degree wasted. Work feeds on itself, of course, and I think that if you have something valuable to convey about your view of the world, and your temperament, you'll do that anyway, no matter what state of mind you are in at the moment.

John Harbison, Selected Works

SMALL ENSEMBLE

Between Two Worlds (1991)
soprano, two pianos, two
    cellos
text: Robert Bly, Jacob Boehme

The Rewaking (1991)
soprano and string quartet
text: William Carlos Williams

String Quartet no. 1 (1985), no. 2
    (1987), no. 3 (1993)

Words from Paterson (1989)
baritone and six players
text: William Carlos Williams

LARGE ENSEMBLE

Concerto for Cello (1993)
cello and orchestra

Concerto for Oboe (1991)
oboe and orchestra

Concerto for Viola (1989)
viola and orchestra

The Most Often Used Chords
    (Gli Accordi Piú Usati)
    (1993)
chamber orchestra

Symphony no. 1 (1981), no. 2
    (1987); no. 3 (1991)
orchestra

Three City Blocks (1992)
wind ensemble

Two Emmanuel Motets (1990)
a cappella chorus

Publisher: Associated Music
    Publishers, 257 Park Avenue
    South, 20th floor, New York, NY
    10010. Tel. 212-254-2100;
    fax 212-254-2013.

John Harbison, Selected Discography

Concerto for Double Brass Choir
    and Orchestra
Los Angeles Philharmonic/
    Previn
New World 80395-2

The Flight into Egypt
Roberta Anderson, soprano;
    Sanford Sylvan, baritone;
    Cantata Singers
and Ensemble/Hoose
New World Records CD 80395-2

Mirabai Songs for soprano and
    orchestra
Dawn Upshaw, soprano; Orchestra
    of St. Luke's/Zinman
Nonesuch CD 79187-2/4

The Natural World for mezzo-
    soprano, flute, clarinet, violin,
    cello, and piano

Janice Felty, mezzo-soprano;
    Los Angeles Philharmonic
    New Music Group/Harbison
New World Records CD 80395-2

Sonata No. 1 for Piano, *Roger
    Sessions in Memoriam*
Robert Shannon, piano
Bridge BCD 9036

Songs of Solitude
Curtis Macomber, violin
CRI CD 706

Symphony no. 1
Boston Symphony
    Orchestra/Ozawa
New World Digital NW 80331-2

Symphony no. 2
San Francisco Symphony/
    Blomstedt
London 443 3762-2

Three City Blocks
Cincinnati Wind Symphony/
    Corporon
Klavier KCD 11059

Variations for violin, clarinet, and
    piano
American Chamber Players
Koch International Classics
    3-7027-2/4

JOAN TOWER

$(\text{B. }1938)$

J oan Tower was born in New Rochelle, New York, spent her childhood in
South America, and returned to the United States to study at Bennington
College and Columbia University. In 1969 she founded the Da Capo
Chamber Players, a new music ensemble that won the Naumburg Award for
chamber music in 1973. Tower continued to perform as pianist with Da Capo
until 1984, and many of her chamber works were written for members of the
New York–based group, which continues to flourish.

From 1985 to 1988, Tower was composer-in-residence with the Saint Louis
Symphony as part of the Meet-the-Composer Orchestra Residency program.
Silver Ladders, written in 1987 as part of her three-year residency with that
orchestra, won the 1990 Grawemeyer Award for music composition. Joan
Tower's music has been performed by the Chicago Symphony, the New York
Philharmonic, the Los Angeles Chamber Orchestra, pianist Ursula Oppens,
clarinetist Richard Stoltzman, the Chamber Music Society of Lincoln Center,
and others. Among her recent commissions are those for the Pittsburgh Symphony, pianist Emmanuel Ax, and violist Paul Neubauer. Joan Tower has
taught at Bard College since 1972. This interview took place in Vinalhaven,
Maine, in June 1995.

·   ·   ·

The reasons why I compose are tied up with so many issues. I started as a pianist, and I played the piano for many years. Then at Bennington someone

asked me to write a piece. I was eighteen, and I wrote this piece, and when I heard it, it was such an incredible experience—as if I was looking at my musical soul hanging on the wall. Boom! There it was with all its problems: too long, too high, too loud. I was very vulnerable to this external object coming back at me.

So I was hooked. I had to do it again and again and again. Except that getting up and playing Beethoven was a lot easier—it was this powerful music, and all I had to do was read the directions to get it to come alive. It was much easier than trying to produce my own music. So I underwent a long conflict between playing and composing. Big conflict! That went on for many years. I actually gave up composing several times because it was too hard. Once I even announced to my friends: "That's it! I've had it with this, I am not composing anymore!" And they looked at me and said, "Right. Sure. You'll be back."

What happened to change this was that my pieces started to get played, much to my amazement. My first reaction was: "You want to play *that* piece?" I needed encouragement and confidence-building to help me with this tortured relationship I had to composing. Gradually I started doing more. The more encouragement I got, the more I composed and the less I played, and finally I gave up performing in 1985 to devote myself full-time to composing. I was already forty-something years old.

Up until 1976 lots of my pieces were for my group, the Da Capo Chamber Players, or its individual members. Da Capo gave me the chance to be in an extraordinary relationship with players. I could work with them, I could argue with them. It was like having a laboratory, but also a family, because we were like siblings. Making music with them and for them, in addition to lifting the music of the other contemporary composers we worked with off the page, was an invaluable musical education for me. It taught me how to think about written music in relation to the players—how to try to make a very finite set of notated instructions come alive for a performer.

I don't usually use external sources as inspiration. I've never even written a song. It's usually just me and my notes. Every piece has a personality that takes hold, and I try to respect that, "listen" to it very carefully before I go forward.

There are all kinds of therapeutic things I do around composing. I used to draw or play with words, but these were just ways of getting started. I don't think any of that had a direct impact on the way I wrote. The actual stuff of composing music, once it starts happening, is a hard thing to articulate. Music has a life of its own, no matter what kinds of "outside" things you bring to it. Berg, for example, was (in some of his works) a numbers man. His theory is mind-boggling to me, because his luscious romantic pieces sound like they're coming from the heart. If he's got the number thirteen organizing a certain part, I don't really want to know about it. What I care about is the musical result. Cage used to throw dice, and other composers have tried to depict nature in some form. But music still has a separate life apart from all that. I try to reach the core of my "voice" any way I can.

I'm a very hands-on person. I start with an idea, two notes, four notes, and then I start sculpting it. I distrust precompositional thinking, because it can never be all-inclusive; it forces you by definition to think about one thing at a time. Precompositional thinking would be like laying out your materials for a house. You could say, "Well, I'm going to have bricks—how many bricks do I need?" I have real trouble with that, because in writing music, you're dealing with a whole range of complex parameters at once, right from the start. You have to consider time, space, rhythm, dynamics, pitches, color, all of which together create the personality of the piece. If you isolate one element, you don't have a personality formed. You only have a brick. I like to start with the identity right away, using everything I have.

My ideal setup for work is a quiet place. I have a beautiful view from my small studio, where I spend about five hours a day, when I'm not teaching or traveling. I write on the average about two-and-a-half minutes of music a month, which is slow, but I need that much time to let my original idea settle down into a consistent response.

I don't show my music to anyone until after it's been premiered.

I made the mistake of doing that—once. I took my first orchestra score, *Sequoia*, to Bill Schuman. He was a very charming man, but when he looked at my score, he said, "Piano won't be heard there. You won't get any horns there—you won't get *any* horns." I was so vulnerable because it was my first orchestra piece, and I was showing it to a really good orchestra composer. I was really nervous, something he didn't seem to notice.

Once I hear a new piece played, I may make cosmetic changes, usually orchestration or dynamics. Very rarely will I rewrite a section of the piece, because once you start doing that, it's like balancing a mobile. You take weight out of one place, and it shifts here, and pretty soon the whole thing has to shift somewhere else. Revising is complicated. You have to be very careful how you do it. It's better to solve a problem in the next piece.

I try to learn from the strengths and weaknesses of those pieces I've already written, and grow with the next one. It's one of the many reasons I keep writing.

Composing for me used to be an agonizing process, and now it's a challenging process. I took the torture out of it because after years and years of saying to myself, "The only way you can do this is to be tortured eight hours a day," I realized I was being ridiculous. So I backed off a little with the torture. It's still very difficult work. You have to be infinitely patient, and you have to be a very good listener. You have to be alert to every little move you're making.

I tell my students you have four perceptions of your work, and all you have are those—it doesn't matter what anyone else tells you. The first perception is: "This is great." Second one is: "This is horrible." The third one is fickle: "Oh, this is great," followed immediately by "This is terrible." The fourth one is the worst: no reaction. You write something, and it leaves you blank. That's the hardest one to deal with. Since all you really have are your own perceptions, you have to trust them enough to let them take hold.

In spite of all the success I've had with my pieces, composing hasn't gotten any easier, except in one sense: the fact that the music is played gives me confidence that my decision-making process is not as bad as I think it is.

Humility is important. Even if you win prizes, they actually don't do much. They really don't. They may go into a résumé or a book, and somebody may be impressed. But what's much more important is that the music gets played. That means that musicians like it, and they're picking it up, and that gives me a kind of inner fuel. Prizes do not contain that fuel.

I think the best composers tend to be the most self-critical, and really good musicians tend to be survivalists. Somewhere in their past they were challenged to survive in some capacity, probably emotionally. They need to express themselves through music.

It was that way for me. When I was growing up, I had a mother who talked a lot, and I became quiet. I was a rebel, but I couldn't get a word in edgewise. My father was very musical, so I inherited his talent, I guess. When I started the piano, I found I could express myself. And then after a lot of therapy and all kinds of other experiences I found I could convey strong emotions— anger and energy and love—this way. Music was the place where I could say whatever I wanted. It was very important for me to do that, and it still is. I was talking about this with a couple of players yesterday. They had the same experience. The instrument became a way of expressing themselves because they couldn't do it any other way. Then it became their life.

Composing is self-discovery, too. When you start writing as a young composer, you write the way you think you should be writing because that's the way your teacher or your colleagues write. When I first got out of school, I hung around a lot of serial composers and was into the twelve-tone stuff, heavily. I was playing it, so my music was fairly twelve-tone-based at that time.

But after about ten years I found my own voice. My piece *Black Topaz* [solo piano, flute, clarinet/bass clarinet, trumpet, trombone, percussion; 1976] was a real honest-to-God, raw attempt at being myself. It was first done at one of these uptown [New York] concerts. I'll never forget it. My composer colleagues thought I had flipped out, gone totally nuts. They hated the piece, and the conductor hated the piece, and everybody hated the piece except the pianist. I wanted to fly to Australia, you know? But it was a real gutsy move for me. It meant that I had to stand up for myself and say, "Hey, I *like* drums— I *like* rhythmic energy—I *like* simple colors!" This was at a time when you didn't do anything simple. It was a real door-opener for me, because after that my own voice started to take shape. It's a move everyone has to make if they're really serious, and it's terrifying, because you have to stand alone.

And it was a *necessary* act—as a pianist, I was bored with being an acrobat. I'd been playing a lot of material where I was counting seven in the time of six and trying to get the grace note with the flutist, you know? After ten years of this, I just said, "I don't want to be an acrobat anymore."

I remember going out to hear a piece by Messiaen: the *Quartet for the End of Time*. I attended this concert at a point when I was heavily involved in serial music, and I thought, "My God, this Messiaen guy is so gutsy—I cannot not believe how gutsy he is." Then I heard another piece, George Crumb's *Voice of the Whale*. He had the *guts* to write such simple music! That had a profound effect on me. From that day on I started being less and less impressed with all the heads around me, like Milton Babbitt, Charles Wuorinen, and all those people. I didn't belong in that crowd! They just happened to be the people I hooked up with when I was coming out of school. It's amazing, the circumstances—it's like I took a ten-year detour.

I think I could have come out of that a lot sooner. I also think I should not have gone for a doctorate, which took me fourteen years and was generally a waste of time. But at that time, you had to have a doctorate to get a teaching job. I did it as slowly as possible, because I hated being in the library. I wanted to be out making music. That's what kept me going.

Working with performers really feeds me. When I hand a piece of mine to performers, and they love the piece, that is the most beautiful thing in the world. They don't know me from Adam, they have no agenda other than making music. When that happens, I feel like I've contributed something to their lives.

Here's a story I like to tell to show the power of music, and also the power of the blueprint, the notated page. I went to Arizona to listen to a concert of my music, and I was supposed to meet a student who was going to play my guitar piece *Clocks*. It's a very hard piece. So I went to the hall. The first meeting with a performer who has been working on your piece is telling, you know. It was very dark, and he wasn't there, and I sat there waiting, and finally he came on stage. He was a tall Native American man with a black ponytail. So I said, "Oh, *hi!*" And he just looked at me and said, "Mm."

I thought, "Well, either he can't play the piece or he doesn't like it or he just wishes he could get the hell out of here." So I said, "Do you want me to sit in the audience and listen?" And he went, "Mm," opened his case, and took out his guitar. He didn't have any music. Then he sat down and played the holy bejesus out of my piece. I realized then that he had spent at least three months, three hours a day, on this piece. He knew every corner of it by heart, he had shaped every phrase. I was in tears by the time he finished. I wiped my eyes and went up to the stage and said, "That was one of the most beautiful performances I've ever heard." And he went, "Mm," and put his guitar back in the case and left.

We'd had no contact, except through the music. There wasn't much I could say to him about anything, and he obviously didn't want to talk about it. But he knew me very well, and I knew him very well, through that performance. It was like our souls had met through the printed page.

I run a course at Bard College called "Composition Seminar," but I don't think you can teach composition. What I do is act as a traffic cop, a facilitator. I set up a situation where I bring players to the school to tape student works. I just make sure that the students know what they have on paper, that they care about it, and that it expresses something about them. That's all I do, and that's a lot of work right there. I think the best teaching of composition is through listening, so I just try to keep that opportunity rolling in the curriculum. I try to keep myself as a personality out of the picture as much as possible so the students can hear themselves.

Right now I'm trying to understand the whole process of becoming a composer, and a woman composer in particular. We're all taught by males, basically, and the books and the curriculum are all-male. There's an incredible network of structures—in terms of the way things are taught, read, published, reported—which are all-male. There are also all-male networks of funding. I always felt like an outsider, but I never understood quite why. I'm just beginning to piece this together.

It looks to most composers that I am not an outsider, because I used to travel with the uptown crowd in New York. That's where I went to school and where I performed. But I stepped away from that, and I've been pretty independent ever since. When you get tossed around in the world you have to hold onto something, and what I've been holding onto is my music. Now that I have more internal confidence and some leverage, I can try to help other women composers.

In the 1940s, Copland was asked why there were no great women composers, and he said it was because they couldn't think in long forms.

Well, Da Capo did a concert of his music on his eightieth birthday, and I asked him, "Do you have a different opinion now?" He didn't answer.

Women have certainly had a very hard time in the arts, though the situation is changing. It's changing in the academic curriculum because there's a lot of pressure on musicologists to revise their thinking about women in the canon. But even though a woman may be encouraged to get a degree, once she's out of school she's less likely to be in the network her teachers are part of. I see a lot of good woman composers out there who are floundering— they can't get jobs, they're not getting their music played. We're talking about very isolated people. It's true that over the last fifteen years more women composers have been included in books and there have been a few more recordings and publications of their work, but we still have a long way to go.

Joan Tower, Selected Works

SOLO, SMALL ENSEMBLE

Black Topaz (1976)
piano, flute, clarinet/bass clarinet,
    trumpet, trombone, two
    percussion

Clocks (1985)
solo guitar

Night Fields (1994)
string quartet

Petroushkates (1980)
flute, clarinet, violin, cello, piano

Turning Points (1995)
clarinet and string quartet

LARGE ENSEMBLE

Concerto for Orchestra (1991)

Music for Cello and Orchestra (1984)

Rapids (1996)
Piano Concerto no. 2

Sequoia (1981)
orchestra

Silver Ladders (1986)
orchestra

Publisher: Associated Music
    Publishers, 257 Park Avenue
    South, 20th floor, New York,
    NY 10010. Tel. 212-254-2100;
    fax 212-254-2013.

Joan Tower, Selected Recordings

Black Topaz for piano and six
    instruments; *Night Fields* for
    string quartet; *Snow Dreams* for
    flute and guitar; *Trés Lent* (in
    memoriam Olivier Messiaen)
    for cello and piano
Muir Quartet; Sharon Isbin,
    guitar; Carol Wincenc, flute;
    André Emelianoff, cello; Joan
    Tower, piano and conductor
New World Records 80470-2

Breakfast Rhythms I and II for
    clarinet and five instruments;
    Concerto for Clarinet and
    Orchestra; *Fantasy . . . Harbor
    Lights* for clarinet and piano;
    Wings for clarinet solo
Robert Spring, clarinet; Eckart
    Sellheim, piano; Ensemble
    21/Weisberg
Summit Records CD DCD 124

Concerto for Clarinet and Orches-
    tra; Concerto for Flute and
    Orchestra; Concerto for Piano
    and Orchestra; Concerto for
    Violin and Orchestra
David Shifrin, clarinet; Carol
    Wincenc, flute; Ursula Oppens,
    piano; Elmar Oliveira, violin;
    Louisville Orchestra/Bragado-
    Darman, Silverstein
D'Note Classics DND 1016

Island Prelude for oboe and string
    orchestra
Peter Bowman, oboe; Saint Louis
    Symphony/Slatkin
Nonesuch CD 9 79245-2

Island Rhythms overture for
    orchestra
Louisville Orchestra/Smith
First Edition Recordings LCD006

Music for Cello and Orchestra;
    Sequoia; *Silver Ladders*
Lynn Harrell, cello; Saint Louis
    Symphony/Slatkin
Nonesuch CD 9 79245-2-ZK

JOHN ADAMS

$\left(\text{B. }1947\right)$

John Adams grew up in Vermont and New Hampshire. As a student at Harvard University he was active as a conductor, clarinetist, and composer. His composition teachers included Leon Kirchner, David Del Tredici, and Roger Sessions.

In 1971 Adams left the East Coast to establish his professional career in the San Francisco area, teaching at the San Francisco Conservatory of Music and serving as new music adviser and composer-in-residence for the San Francisco Symphony. His output spans a wide range of media: orchestra, opera, video, film, and dance, as well as electronic and chamber music. Such pieces as *Harmonium* and *Harmonielehre* (written for the San Francisco Symphony) and *The Chairman Dances* (from his opera *Nixon in China*, commissioned by the Houston Grand Opera) are among the most frequently performed contemporary American works. In 1995, he received the Grawemeyer Award for his violin Concerto, commissioned by the Minnesota Orchestra. Although he is often termed a "minimalist," Adams feels that his music can't be so exactly defined.

In addition to his work as a composer, John Adams is often on the road conducting twentieth-century music. He has been creative chair of the St. Paul Chamber Orchestra and music director of the Ojai Festival, led several tours with Ensemble Modern, and conducted major orchestras in the United States and Europe. John Adams lives in Berkeley. This interview took place in Cincinnati in April 1997.

•   •   •

I imagined a life as a composer at an almost alarmingly early age. At about seven or eight years old, I had a very highly defined imaginative life in which I thought of myself as a fully active adult composer.

I think the signal event of my youth was the bicentenary of Mozart's birth (already a depressing thought, because the bicentenary of his death has already come and gone!). I was in the third grade at the time, going to a very small grammar school in a tiny town in New Hampshire, and the third grade teacher, who was a rather sophisticated woman, read a child's biography of Mozart to the class. All the other kids were probably bored out of their minds, but I was completely enchanted by the idea of a young boy who could compose symphonies and concerti. I think that was the beginning for me of a very strong fantasy life.

My parents were both musicians but not professional musicians. My father played in big bands during the depression, and my mother was a very gifted amateur singer and actress. They had enormous love and respect for all kinds of music—not only classical music, but jazz and folk music. It was a very supportive environment to grow up in. When I was about seven years old, I wanted to study the violin, but the program for teaching instruments in the public schools wouldn't allow me to take lessons at that age. So I reluctantly took up the clarinet, because my dad could play it, and he taught me, and that became my instrument. I played it straight through until I was about twenty-five, and then I gave it up. I got bored with it.

I think early on, composing became associated in my mind with my development as a human being—with the deepest aspects of psychological and spiritual growth. I feel that if I go for a significant period without composing, I've somehow lost something irretrievable. For me, creative work is a mirror of my spiritual evolution, and it's been that way for many, many years, even though some of the results of my creative activity can seem to be pretty far from divine revelation—*Grand Pianola* or whatever! I'm not talking Arvo Pärt here, or Gorecki or Holy Minimalism. But I have never been tied to one essential way of expressing myself, and my work can be not only earnest but also ironic and raucous and vulgar. Whatever the mood I may be writing in, composing music remains a kind of measure of my "pilgrim's progress." I guess it's a very Puritan attitude, considering the New England Protestant environment that I grew up in. I can see that in Ives as well. Ives means a great deal to me, because I understand the environment and the spiritual milieu in which his work was created.

I was a very serious churchgoer when I was a kid. I went to the Episcopal Church and then the Unitarian Church. At some point in my late adolescence I stopped being a practitioner of organized religion, and I think at that point music became the substitute for that need. I've always had a very philosophical bent. I'm very interested in the history of American Buddhism, and particularly in the way that Buddhism has developed in California, something that has harmonized very much with my worldview. I think that in many of my pieces, even the ones that seem rather rowdy on the surface, there is always an underlying sense of a transcendental quest, the kind of feeling that you find in the Ives Fourth Symphony, or the *Concord Sonata*.

I recently recorded *Harmonium*, which is an early work. I was afraid when I went back to it that I would find it a little too dreamy and romantic, but in fact I found it still a very direct and genuine piece. If anything worries me now, it's whether my recent pieces have the level of passionate commitment that my earlier pieces had. I have to ask that of myself all the time. There's always a danger of overcommitting, of wanting to please. You can find yourself in a day-to-day grind, where composing begins to be a matter of racing the clock. I'm always having to step back and say to myself, "Don't do this unless it really has an absolute need to exist."

During the mid- to late 1960s, when I was an undergraduate, I felt very frustrated with the world of composing because at that time, the models were essentially the European avant-garde, particularly Schoenberg and Webern. I felt very alienated from that. I'm sure I wasn't the only young student who was trying to find a way to make a separate peace with this kind of music. That may have been the period when I became more interested in conducting, because it was a way out of what I felt was a really depressing orthodoxy. It was also one of the main reasons that I finally left the East Coast and academia and went to California.

I consider *Phrygian Gates* [for piano, 1977] to be my first really complete and unified piece, and it also marked the beginning of a style that people could associate with my work. That came about as a result of my exposure to minimalism, which was a key discovery for me. I had always experienced music tonally and was very drawn to certain aspects of American music— pulsation, beat, the sense of movement that characterizes a lot of ethnic music and jazz. I heard my first minimalist pieces at the perfect point in my compositional life—I was in my late twenties, and just beginning to take cognizance of who I was as a composer. This music suggested a way out of the old European models, and even though most of the examples available then were simplistic, it seemed fresh and very much in tune with the way people were feeling at the time. It certainly seemed to have a lot more in common with my life as an American living in California in the 1970s than did the music of the European avant-garde composers like Berio or Xenakis or Stockhausen.

My style has never been as pure or refined or isolated in its own language as some other modern composers, like Reich, for example, or Conlon Nancarrow or Morton Feldman. I like to think my music is much more promiscuous. I don't think that that's a negative characterization of it. In fact, I think that's the defining position now with composers who are younger than I am. I can think of almost no composer now in his or her thirties whose music is as rigorously pure as what was being created twenty years ago.

Everyone has unique work habits. Some composers go to work like it's a blue-collar job. Others, like Schoenberg and Rilke, may go for months, if not years, and then have a fantastic white heat and create something like *Erwartung* or *Dueno Elegies* in a very short period of days or weeks. But I am the sort for whom a daily contact with my art is essential. For me, the creative act is not unlike being an athlete. If you're in shape, things tend to flow, and if you're out of shape, it takes some patience and effort to get back in. If I've been away traveling for two or three weeks, I can often have a difficult, stubborn time getting going again.

The process is very private, actually—it's easier to say what I don't do. I am not the kind of composer who sits at a table with nothing but a pencil and paper, although I very much admire that kind of composer. I need to have the sound in front of me, in my hands as it were, like a sculptor. So I've always worked with some kind of mechanism, the piano or a tape recorder or a synthesizer, in order to hear and feel the sound as I make the piece. My principal ideas are often as much physical as they are acoustical. In that sense the initial stages of a new work are often very choreographic. They're felt in the gut, so to speak.

In some respects, the process depends on what kind of piece I am writing. If it's a stage work, of course, I'm working from the text. With both *Nixon in China* and *The Death of Klinghoffer*, my two operas, and also with *I Was Looking at the Ceiling and Then I Saw the Sky* [a song play in two acts] I made a short score: a very stripped-down piano/vocal sketch. That was a practicality, because the singers needed their music long before the orchestration was even begun. When I went back to flesh it out I not only orchestrated, but I actually composed, very thoroughly and in great detail, the rest of the music.

In the cases of orchestra pieces or string quartets or other pieces that don't involve a text, I tend to do everything in full-blown detail from the start. I don't make a rough sketch.

I wish I could say I cogitate a great deal before I begin a piece, but it's not necessarily the case. The way I work probably goes back to my Puritan roots. I work daily, and on commission, so I have this strange, subconscious blue-collar attitude: "Oh! Got to get to work!" I often start with an image. It could be a very strong image, like the image of the ship taking off into space like a rocket (the beginning of *Harmonielehre*). At other times an idea just seems to slide in almost unannounced, a very simple, pulsing wavelike motive that gradually gives birth to a much larger image or set of images. That's certainly the case with *Harmonium* and also with the piece I am working on right now, *Century Rolls*, a piano concerto of sorts. Once a piece gets going, I'll have ideas about what's coming on later. In both cases, that opening gesture leads to something else, which leads to something else, which leads to something else.

Starting a new piece is very hard, because I have very high hopes that this is really going to be the piece. What usually comes is a terrible disappointment. At some point—a week, or two weeks, or even a month later—I might still be sketching and throwing away, and sketching and throwing away, and finally I have to say, "Well, today, no matter what, this has gotta be it." Then this terrible sense of depression comes over me, and I think, "Is this really all it's going to be? Can't I come up with a better idea?" But I have to just go ahead, and this is why I always work with a deadline. If I didn't have that date, not too far in the future, a crisis of confidence might overwhelm me, and I'd simply stop.

Beginning a new piece is like the sperm and the egg coming together. When the genetic profile is set, it's a very delicate moment. And since my creative life has become so tied up with my feeling of spiritual growth, I take this terribly seriously! It isn't so much what other people think about the work; it's what I think about it. But I know that once I get going, the piece will take on forward energy and pick up steam as it moves along. Very often I go back and rewrite the opening. I can think of three or four pieces where I completely trashed the opening or added one. The original version of the *Chamber Symphony* didn't have that ten- or twelve-bar introduction. I realized after I finished it that I needed some little bristling, brisk fanfare to kick the thing off.

I had a wonderful experience when I wrote *Ceiling/Sky* because I was working in the pop song mode. This was a tremendous education for me, because as a minimalist, I had become very self-indulgent—people expected a piece of mine would take five minutes to get off the runway, you know? Working in the pop song mode, I realized that my very first idea had to be really good, and that I had to get to the point within the first twenty seconds of the song, or it would flop. I'm very proud of the songs.

I used to outline all of my pieces at the beginning, particularly when I worked at the piano. I would write a short score with four or five lines and then go back and make a more detailed score. But nowadays I use the MIDI system, and because my music still bears traces of minimalism and tends still to have a pulsation, a sequencer program works very well for me. It's quite easy to enter what I've done into a sequencer and play it back via MIDI. I find it a very creative environment to work in, because I can cut and paste, and invert, and try things out. I have a little software module that I've created which I call my Earbox. It has a large number of transposed scales and modes in it, some of which I took straight from the Slonimsky *Thesaurus* [Nicolas Slonimsky, *Thesaurus of Scales and Melodic Patterns*, 1947] and others that I made up myself. It exists permanently in my software system, so I can take any passage that I've composed and multiply it by one of the modes in the Earbox to create a different color or emotional effect. I first employed this Earbox in the second movement of the *Chamber Symphony* [1992], and I made extensive use of it in the violin concerto. I even named a recent piece *Slonimsky's Earbox* partly out of homage to Slonimsky.

I listen back constantly to what I've done. In the old days I'd slug through it on the piano. But because I am a very bad pianist, I've developed other ways of surveying my music. For years I worked with an eight-channel tape recorder that allowed me to make an extremely primitive version of what I was doing. A lot of *Nixon in China* was tried out by laying down tracks on an eight-channel tapedeck with a piano, which was very laborious. Nowadays MIDI makes it a lot easier for me. I can listen over and over to something, and make judgments about the architectural scale of the piece. Often I will discover that I have made a wrong turn and will have to scrap a long section or seriously redesign it.

You can make wrong turns in many directions. You can make them on architectonic levels; you can make them on — God forbid — levels of taste. One day you're in an insouciant mood and you think, "Oh, what the hell, I'm gonna do this." Two days later you come to your senses and say, "No, that's just not right for the piece."

I get a lot of ideas by listening to other music. I'm always aware of that famous quote of Stravinsky, that the talented composer borrows, and the genius steals. But when you get an idea from another piece, it doesn't necessarily lead to a whole-cloth case of theft. You hear something — it may just be some tiny detail in someone else's piece, or even a pop song or a piece of ethnic music — and you think, "What an interesting connection that is. What if I took that one little idea, and turned it around, or expanded it, or took what is background and made it foreground?" Often the "borrowing" or the "stealing" is so attenuated and so transformed that it has nothing to do with its original source. I'm sure that that's very much how Stravinsky operated, and why he never felt the need to repress his wonderfully omnivorous appetite for all kinds of music.

Over the years I have come to trust my subconscious when it comes to making really important musical decisions. In fact, my principal criticism about the modernist movement in music is that it seemed to deny the unconscious (unlike modernist painting, which was all about the unconscious). We had Milton Babbitt, and Peter Maxwell Davies, and Pierre Boulez, each with an above-board, rationalized method of how a piece is composed, and each with an apparent discomfort about the unknown that lies beneath. This is, for example, why I'm far more attracted and continue to be far more attracted to the pre-twelve-tone Schoenberg. The Schoenberg of *Erwartung* or the Second String Quartet or *Pierrot Lunaire* is to me far more spontaneous and effective than the more didactic, rational Schoenberg of the opus 23 Suite, or the Piano Concerto.

I'm extremely critical of my new pieces. They inevitably give me enormous pain. I hear nothing but what's wrong with them. Fortunately, if one stays around long enough, one gets to hear one's earlier pieces and be satisfied with them—they can often surprise you and give you great delight. I feel that way about *The Death of Klinghoffer* now, and for years I wasn't sure about it.

I have withdrawn several pieces, and I live in terror that after I die somebody's going to dig them out and play them. If a composer has withdrawn a piece, the rest of the world should have the courtesy not to find it and play it. The most notorious example of a piece that I had to call back and completely rework was *Shaker Loops*, which began as a string quartet, under a different title. I was a very young composer at the time, just beginning to feel my way into my own personal language, and I didn't quite know how to achieve it.

This piece was performed publicly in 1977 by the Kronos Quartet in their previous embodiment. It was a dreadful experience. I was sitting in the back row and was so embarrassed and ashamed that I fled the hall—an act of sheer cowardice! I did not even go to the stage to stand and bow with the string quartet. But I knew that despite the catastrophe, something in this piece would work—I just had to struggle with it. So I went back and worked on it over the next four months. Fortunately, I was teaching at the San Francisco Conservatory at the time, and I had a group of students that played contemporary music. I could bring my piece in and try it with them. It actually took several years for *Shaker Loops* to arrive at a state I was satisfied with [there are two versions: string septet and string orchestra].

I was recently given a tape of a performance of the original version of the Sibelius Fifth Symphony. It's one of the most heartening and encouraging things a composer can hear, because almost everything is wrong about it. It has most of the material, including the noble motives and gestures that we associate with that wonderful piece, but they're all in the wrong place. When you hear it, you can't figure how any one person could take that banal thing, tighten it up, rework it, and create the absolute architectural masterpiece that Sibelius made it. It's a wonderful example of the composer's will to make something right.

I had difficult collaborations in all three of my stage pieces. I think part of the reason that they were so hard was that, particularly in the case of the relationship between the librettists and myself, we were all riding certain high horses. Artists tend to consider themselves very highly, you know? If I criticized the librettist, or if the librettist criticized me, each of us would get deeply wounded, deeply offended.

I wonder about other creative areas—for example, the software world—where there are all these little start-up companies. People can't afford the luxury of sulking over bruised egos. Money has been invested, and they have to come up with an idea! So things are tried out, and if they don't work, they toss 'em out and try again.

I've often thought about the great Broadway song-writing teams. Maybe people screamed and shouted and swore at each other and slammed the door, but they had to come back the next day and get it right. So it's possible that serious artists sometimes take themselves a little too seriously. I'm as much to blame, if not more, than anyone else, especially if I've labored incredibly hard trying to set a text to music. I'm constantly aware of how much more labor-intensive composing is than writing poetry, just in terms of the handwriting that goes on. But then the poet will come back and say, "I do all my work intellectually—who's to say it's not just as hard as what you do?" It's a very tricky thing.

I don't find anything particularly hard about composing, although if I'm working on a big piece I can get into a labor crunch. That's hard only in the sense of just sweating it out. But other matters can complicate the process, too. I can give an example with the piece I'm working on now. It was suggested by a highly esteemed artist, and commissioned by a prestigious orchestra. When I was asked to do this piece, I felt like I couldn't say no. But I had a hard time getting going, because I was not sure this was really what I wanted to do, and I became very self-conscious about it. I thought, this artist is so esteemed, and this orchestra is so famous, and the conductor is very serious, and the whole thing seemed wrong, because what I was feeling at the time was not particularly highbrow! I was in one of my typical bad-boy moods. So I found myself in a state of terrible conflict between having accepted the commission, which was, in a certain sense, an economic responsibility, and then having a bad case of cognitive dissonance because I really wanted to write something that was not quite proper for these forces. The gestation period for that piece was very difficult. I finally just had to sit down and say, "OK, I'll forget who's playing it. I'm going to go ahead and write this piece, and we'll hope that they can deal with it." It's not a bad-boy piece, but it falls in my more vernacular vein. I have a feeling that the commissioning people were hoping for something like the violin concerto, which is a more austere work.

I think I learned my lesson this time—what I should do is just decide what the next piece is and then look for the commission, which is very often what I wind up doing. I like very much writing for ensembles that specialize in contemporary music and are somewhat flexible in their instrumentation. They can play any number of styles, and do it all with a tremendous sense of élan and excitement. I can write really interesting, wacky pieces, for those groups—that's really the world in which I operate most comfortably.

I admire even to the point of envy a few American composers who have been able to develop a personal language by means of creating and working with their own ensembles. In other words, they've created their ensemble to embody the acoustical, musical image that they had. Meredith Monk's music is highly identifiable, largely because it's written for her one essential group. So in a certain sense, her originality is very strong, as is the case with Conlon Nancarrow. Much of my work is for more traditional forces, so originality, in that sense, is even harder to arrive at. But I've always thought orchestrally, having grown up in a musical world that was completely conceived through the orchestral format. Fortunately that's been enriched by my long-standing romance with electronic instruments.

I need as much silence as possible to compose. For several years now, my neighbor has had a gardener come over on Thursday afternoons, and this gardener uses a motorized leaf blower to clean the yard. I actually plan my Thursday afternoons so that whatever I'm doing can be done in spite of that annoyance. But every Thursday I find myself grinding my teeth! I've never been able to work at artists' colonies, although I know many composers and writers who thrive in that environment. But I've had a cabin in the Sierras for almost twenty years, and in the summer I take my children there. In the mornings I work in another cabin that's not far away. I always do high-quality work there, because there are absolutely no distractions. I wish I could do that for the majority of the year.

I'm a morning composer, generally, and I do fairly well in the afternoon as well. My biggest bête noire is my "career," which has become a genuine annoyance to me. I haven't quite figured out how to deal with it. It's one thing to pack up and disappear into the mountains for three or four weeks in the summer and work, but it's another to try to carry on a daily life as a creative person and have to deal with the amount of human relations that goes into being a moderately successful composer and, in my case, a conductor as well. Every concert that I conduct and most performances of my pieces always involve some kind of contact, the kind of secretarial time that is a real burden for me, now. I don't have an assistant; I've resented bringing another person into this because I think doing that would break up my time and concentration even further. But at some point I'm going to have to get someone. I already have an assistant who works with me on my electronic and computer things, but I need an Imogen Holst [Benjamin Britten's musical secretary] or someone who can just help me deal with the outside world.

I do twelve or fifteen weeks a year of conducting, and although I always resent having to stop work and get on the plane, as soon as I do I'm usually very energized by the experience because it forcibly draws out an extroverted side of my nature, which I otherwise would bury. Composers tend to get very moldy and introverted and difficult and paranoid, and I fall right into that type after two or three months of working alone. You know—I realize I've worn the same holey sweater for four days in a row; I haven't cleaned up the mess of scores and books I've thrown on the floor. When you're composing, you can always stop and take a walk, have a cup of tea or play with the dog, whereas when you're conducting you're locked into limited time and players' needs. It's a wonderful balance for me.

A lot of young composers are very enchanted by technology. Things like MIDI allow very rudimentarily skilled composers to make recordings of their works that sound alarmingly finished and polished. There is a ten-year-old boy (not a student) who comes over to my house every week or so and plays his music for me. He has a MIDI sequencer at home, and his pieces are all polished and notated with his print software. I don't discourage him for doing that, but I also point out that there's no substitute for having plain, awesome musical chops: having a great ear, being able to perform well on an instrument, and having a huge, encyclopedic knowledge of music. Composers should know everything. Nowadays there's no excuse for not being at least aurally familiar with medieval music and Renaissance music, and they should know jazz and pop music, too. It's all possible to do.

More so now than ever in my life, I have come to lament the way in which classical composers have marginalized themselves over the last seventy years. It seems that they are now almost non-entities, unknown in the culture, as opposed to the nineteenth century, when we had figures like Wagner and Verdi and Beethoven and Chopin, some of whom may have lived frustrating, tragic lives but were major figures in the culture of their eras. Maybe Mozart was only speaking to a very refined slice of the culture, but at least his name and reputation were beyond dispute. Now, particularly in the United States, culture is, even among serious, college-educated people, defined by popular culture, and "serious" composers have become ever more incomprehensible to even the more informed listeners. As a result, the composer has retreated further and further into an isolated, bunker mentality. It's the syndrome that Milton Babbitt embraced in the 1950s—that he was a nuclear scientist and only other nuclear scientists could possibly understand what he was saying. That to me was an arrogant stance that brought about its own karmic results. Unfortunately, audiences have come to the point nowadays where they expect trouble whenever a new work is on a program. How different this is from the world of modern painting or sculpture! If you go to New York and want to see what's at the Museum of Modern Art, you have to wait in line for an hour just to get in.

In my own work, I try to find a way to create something that is on the one hand fresh and new and has the feel and sensation of being written in my time, and on the other hand can have a larger cultural impact, be comprehensible to a level of educated people who are not musical specialists. I see myself in the line of the American half-vernacular, half-classical composer, someone like Ives, or Copland, or Bernstein, or even Gershwin. I find as I get older that my music tends to be part of that tradition, which I think is a very strong one. The great thing about that tradition is how much pleasure it gives people. It defines so much the American experience.

John Adams, Selected Works

SMALL ENSEMBLE

Chamber Symphony (1992)
fifteen instruments

Hoodoo Zephyr (1993)
MIDI keyboard (recording only)

John's Book of Alleged Dances
(1994)
string quartet and foot-controlled
sampler

Road Movies (1995)
violin and piano

Scratchband (1995)
amplified ensemble

LARGE ENSEMBLE

Lollapalooza (1995)
orchestra

Short Ride in a Fast Machine
(1986)
orchestra

Violin Concerto (1993)
violin and orchestra

The Wound-Dresser (1988–89)
baritone and chamber
orchestra
text: Walt Whitman

STAGE WORKS

The Death of Klinghoffer (1990)
opera in two acts
text: Alice Goodman

Nixon in China (1987)
opera in three acts
text: Alice Goodman

Publisher: Boosey & Hawkes, 24
East 24th Street, New York, NY

10010-7200. Tel. 212-228-3300;
fax: 212-979-7057.

John Adams, Selected Discography

The Chairman Dances
Baltimore Symphony/Zinman
Argo 444 454

*Chamber Symphony, Grand
Pianola Music*
London Sinfonietta/Adams
Nonesuch 79219

China Gates
Alan Feinberg, piano
Argo 436 925

Christian Zeal and Activity
San Francisco Symphony/de Waart
Nonesuch 79144

Eros Piano
Paul Crossley, piano; Orchestra of
St. Luke's/Adams
Nonesuch 79249

Fearful Symmetries
Orchestra of St. Luke's/Adams
Nonesuch 79218

Harmonielehre
City of Birmingham Symphony
Orchestra/Rattle
EMI 55051

Harmonium
San Francisco Symphony and
Chorus/de Waart
ECM New Series 1277; Warner
25012

Hoodoo Zephyr
Nonesuch 79311

Phrygian Gates
Ursula Oppens, piano
Music and Arts 604

CLAUDE BAKER

$(\text{B. } 1948)$

Claude Baker grew up in Lenoir, North Carolina, and majored in music at East Carolina University. He studied composition with Samuel Adler and Warren Benson at the Eastman School of Music, where he completed his doctoral studies. His music has been commissioned by the Louisville Orchestra, the St. Louis Symphony, and the National Symphony, among others.

Baker often composes under the impulse to pay homage to music of the past, and he sometimes quotes the music of other composers in his work. "I'm a very referential person," he says. "Perhaps I show my musical personality best through allusion to others' music." Baker also finds inspiration for nontextural music in literature. His prize-winning orchestral work *The Glass Bead Game* is based on the novel by Hermann Hesse, and *Shadows* (for orchestra), along with its companion *Whispers and Echoes*, is based on Japanese haiku poems. Among his recent commissions is a solo piano piece based on the poetry of Whitman for pianist James Dick and the International Festival at Round Top.

Claude Baker teaches at Indiana University and has been composer-in-residence of the St. Louis Symphony Orchestra since 1991. He lives in Bloomington. This interview took place in Bloomington in April 1997.

• • •

I think that I compose for the reason that most people in the arts pursue the activities they do. That is, they derive a level of gratification from those pursuits that they can't get from any other means. And nothing in music—in performance or teaching, or any other aspect of the profession—gives me the same degree of fulfillment and gratification that composition does. The process is incredibly masochistic at the time I am doing it. It's painful and frustrating and humbling and maddening, but at the end of it all is this product. It's almost as if I don't care if my composition is performed or not, because it's the journey, going through the whole process, that brings about the greatest satisfaction.

I started composing by accident, really. I was in my junior year of college, a music theory major. I had to take composition as part of the degree, and in the first semester I did it grudgingly and therefore produced nothing of any substance whatsoever. But in the second semester I said to myself, "Look, if I'm going to have to take this class, I might as well try my very, very best to make this worthwhile and legitimate." So I threw myself into the first assignment, which happened to be a work for string quartet, and when it was finished, I experienced a feeling of contentment, fulfillment, and gratification I'd never encountered before. Here was something that I had created, and in which I could take pride, unlike any paper I'd written or any recital I'd played.

I can't offer a Wagnerian rationale for composing, such as "the role of my music is to elevate all mankind." But I hope that people who listen to my music will ultimately feel the joy that I felt while writing it, and will perhaps understand more about me, personally, or perceive what I might understand about them.

The way a piece evolves very much depends on what type of work it is. If it is programmatic in nature, extramusical associations will provide the impetus. For works like *Shadows* [for orchestra] or its companion *Whispers and Echoes*, the starting point was Japanese haiku poetry, on which each of the movements is based. The poetry conjured up images, both visual and aural, and in turn helped dictate the form of each movement. If, however, I'm writing a piece of absolute music, I may take as a starting point an actual musical fragment—either a harmonic progression, or a melodic motive—and then look at the implications of what this motive contains.

I have to see a piece from beginning to end. I have to be able to move through the composition in real time before I can actually sit down with pencil and paper and pull it into reality. I also need to have a sort of plan, a structure, in order to begin work. I might make time lines, graphs, or little sketches having to do with various parameters of the piece, not necessarily with reference to specific pitches or sonorities. Still, the image I see of the piece at this point is very diffused. It's not specific at all, but I know I want a certain type of activity that will in turn, at a certain tonal level, move to another type of activity. It takes me many months to get to the point where I can see and then hear this piece in its ideal, and admittedly vague, form.

Proust talked about the great disparity between the ideal and the real world: the ideal world that he perceived, and the outcome of trying to make that ideal world real. It's the same thing with the composing process. To try and make that ideal the way that I see it, as I look up, and the way I hear it, as it passes in real time, is a disappointing project in and of itself. And yet it's exciting too, because once I get to the point where the whole piece is completed in my imagination, I can *see* it! I want to say, "Well, look up there! There it is! Just play that! Here, copyist, look up there, copy this down." But of course it doesn't work that way. As a piece becomes tangible, inevitably something is lost. I realize how many things I have not thought of, or I'll suddenly have no ideas for materials to use. It's never as complete as I had thought. I will spend countless hours working on a minute detail, to get it closer to what I thought I conceived of initially.

With *Whispers* I wrote the last movement first because I wanted everything to lead to it. I completed the first movement next, then the third movement, and the second movement. Not every piece is written like that. I have a little fiddle piece that I wrote chronologically, without knowing how it was going to end, groping my way along. It worked out OK, but it's also short, only seven minutes. With a large piece you don't have the luxury to sort of play around and think, "Well, this is kind of fun . . . and what about this?"

I'm always suspicious of composers who say, "I let the music take me where it will—wherever it leads me, I will follow." I don't buy that statement for a second. I know that somewhere they're organizing this piece, and they have a long-range vision. Maybe that vision isn't quite clear at the time they start, and yes, the material itself will suggest certain things. It's very possible to start in a certain direction, hit a brick wall, crash and burn, retrace your steps, and start in a different direction. Many times I've gone through this elaborate process of making diagrams and graphs and realized as I've gotten into the piece that it's just not going to happen that way, while at the same time something even better is suggesting itself.

I know other composers work differently. I have a student, for example, who will have an initial idea, like a single block of modeling clay. He'll then get another glob, the same color, the same shape, but he'll twist it a different way. Then another glob, molded slightly differently, and pretty soon he has a whole table full of globs and it's a question of arranging them in a way that makes structural sense. I can never see the development of his pieces during this process, nor can he. He will bring in reams and reams of paper and just sort of look at them and say, "I have no idea what to do with all this." Finally the subconscious will make all the connections for him, because nothing is ever far removed from anything else. Inevitably his pieces wind up sounding so spontaneous, so carefully conceived, so logical and inevitable. Zoom!

There it is! The work goes from here to there, and I ask him, "Is this the same piece you struggled with, the one made of little bits of molded clay?" I try to get him to think of other ways to approach composition because it takes him forever to write a short piece. But it's the way that his mind works best, and it's the way he feels comfortable. The results are always, always wonderful. I think that many young students tend to work with this add-on technique. But as people get older and the musical forces they write for expand, more parameters have to be carefully considered, within a greater structure, a greater plan. When this student comes to a point where he has to produce a longer symphonic piece, that sort of playfulness might not work—or it might take him ten years to write the piece.

I'm always amazed at the facility of some of my colleagues who don't hesitate to make small decisions very quickly, and instinctively. I second-guess myself at every turn. I ask myself, "Is this the best it could be at this point, or is there another alternative?" Maybe it just boils down to sheer indecisiveness on my part, but writing is a constant struggle, yet with a great deal of joy in that struggle, in the whole process itself. You see, I'm the kind of person who, if I'm not stabbing knitting needles into my eyes, wonders if he's doing the right thing. Even the choice of a dynamic marking causes me great angst. "Is this passage going to be *piano*? Maybe it's *poco piano*. Maybe it's *mezzo-piano*. No, *mezzo-piano*'s too loud, maybe it's . . . " I will also spend countless hours deciding on just the right articulations. I don't think there is anything easy about composing, for me. It's got to hurt or it can't be good.

There have been times when I've had to work faster because of deadlines, but somehow I've never felt as connected to those pieces. If you asked me what is happening in measure 25 in the first movement of *The Glass Bead Game*, I could tell you, because I spent *hours* on measure 25! I know *exactly* what it contains! But there are a couple of pieces where I had to work very fast and I couldn't really tell you what's happening in measure 25. For some reason I feel that since I took a shortcut to finish those works, they don't deserve to exist, because they didn't go through a torturous birth. And yet shouldn't composing become easier? Maybe not.

I do tend to isolate myself to compose. In the first few months, sometimes, I wonder if anything at all is going to manifest itself. The initial concept may seem very clear, but bringing it to fruition seems an impossible task. I think, "I'll never get this, it will never happen—it's hopeless! I don't have a clue to what I'm doing!" And this angst will go on for weeks, maybe even months, I blush to say, while I'm doing other activities, walking, doing mindless chores. The subconscious, of course, does remarkable things. It takes over when I'm asleep or involved with other activities and reorganizes the information in its own way. But eventually I do have to be isolated to make this new piece almost an obsession, to the exclusion of other things.

There are many other composers who can compartmentalize well. They can say, "This is the amount of time I have to devote to this project. I will go into a compartment, I will shut the doors and draw the blinds and think of nothing else for this certain period of time." And they do it beautifully. They can walk out of that compartment and leave that work behind and go on to the next project. I can't do that. My compartments leak all over the place.

So I don't make as efficient use of my time. I've gotten better at it, but it's still very difficult for me to maintain that sort of mental discipline. I tend to go in and out of concentrating on my work at various times of the day when it's most untimely and most inappropriate. When I really should be dealing with some other task, I find myself going back into the composition compartment. I can't seem to control that. The new piece begins to occupy not only every waking moment but also maybe every unconscious moment.

During the course of the school year the amount of time that I have for composing is very limited. In the summer months I spend all of my days trying to get to the point of lassoing the ideal world and dragging it, kicking and screaming, onto the page. By the time the concert season and the school year start, I hope to be to the point of dealing with issues like orchestration and the preparation of score and parts for a performance, things that I can accomplish when other responsibilities have my attention. Mahler also devoted his summer months to composing, because his demands as a conductor during the year were so great. Many other people in academia work the same way.

Many of my pieces use quotation. In the two pieces I alluded to that are based on Japanese poetry, quotation plays a crucial role, because in classic haiku writing, a poet will often refer to a work by a previous master. It's part of the established technique. So not only does the poet create a whole world of imagery, but that world is expanded with additional associations, since the reader also moves into a previous poet's world. One begins to see the same object or the same scene from several different perspectives. The web of associations makes the work more complex.

Essentially, I'm a very referential person. I pun a lot. I make allusions to literature, to quotations from plays, novels, or popular culture. As a composer, too, I'm highly referential, not just in the conscious use of quotations but also in influences, from music that I know and love. There may be in my original conception of a piece the notion that I'd like to have a section, say, very much like the opening of Lutoslawski's Third Symphony. Or maybe I'd really like something to be very similar to the structure of the "Myth" from Crumb's *Makrokosmos III*.

I used to feel very bad about referring to others' work in my music, until I attended a lecture Ligeti gave when he accepted the Grawemeyer Award in

Louisville. He was talking about one of the piano etudes that had received the prize that year. Using an overhead projector, he showed us a numerological construction he had used as a precompositional basis for this particular etude. On another screen, he projected the etude itself—he was demonstrating to us the connection between the etude and the number system. Then he said, "I want to show you where I got this idea." He took the music off the screen, put up another series of numbers that was almost identical to the one that he had originally presented, and said, "This is the system Conlon Nancarrow used in one of his piano roll pieces. This is where I got the idea for my etude, and I want to acknowledge Conlon Nancarrow and to say that I think he's one of the great composers in the world and that he's been a great influence in my life." Here was Ligeti, obviously well established and not a young man anymore, yet still willing to acknowledge his influences, and proudly.

I think that I show my influences very clearly, and as I get older, I see less and less wrong with that. "Originality" is a self-deluding concept. Ned Rorem said that the very best composers are those who are best able to disguise their thievery. We all keep, consciously or unconsciously, a treasure trove of information. It's that mine of information, of past history, that you're drawing from when writing. All the composers you have listened to, and loved, and been influenced by, constitute this vein that you tap into. Pieces don't magically spring forth in full armor from our heads; they come from a wellspring of different sources. Whether we acknowledge those sources or not, whether we're aware of them or not, is almost inconsequential to the process. Try to name a composer who hasn't at one time in his or her career shown the influence of someone else. Stravinsky's most popular piece is probably *Firebird*, even today, and his debt to Rimsky-Korsakov is enormous.

There's the danger, of course, of making your music sound too much like the work that provided the initial spark. Sometimes I've been totally unaware of the connection or just forgotten the similarity because after a time, the source fragment becomes mine. It's not until someone else points out the correlation that I go, "Whoops! Yow! Oh, my God, yes!" And I feel myself blushing! Other times I'm aware of the connection but I can't seem to do anything about it. It's *le mot juste*, the right word for that occasion, and it can't be any other word. Besides, I have thought about this particular section of my piece for so long, and the reference source has become part of my whole thought process. I can't dislodge it. It's got to be there, and that's all it can be.

Vaughan Williams talked about this in his autobiography. He didn't care if the word had been said a thousand times before—if it was the right word for that occasion, it had to be used. My orchestra piece *The Glass Bead Game* has a big collage in the last movement, and when I was getting permission from various publishers and composers for the pieces I used, I was turned down by only one, Mrs. Vaughan Williams. I had used a passage from her husband's Fourth Symphony that *had* to be there. The way I had juxtaposed and superimposed these other quotations all led to, from, and supported this fragment from the Fourth Symphony.

Now I could have just written in the style of Vaughan Williams, but that would have defeated the whole philosophical point behind this collage, and indeed the Glass Bead Game itself in Hesse's novel. So I wrote to Mrs. Vaughan Williams, quoting from her husband's autobiography about *le mot juste* and his view toward musical citation, borrowing, and the influences of other composers. And she wrote back saying, "Blessings on the use of *le mot juste*. Your quotations from my husband's autobiography won the day. And of course, the passage from the Fourth Symphony is yours."

I don't deny that I have come under a lot of criticism from composers and critics for conscious musical quotation. Performers frequently consider musical borrowing to be a sign of creative inertia. "So, what's wrong, Baker—couldn't think of anything else to write? You had to steal from somebody else?" Composers oftentimes consider musical borrowing, particularly of a fairly well-known source, as a way of pandering to an audience: "It's something they'll recognize so they'll like your piece." And what does the audience think? If you've borrowed from a well-known piece, something near and dear to them, they consider its use a sign of blasphemy.

It's a no-win situation from any standpoint. And yet the irony here is that I think when I use musical borrowing, I am actually more original than I would be if I were not using borrowed elements. I know that it sounds paradoxical, but I really do believe that I can give greater vent to my imagination by using as a basis of a section or a piece a quotation that is salient to what I'm trying to accomplish, either programmatically or even structurally.

That said, I want to add that I find myself less and less attracted to quotation now. Maybe it's because I've been beaten up so badly over it. There is a part of me that still longs to do it, and I can't help that. I'll be thinking about a new piece, how a particular section is going to be constructed, and almost invariably another work will come to mind. And I'll say, "That would be perfect! I can make this little reference, and it will be very subtle, and . . ." It's the same temptation I have to pun, which is why I have no friends left, because people are so tired of me punning. But it's the way my mind works—someone will use a phrase that will remind me of a pop song, and I'll sing it. Something else will remind me of a quote from Shakespeare, and I'll blurt that out.

Joan Tower once said to me, "I couldn't understand why you loved quotation until I got to know you. You are such a referential person; everything reminds you of something else—it's just part of your personality, isn't it?" I think there's a great deal of truth in that observation. Yet when I hear another composer use quotation, I often feel uncomfortable. It's like looking at myself in the mirror, seeing something in someone else that raises misgivings about what I do. I'm hearing the aesthetic of musical borrowing from a very objective standpoint. It's not so close to me.

I'll give you an example of the tightrope I sometimes walk when quoting other composers' music. In the last movement of *Whispers and Echoes* there is a section quoted from "Der Einsame im Herbst" (from Mahler's *Das Lied von der Erde)* that suddenly erupts from my music and then subsides back into it. In my original concept for the movement, I knew that I would lead up to and away from that point with material derived from other facets of Mahler's score. In my ideal world, the inclusion of the literal quote seemed perfect. But when I actually wrote it out, then stepped back and looked at it, I felt queasy. I said, "This is all wrong, this is over the top! It's too much!" Yet I couldn't let it go. Everything before had led right up to it. What was I to do? The whole concept was skewed from the beginning.

So I did leave the section as it was, and at the first rehearsal, when the Mahler quote came bursting forth, I thought, "Oh, God, no." But the players loved it. They thought it was just beautiful. And I hoped that perhaps its inclusion was going to be OK. But I know now it isn't. It's way too much. And I got blasted in the press for it. The orchestra took the piece on its 1995–96 Midwest, East Coast, and West Coast tours. It was performed nineteen times in that season. There was only one good review, from L.A. All the other critics went: "*What?*"

In the same movement I also make a number of references to "Frühling" from the *Four Last Songs* of Strauss. There's only one literal quote, however, of four chords, which I use as a recurring motto. The Strauss fragment combined with the Mahler seemed to bother people. The critics I've talked to say it's not the use of the material itself, and not the way I've used it—it's the fact that the material was from the *Four Last Songs* and *Das Lied von der Erde,* which are almost religious icons. I tried to treat these works very religiously, with great restraint. I wanted to embrace them, to show nothing more than the utmost respect. It's interesting, because in the same piece, I quoted a fourteenth-century rondeau of Baude Cordier, and no one said a word about it. No one cared. My use of it was more blatant, but with Baude Cordier, I wasn't dealing with a god. With Strauss, perhaps I was.

I tend to withdraw my pieces or do major revisions, although in truth I think it's very difficult to make anything except minor revisions without rewriting something completely. But because I have this obsessive-compulsive personality, I tend to go back, to pick at things. I don't usually rewrite entire pieces, but whole sections, I do. If there's something wrong with the initial concept of a piece, as I think there was with the last movement of *Whispers and Echoes,* it's hard to deal with—I'd have to take out that movement and start the composition all over, since the whole work hinges on that last movement. That's why I left the piece as it is—I'll just have to suffer the slings and arrows of outrageous fortune.

Sometimes revised pieces manifest themselves in different forms. Early on I subscribed to the "dance of the sacred life cycle," where you can reincarnate your work. And for a long time I wanted to carry something very tangible from one piece to the next, so there would be a sort of reincarnation. But even though I am self-referential to a great degree, I could play ten of my pieces for you and you might not be aware of a connection, from one to the next.

There's great disdain in this country for composers whose style is easily recognizable, or who borrow elements from one piece and bring them into the next one. I think that attitude is uniquely American. When [Luciano] Berio took *Sequenza VII* [for solo oboe] and turned it into *Chemins IV* [for oboe and chamber orchestra], people wrote articles about his mining of the material from *Sequenza VII*. He himself frequently talks about mining materials from early pieces and bringing them into later ones. Another example: when [Bernd Alois] Zimmermann took an entire section—whole, same orchestration, everything—and dropped it into a completely different piece, scholars talked about his adherence to a *Grundgestalt* that is so important to him he could not let it go! In Europe, not only is it considered proper to do this, it's almost expected that you will take, let's say, a piece for orchestra, and arrange it for a wind band. Maybe there'll be a chamber version of it, too. One piece will have several different outlets, different manifestations, different lives. But if a composer in this country dares to bring a section from one piece into another, he or she is blasted by other composers, by critics, by performers.

We have the "new model every year" mentality—and yet, nothing is completely new. If you listen to the music of any composer, particularly a prolific one, you will hear many of the same gestures, again and again and again. There is nothing wrong with that. There's a sort of fingerprinting in the music of most composers, and because of this, for example, you *know* when you're listening to a piece of Brahms, you *know* when you're listening to Tchaikovsky.

The romantic concept of the composer, the *artiste* apart from and above the rest of the madding crowd, does not apply anymore. Today, at least in this country, there is no such lofty vision of the artist! We're all perverted scum, as far as many of the politicians are concerned. The role of the artist in today's society cannot be that of the lonely wanderer. If an artist of whatever sort doesn't operate in the everyday world, he or she is sunk. We have a greater responsibility to society than ever, perhaps. In addition to providing new creations, we have a social role that we've adopted for ourselves, which may be equally important. Who knows?

When I first became composer-in-residence in St. Louis, I used to try, for what I thought was the sake of the audience, to demystify the process of composition. People would ask the same questions: "How do you do this? How does it work?" And I'd say, "Oh, you know—it's like writing a paper for your college or high school class. You draw an outline, list the salient points you want to emphasize or touch upon, and gradually flesh out your outline until you are able to write it."

Well, that's just not the truth. I've since come to see the fallacy and the harm in that assertion. I was trying to create a closer bond between the composer and audience, trying to show that the compositional process is not mystical. And yet it is. It *is* mystical. It is special, it is unique, it is unexplainable. Sometimes I look back at a piece I've written and wonder, "How in the world did I do this? How did this ever come to pass? I just don't understand." And the memory of all the hard work is completely gone. Mahler said that with each new piece, he had to learn the art of composition all over again. There is a lot of truth to that.

Claude Baker, Selected Works

SMALL ENSEMBLE

Banchetto Musicale (1978)
clarinet, violin, piano,
    percussion

Concertino (1970)
three quintets, piano, percussion

Divertissement (1980)
clarinet, violin, cello, piano

Fantasy Variations (1986)
string quartet

Tableaux Funèbres (1988)
piano and string quartet

LARGE ENSEMBLE

Awaking the Winds (1993)
orchestra

Awaking the Winds (1994)
chamber ensemble

The Glass Bead Game (1982,
    revised 1983)
orchestra

Into the Sun (1996)
high voice and orchestra
text: Kenneth Patchen

Shadows: Four Dirge Nocturnes
    (1990)
orchestra

Speculum Musicae, Pars II (1976)
orchestra

Whispers and Echoes (1995)
orchestra

Publisher: MMB Music, 3526 Washington Avenue, St. Louis, MO 63103-1019. Tel. 314-531-9635.

Claude Baker, Selected Recordings

Awaking the Winds
Indiana University New Music
    Ensemble/Dzubay
Indiana University IUSM-05

The Glass Bead Game
Louisville Orchestra/Bernhardt
Louisville First Edition LS-789

Omaggi e Fantasie
Michael Cameron, double bass;
    David Liptak, piano
Gasparo GSCD-286

Shadows: Four Dirge Nocturnes
St. Louis Symphony
    Orchestra/Slatkin

St. Louis Symphony Orchestra,
  "The Slatkin Years"; six-CD set
  (not for commercial sale)

Vier Nachtszenen
Ruth Inglefield, harp
Gasparo GSCD-286

DAN WELCHER

 $\left(\text{B. 1948}\right)$

*B*orn and raised in Rochester, New York, Dan Welcher was trained at the Eastman School of Music and the Manhattan School of Music. His composition teachers included Samuel Adler, Warren Benson, and Ludmilla Ulehla. For six years he was principal bassoonist of the Louisville Orchestra, and from 1976 to 1990 he was a member of the artist faculty of the Aspen Music Festival, teaching bassoon and composition. Welcher was composer-in-residence with the Honolulu Symphony Orchestra from 1990 to 1993. He is professor of composition at the University of Texas, where he directs the New Music Ensemble.

Welcher's music has been performed by the Chicago Symphony, the St. Louis Symphony, the Los Angeles Chamber Orchestra, the Dallas Wind Symphony, the Chamber Music Society of Lincoln Center, and the Cleveland Quartet, among others. His recent commissions include *Bright Wings: Valediction for Large Orchestra* for the Dallas Symphony and an oratorio on the life of President John F. Kennedy for the Handel and Haydn Society of Boston. His catalogue also includes several wind ensemble pieces inspired by American themes. *Three Places in the West*, for example, pays homage to Arches, Yellowstone, and Zion National Parks.

Dan Welcher lives in Austin, Texas. This interview took place in Sooke, Vancouver Island, British Columbia, in December 1996.

•   •   •

If I weren't composing I would be doing some other kind of inventing, because that's how my whole life has gone. I've always liked to make things up, and for awhile I was creatively involved with words, as well. I was an amateur journalist as a kid. I had a monthly newspaper called the *Lakeshore Community Press* that I started with two friends when I was twelve. The paper lasted for about sixteen months, with more than 150 subscribers, and we were everything—paperboys, editors, reporters, news hounds. We just looked for things to write about, then went out and did it.

For me, the newspaper was somehow tied to my musical activity. I was taking piano lessons at the time. Then in the seventh grade I started bassoon lessons because I wanted to be in a group—I was jealous of my friends who were in the band or orchestra. I got into the band after three weeks of lessons because it didn't seem to matter how well I played the bassoon, as long as somebody was there to hold the thing. By my senior year in high school I had composed a wind quartet for my friends to play, and my opus 2, *Essay for Band*, which the band played for commencement. But I was also editor of the school newspaper and the literary magazine, and not certain at all about a career in music. It wasn't until the summer before I started college that I finally decided to go with music, not journalism.

Writing music, like writing words, comes out of a need to communicate with people. It's not an inner need to just express into the void. I don't like that motivation in other artists—I think a new piece has to be something that you want other people to "get." Writing music does what writing poetry used to do for me, and the way I always imagined writing short stories and novels would function if I'd ever stuck with words that long. It's a way of getting into somebody's ear, of saying something that will move people, do more than just keep them awake. I want to spark an emotional or internal change that would not take place without my music. Of course, I also compose because people pay me to do it, and the creative impulse can be generated by the commission as well as by an internal need. However, the professional parts of this life are forgotten in the moment of writing. The same old excitement kicks in, and the music just comes—who knows why. If I stop to think about it, the flow stops. I don't analyze the impulse; I just let it keep coming.

The first few days of working on a new piece are always the worst. The first few scratches, the first few "What am I doing here?" emotions, the first feelings of inadequacy can nip a new work in the bud. Commissions can help get you past that point, because you know someone wants your piece even before it exists.

I've written only two pieces where I didn't use the piano at all. One was a song that followed a text, and because I had created a sound of two superimposed perfect fifths—a kind of a hyper guitar motive that would carry the piece—I could work without a piano. But I prefer having a keyboard, not just to test things, but to noodle on, try my materials out. I go through two drafts, because I always recopy the first one. Recopying is really editing. It forces me to slow down, to find places that need more attention or necessary changes. I don't show anything to anyone until I've finished the first draft, because the slightest hesitation on the part of a listener I respect might derail me completely. There aren't that many people I trust, whose tastes are that close to mine.

Deadlines are good for me. When I first started composing and didn't have commissions, I always gave myself deadlines, anyway—I'd make a big red mark on my calendar and write, "First draft finished by this day," and I always beat my deadline. That's probably an anal thing with me. Sometimes the deadline pushes me to get a piece done too soon, and I wind up having more time to polish than I really should have. In some cases it would have been better to take more time in the writing.

Now that my composing schedule is laid out in advance, I usually know that, say, three months from now I'll be writing a particular kind of music. It gives me three months to be receptive, to think, to have experiences suggest themselves to me as potential pieces. Having a title ahead of time always helps. Sometimes I collect them. I've held onto ideas and titles for years, not knowing what the medium would eventually be.

I'm best if I write first thing in the morning—two to three hours max. I can get a lot done then, "from scratch." A few years ago I was on a real production line, orchestrating a symphony at the same time I was writing a violin concerto. I would compose two or three hours in the morning on the concerto, and in the late afternoon and evening, when I had finished teaching, I would orchestrate the symphony (flesh it out from a four- or five-line short score to a twenty-eight- or thirty-four-stave orchestra score). I can orchestrate without having to be absolutely fresh, because I treat it as a craft, like woodworking. I always compose in short score, but those sketches are carefully annotated—I always know what instruments I'm using at any point.

I can remember exactly how it felt to write the clarinet concerto, because I wrote it at the MacDowell Colony, start to finish. That doesn't include the orchestration, but all the notes of that piece were written in nineteen days. For a lot of my time at MacDowell I was actually miserable—lonely, anxious, and just not terribly happy. But by God, I wrote tons of music. It just came pouring out, to such a degree that by the end of the second week I had basically sketched the piece.

After that I still had six days at the colony, and I thought, "Why don't I make fair copy and really polish it so that if I have to, I can put it away for months and just open it up later and go to work on the orchestration." So I recopied the entire thing, polishing as I went along. I changed one little passage in the first movement, which I played through for another colonist, [the composer] Mike Schelle. He said, "You know this one little transition, where you get to this great climactic peak in the slow theme in part two—it's over too soon! I think you need to do a sequence there. You need to do that phrase twice." So I worked on it, added three measures and a modulation—the same two-bar thing, at a lower pitch level, with a bar of connective tissue. That was all it needed, and Mike was right. That was the place where my initial rush to finish was a little bit off.

At that time in my life the colony experience must have been ideal. It didn't feel all that good, but when I look at the results—and that's really what matters—perhaps putting oneself into a situation of deprivation, where there is some kind of longing, is good for creative work. It forces the mind to channel the longing into the work instead of giving it release through companionship or cooking a meal. In my normal life those are pleasant activities, but they do take me away from the excessive focus that a piece like the clarinet concerto profits from. I've written pieces where I wasn't feeling that way, and they came out well, too. My piano concerto was written largely in a little log cabin one summer in the mountains of Colorado. We had one of those Richard Strauss arrangements, where the couple has breakfast and then the wife pushes the husband downstairs and locks the door, which is what Pauline used to do to Richard. You produce, you come back upstairs, make your lunch, and go back to work again. I guess for me, the ideal situation means not having to teach. But that doesn't necessarily translate into absolute solitude.

Pieces in my "late middle maturity" are coming out with a lot of forethought and planning. That wasn't always the case. With my early orchestra pieces I just sat down and started writing. I remember full well how my flute concerto [1973] began. I wrote a tiny motive, this little *duk-a-da-dah* in the xylophone, sustained in the high winds and strings. Then the flute comes away from a unison in that high note into a downward spiraling motive. That was one of those "upper left" pieces, where you just start writing. But when I listen to those pieces now, I hear dead spots where I'm being rhetorical, spinning my wheels. I didn't really know where the music was going, I just hoped it would find its own way. Now, the first thing I do is make a piece inevitable. I have to find a real reason for each piece to be. I don't want to finish something and then wonder what or who it's for.

We could look at a piece that I wrote with perhaps a little too much forethought: the Second Symphony, commissioned by the Flagstaff Symphony and the Lowell Observatory, which was celebrating its hundredth anniversary. I wasn't told what to write, but there was a clear message that they wanted something they could feel personally attached to. It seems artificial at first, to go looking for extramusical reasons to connect a piece to a commissioner, but usually by the time the piece is finished, it works and seems more interesting than it might have been otherwise.

With the Second Symphony there were two forces working in my imagination: the Lowell astronomers, and the environment of northern Arizona and the native peoples there. What I did was try to combine the astronomer's science with the Native American and his spirit, and I came up with a piece called *Night Watchers*, which is vaguely "about" man looking upward. It's a four-movement symphony that moves chronologically through the ages, beginning with primitive man, moving on through three eras of scientific discovery, and ending with primitive man and scientific man together, agreeing that the universe can't be fathomed.

In the first movement I decided to musically depict the creation of the universe, which is a heady thing to try. I made a "big bang" that created all the musical materials for the symphony: three Hopi Indian chants with pentatonic motives, and also Ptolemy's idea that the planets have their own intervals, which they hum. I made a scale out of the planets' intervals and made my big bang erupt by pressurizing all the little motives until they burst. What was left was a huge artificial overtone series, which created a chord. The second, third, and fourth movements came from that chord and those notes. Of course, it doesn't sound like the same music for thirty minutes, but everything in the piece is related and integrated.

To plot the symphony I made a graph, a time-line picture chart of all four of the movements showing major divisions, textures, keys, or key centers, where there's counterpoint and where there isn't, where there's rhythmic pulse and where there isn't. The graph also showed clock time. In the case of the big bang in the first movement, I allowed one minute from initial rumble to cataclysm. Coming down from the crescendo, I planned on taking two minutes to "set up the world." Of course, when I begin to write the notes, I'm free to alter any plan I've made. If something doesn't feel right, I can always change it.

The *Night Watchers* commission came in December, and the piece had to be written and sent to my copyist by the end of the following summer. I was teaching in the spring, and it was impossible to work on a piece of this scope for just an hour or two every morning. So from January to March I only read, looking for a raison d'être for this piece. It wasn't called *Night Watchers* at that point. It wasn't even called Symphony, it was just "orchestra piece." I read Frank Waters's *Book of the Hopi*, then Carl Sagan's *Cosmos*. The astronomers sent me books about and by Percival Lowell, the founder of the observatory. Also, someone in Flagstaff sent me a painting of Hopi kachinas standing on their kiva, throwing stars up into a dark sky [*Putting Up the Stars,* by Clifford Brycela]. That painting turned out to be the spark, the seminal gesture of the piece itself. The first notes I wrote were the "star-thrower" motive, but I didn't actually write them until March.

I finished the first movement in late March, the second movement in June, and sketched and orchestrated the other two movements during June and July, which I spent in Flagstaff. To me, this piece shows some of the strain of having been produced a little too quickly. The last movement, especially: the proportions are right, but I was really fighting the clock to finish it. Sometimes it was just pure torture to make myself sit down and work. I was tired.

I'd just been through the birth of a piano concerto that had taken a year to write, and I really wanted a vacation. But a commission like that for a large-scale piece with a generous budget can't be turned down because the timing isn't perfect. I still like the piece and probably will eventually forget the trouble it gave me.

Some people might imagine *Night Watchers* as a movie score because it has a preexisting script. I don't always write this way, but in this case I did, and I knew where to stop following the script because ultimately I was writing abstract orchestral music. For example, the second movement, "The Music of the Spheres," is based on Ptolemy's theory of the universe: Earth is the center, and there are seven crystal spheres surrounding it like ever-larger nesting dolls; six of them contain the known major planets and the sun and the moon, and there is an outer sphere containing all the stars (hence the term "seventh heaven"). The music comes from the ancient idea that each celestial body has its own sounding interval, Earth's interval being "fa-mi." I made a scale from the intervals of the six known planets and outlined a three-part form. Each part of the form contained the same melody plus a bass line and a countermelody, but with radically different orchestration in each new appearance. It's as if, for instance, you were standing on Earth to hear it the first time, then standing on the first sphere, which is the sun, and then on the moon. One view would highlight the "fa-mi" interval and its little melody, another would highlight the longer "universe" melody that comes from the rest of the scale, and the third would look at the scene from the point of the harmony. So the layers of sight, in terms of musical form, are A, A-prime, A-double-prime, with little interludes in between that we could call X and Y, one being the reverse of the other, plus a coda. That was a simple way of setting up a piece that is totally abstract, but that is derived from an extramusical narrative.

One can talk about this piece without referring to plots or outlines at all. In the first movement, for instance, the "form" could be described this way: dissonance and chaos explode into a cosmic chord, which generates a stately and noble theme, heard three times. The character and effect of that theme are not accidental. I know what kinds of intervals and melodies tweak people —I know how to make people's skin crawl, how to make them shiver. I can't say it works on all listeners. There are some people, such as overly trained composers and theorists, who aren't moved by a third relation or a delayed resolution. But the average listener is, even without knowing why.

My harmonic systems for pieces are individual entities. The wind ensemble piece *Zion* is entirely written from the pentatonic scales of two hymns, "The Walls of Zion" and "Zion's Security," one being a minor pentatonic scale and the other being a major pentatonic. When I overlaid the two scales, it made a nine-note scale, so that the fifth note of the first five-note scale is the beginning of the second five-note scale. With that I was able to make linear passages for instruments like saxophones and clarinets without cheating or going outside the system. In writing twelve-tone music, especially for strings, you always find after awhile that the intervals of the row you've made are impossible to play fast. That's where people usually abandon the system.

But if you're careful when you make a system, you won't have to abandon it. It takes some time and planning, but that's why the "Zion sound" came out so harmonious. Those overlapped pentatonic scales make great runs. The piece is full of notes, flash and dazzle, because there's always somebody running up and down one of these scales. It was all correct within the system; it all came from those two hymns, which was a neat thing to do. This is how we're taught to work when we learn to be composers, but it feels artificial for the longest time. When many people learn the twelve-tone system, they get stuck in it and can't leave because everything in the little matrix box is preset. Most—not all—of the music that's been written with that system sounds arbitrary, because it is—the ear plays very little part in it. You have to adapt whatever system you're using for your own needs, temper the means to meet your end.

I don't think that setting up a tonality system means that your music is cerebral, or that it can't possibly be heartfelt. I'm always looking for a mood, for an expression of feeling. What Brahms did, with his careful interrelations of every little motive, is no different from what I do with my overlapping pentatonic scales or twelve-tone rows. If you have a sense of what you want the piece to do before you start writing it, then you will consciously or unconsciously make system choices that facilitate your design.

Timing comes partly from experience. When I first started making charts for my music, I'd listen to pieces I knew really well and felt were proportioned perfectly. I listened to a lot of Stravinsky with a stopwatch, to sections of certain kinds of music, and remembered exactly in seconds how long they were. Balanchine taught Stravinsky to work that way: dancers doing certain kinds of motions will be exhausted in this many seconds, and then we bring on the next six long-haired Lolitas who can last fifteen seconds longer because their motions will be less frenetic. In fast music, Stravinsky had about a one-minute limit before a major change. You can listen to *The Rite of Spring* this way, but you can also jump ahead to a nonballetic piece like the *Symphony in Three Movements*, which is supposedly absolute music, and find the same principles at work. Ravel is known for his formal clarity, too. I remember going through the entire *Daphnis and Chlöe* ballet with a stopwatch and finding that the big dance at the end is incredibly short, less than three minutes. The whole second suite is about twenty minutes long, yet the *Danse Generale* never seems too brief. It's a huge surge, a summing up, and it seems just right.

Doing this, I realized that clock time and internal comprehension of time can be very different. I started listening to my own music that way, and now I cringe at how in some of my earlier pieces I allowed myself to go on for so long. It seems so self-indulgent. My bassoon concerto feels that way—I just want to take a pair of scissors and stop it in the middle.

I'm not really sure how I started studying others' music with regard to time. I just remember being unsatisfied with my own music in terms of proportions, and didn't know a better way to improve it. No one really teaches composition—this is the great, unspoken, dirty little secret. You can teach the elements of craft that go with composition, but you can't teach the creative process. Everyone finds his own path, and that was mine, in terms of formal plotting.

I have to get hit by lightning to write a piece in the first place. There has to be some kind of an initial "aha," which is the genesis of the idea. Like seeing the painting of the kachinas throwing stars into the sky—I knew exactly what I could do musically the minute I saw it. But that in itself didn't write the symphony.

The interesting thing about being fifty is looking for the "aha" when there isn't one. I can't just sit down and start at the upper left-hand corner. The music would be stillborn if I did that. The challenge is in casting about for the inspiration, or jump-starting the lightning bolt. That's why I like reading and studying, looking for a title before I write a piece. I did an experiment in 1995, though: *Bright Wings* was written start to finish without a title or a program. I wanted to see if I still could write for orchestra without any programmatic elements. I did make an outline, a picture and a graph, but I did not use any specific images or title or story line to propel the piece. It was a succession of moods—I knew how I wanted it to feel. In the course of writing, some vague extramusical ideas came into play, having to do with loss and memory and a certain kind of unquenchable spirit. But more than that, I couldn't be specific. There was a lot more doubt, waiting, and abstract feeling than I'm used to, but I doubt that anybody hearing this piece would sense anything different from others I've written.

Every piece should have a reason. That's scary to think about, because if you're feeling at all cynical, you could look at the huge amount of music that's out there and say, "Enough, already!" Why does composer X have seven piano sonatas? What was wrong with number five, or what in number five needed to be completed in number six? Why does a person write eight string quartets, if they all do basically the same thing? A lot of twentieth-century music has failed to deal with this question. I've always wondered why Walter Piston kept writing because his pieces all seem to be the same. Once this *chugga-chugga-chugga* thing gets going, it does pretty much what his other music has already done.

Here's what I mean about looking for the reason for a piece. Perhaps one of your sonatas is profoundly romantic, perhaps the second movement is a love duet between the right hand and the left hand. The next sonata might be a scientific piece that holds emotions in check but does fascinating things with sound, where the hands are spaced widely apart and create overtones. A third piano sonata might explore a particular finger motion—it could be an etude where you're dealing with one pair of notes inside another pair of notes. All three pieces are there for different reasons; each has its own reason for existence. Beethoven knew this better than anyone. Although he produced nine symphonies, seventeen string quartets, and thirty-two piano sonatas, he managed to make each piece unique.

I loved what Michael Tippett did when he finished writing his opera *The Knot Garden*, which is a retelling of Shakespeare's *The Tempest*. In the end all the characters pair off, but the Ariel character is left high and dry. One year later, Tippett wrote a set of songs for Dov, this "airie" whom he had grown quite attached to after working on the opera for so long. The songs were meant to help Dov find himself. You could say it was therapy for the composer, but there is a reason for that piece, and a really good one, I think. When Jan DeGaetani asked me to write a piece for her, she wanted it to be for voice, English horn or oboe, and piano. [Mezzo-soprano Jan DeGaetani was one of this century's great champions of American music and American composers. She died in 1989 at the age of fifty-six.] The problem was not finding a good text for Jan. She could sing anything. The problem was finding a reason for that double reed. I couldn't think of one until I discovered Pablo Neruda's poem "Abeja Blanca," which springs from the image of a bee buzzing in the soul. That was it. That was the "aha."

Dan Welcher, Selected Works

SMALL ENSEMBLE

Harbor Music (1992)
string quartet

Quintet (1983)
clarinet and string quartet

Tsunami (1991)
cello, percussion, piano

Vox Femina: A Cycle of Poems by and about Women (1984)
soprano, flute, clarinet, violin, cello, piano

LARGE ENSEMBLE

Bright Wings: Valediction for Large Orchestra (1996)

Haleakala: How Maui Snared the Sun (1991)
narrator and large orchestra

Piano Concerto, *Shiva's Drum* (1993–94)
piano and orchestra

Prairie Light: Three Texas Watercolors of Georgia O'Keeffe (1985)
orchestra

Symphony no. 1 (1991)
orchestra

STAGE

Della's Gift (1986)
opera in two acts
libretto: Paul Woodruff (after "Gifts of the Magi" by O. Henry)

Publisher: Theodore Presser,
   Presser Place, Bryn Mawr,
   PA 19010. Tel. 215-525-3636;
   fax 215-527-7841.

Dan Welcher, Selected Recordings

Abeja Blanca
Jan DeGaetani, mezzo-soprano;
   Philip West, English horn;
   Robert Spillman, piano
Bridge Records CD BCD9048

Brass Quintet
American Brass Quintet
Summit Records CD 187

Clarinet Concerto; *Haleakala*;
   Prairie Light
Bil Jackson, clarinet; Richard
   Chamberlain, narrator;
   Honolulu Symphony Orchestra/
   Johanos
Marco Polo CD 8.223457

*Evening Scenes: Three Poems of
   James Agee*

Paul Sperry, tenor; Voices of
   Change/Welcher
Crystal Records CD 740

Harbor Music; *Seven Songs on
   Poems of e. e. cummings*; *Vox
   Femina*; *The Bequest* for voice
   and flute
Cavani String Quartet; Judith
   Kellock, soprano; Martin
   Amlin, piano; Laura Gilbert,
   flute; Isis ensemble
Gasparo CD GSCD-314

Piano Concerto, *Shiva's Drum*
James Dick, piano; Round Top
   Festival Orchestra/Verrot
Round Top Records CD
   RTCD003

The Visions of Merlin
Louisville Orchestra/Endo
Louisville First Editions Records
   LS-793

Zion for large wind ensemble
North Texas Wind Symphony/
   Eugene Corporon
Klavier CD 11070

DANIEL S. GODFREY

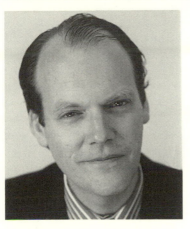

(B. 1949)

Daniel S. Godfrey grew up in Atlanta, Georgia; Ankara, Turkey; and Ardmore, Pennsylvania. His father is a sculptor, architect, and former university teacher and administrator, and his mother led a volunteer career in health-care administration. Godfrey earned two music degrees at Yale and completed a doctorate at the University of Iowa. He also traveled to Europe several times pursuing his interest in transcendental meditation. His composition teachers included Mario Davidovsky, Robert Morris, D. Martin Jenni, and Richard Hervig.

Like many composers, Daniel Godfrey is concerned with the conflict between the artist's inner life and expectations of the outside world. "One of my life's lessons is that the music is going to be better if I don't attach myself to the end product, in terms of the response to it, what it's going to do for me," he says.

Daniel Godfrey is director of the Syracuse University School of Music and coauthor, with Elliott Schwartz, of *Music since 1945* (Schirmer Books, 1993). His works have been played by the Louisville Orchestra, the Honolulu Symphony, the Da Capo Chamber Players, and the Lark and Cassatt String Quartets, among others. He founded and codirects the Seal Bay Festival, a festival of American chamber music held each June in Maine. He lives in Syracuse with his wife and son. This interview took place in Vinalhaven, Maine, in June 1995.

•   •   •

There is a mix of reasons why I compose, which I think—in a kind of fated, inexorable way—work together. Some of them have healthy roots, and some of them have unhealthy roots. Part of the unhealthy motivation, from what I can gather, comes from childhood, when my abilities—whatever they may be—were discovered. The discovery changed my role in the family: writing music became my niche, my way of mattering.

When I started composing, I was eight, the fourth of five children, and we were living in Turkey. I wanted to hear piano music, and my sister, who knew how to play, wouldn't practice when I wanted to listen to it, so I just sat down and played for myself. I didn't know any repertoire, so I had to create my own. I put together one little piece after another, and the pieces actually had shape to them, appreciable content. At some point my parents and siblings heard me doing this and couldn't believe their ears. All of a sudden I had a way of staking out my importance in the family scenario.

So it's become apparent to me, as I've looked back on my uneasy progress and felt it resonate in my parents, that there's a lot tied up there. Yet it's also clear that beyond that, even deeper inside of me, there's a primal necessity to compose. It's so strong that when I listen to a piece of music or go to a concert, I often have a hard time sitting through the experience, because it sets off my own need to create. There's an elemental drive to get my inner self out and make a connection with the larger world. It's like the impulse that drives exotic birds into a mating dance. I mean, why do they do all this elaborate stuff? They don't know, nobody knows, but they do it. And they can't *not* do it. That's the way composing is with me.

I have a much smaller repertoire than I aspire to at this stage of my life, but that's always been the case. There have been so many hurdles, internal and external. There was a period of time when I was just blocked. For years I couldn't leave a single note unrevised, I was so tied up in knots. But I just couldn't give up the idea of composing.

When I was a student, part of what got to me was this: I knew in my heart and mind how I wanted to write, but the message I got from teachers and peers was, "You don't want to write that way, that's old-fashioned stuff!" And so I did what I thought I was supposed to do and wrote tortured, nontonal music. A couple of very good pieces resulted, also a lot of junk.

Then, in graduate school, I wrote my first string quartet, which is a real piece of personal gushing, even though it was pretty cerebrally put together. It was outwardly melodic and tonal, had a voice that I had been repressing for years. It worked because I was young enough not to be self-conscious about what I was doing. I was committing an act of rebellion. My teacher, who'd originally discouraged this sort of thing, heard a phenomenal performance by a graduate string quartet at Yale, and his response was "Look, this is done so well, I can't argue with you."

I think that was the moment when all the escape routes from being a composer became impossible, despite the fact that being a composer in this world, and in this culture, can be so exasperating.

While writing that string quartet, I was on an incredible high. I'd been involved with meditation, was on an austere vegetarian diet, and my physiology was in some kind of rarefied state. I had incredible energy, and it really carried me for about three years. Soon after that I began to have trouble writing, but I was saved by a kind of burst-through that produced a couple more successful pieces. One was a trio for clarinet, horn, and piano. Although it was very short, it managed to get me connected professionally.

I struggled miserably after that. I went back and forth. Composing in that overtly personal voice had brought out so much insecurity. I started to clutch. And right at the middle of it all, still in my twenties, I got a commission from Tanglewood. Now you have to understand: I'd been taught that Tanglewood was the stairway to Nirvana, the one venue to which all should aspire, and I just froze from the pressure of it. I'd been given a big commission, and I simply couldn't finish it. I called up Tanglewood about two months before the deadline, knowing at that point that it was a lost cause. A year had passed and I had gotten nowhere—I'd thrown away a lot of music. Gunther Schuller, who has always been a good friend and mentor, did his best to calm me down and offered to extend the commission for another year. But by then I was completely demoralized, and a second year went by with no progress.

I was working on a Ph.D. at Iowa then, and the people there were thinking, "God, what's happened to Dan?" I didn't unfreeze for about three years, until the statute of limitations on my dissertation was about to expire. Then I was faced with a choice: either complete something or start life over again.

I had to send back the advance for the Tanglewood commission, in increments. It was the most humiliating thing. By the time I finished paying them back I was thirty. There were other kids out there, younger than I, who were winning big prizes and orchestra performances by then. Here I was, paying back a Tanglewood commission, I had no doctorate, I wasn't sure I was going to get one, and that could mean no teaching career, no future in composition, no nothing. But despite everything I'd been through, it never occurred to me to stop being a composer. What occurred to me instead was that I would continue to be a composer and no one would know or care.

I finally started writing again when Steven Schick commissioned a percussion piece from me. The ideas in it seemed quite silly when I wrote them, but I just decided to keep going. I couldn't afford not to. It was painful. I had headaches and nausea, and part of me was writing music, while another part of me was saying, "You can't do this, this stinks, this is no good."

At one point in the process, I had a revelatory moment: I realized that some composers who were getting significant attention were writing music without a lot of creativity or intelligence. I knew that at the very least I wasn't stupid—that even if I pursued what seemed like a really dumb idea, I could do something intelligent with it.

Still, I had headaches, I went through physical pain, it was like being sick. I *was* physically sick. But I pushed through the piece, it was accepted as part of my dissertation, and it turned out to be one of my more successful works. That was a real point of transition for me. A crucial step, just like the one with the quartet. Steve recorded the piece and has brought down the house with it many times.

I want to add that I went out to Iowa as sort of a big fish they had lured from Yale—at least that's how *I* thought of myself. Well, I got humbled fast. Academically I had to work much harder out there. And there was another problem: when you're a composer in your mid- to late twenties, it isn't healthy, no matter how supportive your teachers are, to become a supplicant again, turning up at your lesson every week with scores for evaluation. The time for that is long past. If you haven't developed a committed voice by that time, you're either going to find it on your own without external help or it's too late.

The only reason for continuing school at that point was to earn a ticket to a job. That's not to say it was a waste of time. I learned a great deal, but not about being a composer. After that I had to unlearn the habit of wondering who's going to say what about my music, how it's going to be evaluated.

Evaluation is a loaded issue for me because until my midtwenties, I was a very introverted, withdrawn, angry kind of person, you know? From nursery school to adolescence, for no clear reason, I was generally not welcomed by my peers. It was just this quirky thing—and so I grew up feeling that I simply was not acceptable to whatever group I was with. And since then, of course, my peer group has become other composers. Not surprisingly, I've found myself to be extremely sensitive, oversensitive, to their responses. When I write, I have to consciously put that aside. I usually succeed in the larger sense, but when it comes down to working out details, I often get much pickier than I need to be. That's why I think I write better music when I'm under a huge amount of pressure, a deadline, because I don't have time to fuss.

But despite these struggles, I've been fortunate. When I arrived at Syracuse University to teach, I found a nurturing professional community that supported me and gave me opportunities to support others. There are many difficulties with the academic environment. It can be time-consuming and frustrating. But my colleagues at Syracuse have always been wonderful, and that's made a huge difference. The competitiveness and one-upmanship often found among faculty at other schools has been minimal here. That's given me space to start finding myself as a composer, and I am very grateful for that.

My working process resembles that of the biblical sower of seeds. When I start a piece, there's a kind of sentiment, a body of affects, or a configuration of feeling, that I'm compelled to express. I begin to toss ideas around, mulling things over when I can't get to sleep, when I'm walking to work, when I'm driving, when I'm in the shower (my water bills are spectacular) and at the keyboard. Some of these ideas will germinate, and some will die off.

What often happens is that when I hit on something that seems to have promise, I begin to work with it. It may be the beginning of a piece, or it may turn out to be the beginning of a middle movement, or the beginning of an inner part of the architecture, or something else. Eventually the music begins to take on a localized but very specific profile—an unconscious process gradually becomes conscious. Those ideas have been growing and interacting, and a moment comes when they surface and I realize, "Ah, this is what's happening."

Sometimes it all comes together in a five-, ten-, fifteen-minute period of contemplation. One moment I'm wondering, where is this going? The next moment, just like tumblers in a lock, things sort of fall into place, I see the whole trajectory. Some of it is detailed, some of it not, but there is enough detail so that I know what I have to do. That's when I really begin working my way into the piece. I may realize then that what I'd been working on turns out to be the beginning of the piece, or someplace in the middle, or even a candidate for the trash bin. Often, it feels like the music has been there all along. It's like when two people first fall in love, and they feel they've "always known it."

So I feel I've always known this music, but at the same time, I now feel it isn't *my* piece. If this sounds corny and pretentious, forgive me, but what that moment of discovery feels like is . . . a gift. And the question then is, can I make good use of it? If the piece speaks truly, then I've earned what has been trusted to me.

Composition is a lot like Zen, or other forms of meditation. You allow yourself to fall between the cracks of phenomenal reality, these illusionary boundaries, into a broader and unbounded realm. And the illusionary boundaries for me are my judgmental impulses and my projections of others' judgments. For me, writing a piece, if it's good, is a deliciously paradoxical balance between innocence of heart and intellectual rigor. To get there, one has to give oneself over to the belief that training and experience will do what they have to do, and whatever riches lie within will emerge, come to the fore.

I've been involved with meditation for twenty-three years, and out of a series of personal exigencies have built on that, along with other forms of self-discovery. But I don't document my psychological growth process in music. For me, that process is meant to clear away the detritus so that what's inside can come out. Psychological growth is just a means to an end, and the end is real living, and that's what music springs from. Clearly, meditation has major implications in my view of the world; my outlook is very strongly shaped by the Vedic tradition. But to write music "about" this would make no sense. That would be like focusing on a map of the territory; I'd prefer to explore the territory itself.

For me, lightning bolts, the so-called moments of inspiration, usually follow hard work—they rarely come before it. It's like the moment I was talking about before, where I've worked into a piece and all of a sudden the tumblers fall into place. It's difficult because at first you don't know quite where you're headed, and the clock is ticking, and you begin to doubt what you'll find, or whether you'll find anything, and you have to keep working and looking in spite of that doubt.

But there is finally that delectable moment in some pieces where the whole thing is there, and I think, "Man, if I can get only this piece out the way I hear it!" It can happen: the whole movement goes by in your head. You've got it, you're intoxicated with it, you want everyone to know. But it's only in your head, it's not on paper yet! If it's orchestral music, to get those fifteen minutes down on paper could take you another three months. What you want are just those fifteen minutes that were so full of life and spontaneity and ripeness and clarity. You want somehow to hold onto them and work through the labyrinth of details without losing all that magical vitality. You wonder, will I have this three months from now? Or will I have something that isn't this, and have to live with the fact that once I had it in my head, and lost it?

I find that the work is harder when I'm first starting a composition, because the piece isn't as clear as it becomes after I know where I'm going. The uncertainty brings fear, which makes me procrastinate. I begin to be afraid that the piece isn't going to turn out. I get spaced out, easily distracted—it's a mechanism for not facing the void.

Even after I know where I'm going, there are little battles I have to fight: how to get through the next three measures, how to get through a particularly gnarly bit of counterpoint. I don't want the texture to be too dense . . . the piece has to unfold at a certain rate . . . but it has to incorporate certain ideas, and the ideas can't be covered up. Not only that, the ideas have to balance and flow within a larger continuum that is just as compelling as the ideas themselves. Sometimes I feel there's no way to pull it off. It's as though I'm going into a blind canyon.

It's amazing, though, how the mind works these things out. A lot of composers have the experience of spending literally twelve hours wrestling with a problem that just will not yield. Finally you're completely distraught. It's 1 A.M., the deadline's a day closer, you're only going to get five hours of sleep before you get up to teach that 8:30 theory class, and you've just gotta give up for now. You go to bed, sleep, wake up in the morning, and suddenly realize, "Of course. How obvious! This is the way the piece should go." You sit down and the whole thing's done in an hour and a half.

Those twelve tortured hours may be essential to the process, but in any case, what happens is that when you finally let go, everything gets worked out, and you're ready to move on.

One of my life's lessons is that my music will be better if I don't attach myself to the end product in terms of how audiences or colleagues respond or how it's going to affect my career. The only way one can free oneself is to be in the moment of composing. The great irony is that when you do that, the product is far better—the fruits are richer if you forget about them. When you're obsessed with the outcome, the actual doing is weakened. That's a very hard lesson to learn, because from day one, in this society, we are taught the very opposite. We measure obsessively. All these little mental tape recordings about how we measure up are running all the time.

One thing that energizes me is knowing that the music will be heard. An upcoming premiere means that the door is open for me to make a connection, to close the circle, to complete the social process. Commissions are wonderful, because knowing there are performers interested in what I have to say opens the creative veins in my system. The blood begins to flow.

Composing for a group of people I know personally and admire is especially gratifying. I have a sense of their personalities, and I can allow myself to be influenced by them in a noncerebral manner. I trust that my sense of who they are is going to find its way into the music.

One of the great benefits of working with really good musicians is the opportunity to revise. Revision requires an openness to the necessity for change, the ability to see the holes in your craft. How, for instance, could anybody pretend to know everything about orchestration? All the great composers have said they never stop learning. They learn to the grave. To get really good suggestions from performers, though, there has to be a sense of shared purpose, mutual respect between the musicians and the composer. In a situation like that, I take suggestions as compliments. I relish the opportunity to make improvements—to shift doublings, add a measure, alter pitches, change the instrumentation, omit a beat—to make small adjustments that sometimes change the momentum or pacing of an entire movement.

The usual composing situation for me is at home, sitting at the piano or the drafting table. I can't work at school—it's impossible. When I'm at home, I first have to make peace with Abe and Diana, who, when I'm pressed by a deadline, may feel like I'm not with them. As a deadline nears, I'm generally forced to sacrifice sleep. I don't like doing this, because I'm usually exhausted by nine or ten at night. But then there's a point around eleven o'clock when something kicks in. I resign myself to being up till two or three, and then I realize, to my pleasure, that I have four hours where I get to be a composer. That's when things really start happening, and I feel great about it. This is my dharma.

While a work is in progress, the only people I might show it to are one or two of my closest colleagues. We're mutually aware of how sensitive we are, but we respect each other's opinion. It can be painful—and sometimes disruptive—to get a candid response, and it's just as hard to give one. Composing is so personal, even technical issues carry a lot of voltage.

When you've written a piece, it's like being a parent. You go to the kindergarten to pick up your kid and there are twenty other children there, all quite wonderful. But you look at your child, and you're convinced there's something unique about him. He's not like any of the others, he has something magical, ineffable. You see it—surely the other parents see it, too! But of course they see the same in their own children. With composition the gestation, the birthing process is so intense. You may be the parent to the most wonderful creation imaginable, but even so, you as the composer are not the best person to make that judgment.

I don't want to preach, but sometimes I think we composers need to change the way we think about what we do. We seem to believe that we can decide among ourselves what is important to audiences, present and future. Well, we're dreaming! If what we have to say has meaning for future generations, they'll listen. If it doesn't, they won't. We're not avatars of culture, deputized by God to educate the public.

Our whole idea of originality needs to change, too. Being new and different is neither good nor bad, and it doesn't have much to do with being original. Music is original if it originates deep in the soul. Part of what's stored in the soul is all the music we've heard and loved from childhood on, blended in a unique synthesis with all our other experiences. That's why most honest expression is bound to be "derivative," because it will reflect those inner influences in some way. A composer who attempts self-consciously to diverge from what others have done is focusing on the superficial, and that, to me, is the very opposite of originality.

We are all unique below the surface, but at an even deeper level, we all share the same humanity. In my personal cosmology, we are a mosaic of intelligences emanating from one pervasive intelligence. To me, that means, paradoxically, that the most profoundly original music, coming from the deepest part of the individual, will have the most universal appeal, will resonate with the broadest possible audience. It doesn't matter what style, method, or ethnic sources are involved. The frontier is not in the method but in the mind behind it.

Daniel S. Godfrey, Selected Works

SMALL ENSEMBLE

Arietta (1990)
cello and piano

Dickinson Triptych (1986)
soprano, piano

From a Dream of Russia (1996)
clarinet, violin, piano

Impromptu (1984)
clarinet, cello, piano

Nonet (1995)
wind quintet and string quartet

Numina (1991)
flute, oboe, clarinet, violin, viola,
   cello

Scrimshaw (1985)
flute, violin

Serenata Ariosa (1995)
clarinet, viola, piano

String Quartet no. 2 (1993)

Three Marian Eulogies (1987)
high voice, viola, piano

Two Scenes in Chiaroscuro (1994)
flute, oboe, clarinet, horn, violin,
   viola, cello, piano, percussion

LARGE ENSEMBLE

Clarion Sky (1992)
orchestra

Jig (1996)
concert band/wind ensemble

Lightscape (1997)
orchestra

Mestengo (1988)
orchestra

Sinfonietta (1996)
string orchestra

To the Muses! (1998)
concert band/wind ensemble

Publisher: Margun Music, 167
   Dudley Road, Newton Centre,
   MA 02159. Tel. 617-332-6398;
   fax 617-969-1079.

Daniel S. Godrey, Selected Recordings

A Celebration
James Avery, piano
Orion Master Recordings ORS
   79340

Five Character Pieces
William Preucil, viola; James
   Avery, piano
Orion Master Recordings ORS
   79340

Intermedio
Cassatt String Quartet
CRI 671

*Music for Marimba and
   Vibraphone*
Steven Schick
GM 2041CD

Progression
electronic
Orion Master Recordings
   ORS 77262

Scrimshaw
Linda Greene, flute; Martin
   Wolfhurst, violin
Uni-Pro Recordings SR-327

String Quartet no. 1
Rowe String Quartet
Orion Master Recordings ORS
  77262

Trio
David Ross, clarinet; William Preucil,
  viola; Tom Hundermer, horn
Orion Master Recordings ORS
  79340

FRED LERDAHL

$$\left(\text{b. 1949}\right)$$

Fred Lerdahl grew up in Wisconsin, learned the piano as a child, and played the oboe in his high school band and orchestra. He studied composition with James Ming at Lawrence University, Earl Kim at Princeton, and Arthur Berger and Roger Sessions at Tanglewood. He has been commissioned by the Spoleto Festival, the Orpheus Chamber Orchestra, the Chamber Music Society of Lincoln Center, and others. His works have been performed by the New York Philharmonic, the Pittsburgh Symphony, the San Francisco Symphony, the Boston Symphony Chamber Players, and the Juilliard Quartet.

Lerdahl is also known as a music theorist, notably for his book *A Generative Theory of Tonal Music* (written with the linguist Ray Jackendoff), which models musical listening from the perspective of cognitive science. For him, composition and theory form a comfortable partnership.

"I started evolving my compositional techniques out of my theoretical work," he says. "It's not that I completely invented everything, but I developed a set of compositional techniques that are partly my own, partly out of my music theory, and in some cases related to composers like Debussy and Bartók."

Fred Lerdahl is Fritz Reiner Professor of Musical Composition at Columbia University. This interview took place in New York City in October 1995.

•   •   •

For me, composing is a need. It's something that's been deep in my psyche from an early age. I do music theory, too, and I'm creative in that, though the field's different. But I am always seeking an idea, which I have to think through. I get emotionally invested in it, whether it's a purely musical idea or a theoretical one. I have to think through it for myself and create this thing, which is mine.

I think certain conditions in my family made music important to me, including being exposed to a lot of music early on. Coming from a somewhat troubled family might have driven me to music as a refuge. I think that's not uncommon, actually. So music has always been a comfort for me. It gives me emotional and intellectual fulfillment. If I don't listen to a certain amount of music, I feel deprived.

I grew up in Madison, Wisconsin. My parents got my two older sisters the best piano teacher in town, but since I was a boy and was supposed to play sports, which I loved to do, I got a semicompetent piano teacher. I didn't start piano lessons until the age of ten, but I was the one who was really gifted in music.

There's an amusing and appalling incident I remember from my piano lessons. My teacher had assigned me the theme from the slow movement of Beethoven's Fifth Symphony, arranged for whatever level of John Thompson I was in. We had the record of the symphony at home, so I listened to it and arranged the whole movement by ear. When I went to my lesson the next week, I gave it to my teacher and said, "Look what I did!" And she said, "Oh, that's very nice. But did you practice your assignment for the week?" I quit not long after that.

I improvised at the piano a lot, then started taking oboe lessons. I played in the school band and orchestra and started composing around the eighth grade. I had a friend in the ninth grade who was already writing pieces, and he told me I ought to write some of mine down. By the time I was a senior in high school, I had an orchestra piece that was premiered by the high school orchestra I played first oboe in.

My mother was OK about my musical activities. My father ran an insurance company and loved music, but the fact that I could think in sound was very mysterious to him. He also thought that people with that kind of talent starved. One of his clients was a composer, a professor at the University of Wisconsin, so he had me make an appointment with this professor at his house. The professor looked at my music, checked out my ear, and gave me a thorough examination to see if I had what it took to make a living as a musician. I passed quite easily, and my father relaxed.

The way I compose has changed over the years, and it's had a lot to do with my theory work. When I was in college I would dash off five, seven pieces a year, leave them in whatever state of completion I got them to. But in graduate school I was suddenly faced with the enormity of what it takes to write a *good* piece. I became aware of all the problems that contemporary music has, both sociologically and with its musical language—everybody composes by a different system, or without a system, and therefore by the seat of his pants. So many different aesthetics and syntaxes were going on at once, and it seemed to me very unsatisfactory. I also felt that whenever composers did compose in systems, those systems were arbitrary and not hearable. At the time I started thinking about this, I was studying with Milton Babbitt.

I certainly respect his intelligence and originality, but for me he stands for the kind of arbitrary, essentially unmusical system-making that has typified much composition in this century.

All of this was very much on my mind early on, and I think it got in my way for awhile because I became very self-conscious. I was composing a lot with texts in those days because it helped me overcome problems of purely musical organization. My music was fairly atonal and intuitive, written largely from beginning to end. I found that when I set words, I could project the vocal line well in advance, and build my forms around it.

Then, in the mid-'70s, I started (with Ray Jackendoff) developing this generative theory of tonal music, which is basically a theory about how people hear music. I became deeply involved with cognitive psychology and was trying to make a musical model for how the mind works. The whole point of it, at least at the outset, was to create a foundation for myself as a composer that I could believe in. I wasn't interested in composing by private codes. I wanted to compose by methods whereby somebody could hear everything, where the basic kind of organization was cognitively transparent. Since then my attitude has become more nuanced, but that is where my impulses toward theory-making began.

So building my theory and composing have gone hand and hand. I started evolving my compositional techniques out of my theoretical work. It's not that I completely invented everything, but I developed a set of techniques that are partly my own and partly out of my music theory, and in some respects related to techniques of composers like Debussy, Bartók, Carter, and Ligeti.

By the late '70s and my first string quartet, I started to evolve what I call "expanding variation form." To explain it would be very technical, but it is a way of working that is strict, but quite audible. It involves geometric expansion from variation to variation. As I expand, I keep within the framework of what I created before.

I don't use this in every piece, but I've used it a great deal. There are certain things about it that appeal to me, aside from the fact that it's basically a hearable process. It's also very important for me to have a tonic. I want my music to have a home base, with points of departure radiating from that. The process is expressively powerful. In a sense, I wanted to recover tonality through a method of my own invention. The expanding variation idea creates a form that is uniquely my own.

I use the expanding variation idea in different ways. I might create one kind of variation for one part of the orchestra, then give another kind of music, with different rhythms and tempos, to another part of the orchestra. As the second music develops, the first music might come to a point of completion. I've created a number of pieces that do this—it's like weaving a tapestry.

Whether I'm working in this tapestry-like way or doing one large expanding variation from beginning to end, the process is very controlled. On the other hand, I know only in part where a variation is going to go. Having expanded to one point, I'll build a larger expansion with the next variation, and that expansion has to take place within the framework of what I've already done. At the same time, what I do with this new variation is open-ended. It's constrained by what I did, but it's not constrained in terms of the future. It's like a tightrope or highwire act, having strong constraints and a lot of freedom as well. Composing a piece in this way is an adventure. You're controlled by what you've done, but where you're going could be any number of things.

So when I'm composing this way, I don't plan pieces from beginning to end. What I'm committed to is a process of developing material. I just know I'll go along using a set of techniques. In any particular case I won't know what the piece is until it works its way through. I usually have a sound image early on of what a piece is, and what it expresses, but I often don't know until I'm well along what it's going to look like as a whole. (Sometimes, when I'm starting to conceive a piece, I imagine the performing group on stage. In that way I try to externalize it, visualize what I'm going to do.) It's not a top-down way of composing at all. It's very intuitive. I'm a formalist, but I use an open-ended formalism that allows me lots of fantasy. That combination is something I've always wanted, and struggled for a long time to achieve. I feel like I've evolved a melodic, harmonic, rhythmic and formal language that I could work and evolve within for the next fifty years. My limitations are time and imagination.

I have a store of almost conceptual ideas for pieces I haven't written yet. For instance, I think it would be really wonderful to write an orchestra piece that has no obvious internal boundaries whatsoever, something that's just evolving sound, as in some computer music pieces where you can't tell when a particular event begins and ends. It would be completely different from anything I've ever written. I would make harmonies and colors occur in such a way that you'd never feel any attacks, or any normal boundaries. A few pieces have tried to do that, European ones in particular, but they don't have much structure. My theories suggest ways to overcome this problem.

Marches [for chamber ensemble; 1992] was an "idea piece." I wanted to write a piece that was a bunch of marches, completely in 4/4 time. It isn't an expanding variation piece, but it uses all the overlaying effects that came from that technique. In this piece, marches overlap continuously. One goes into another, or two go on at once, then another emerges from a previous one, and so on. The mood alternates constantly between passion and humor.

For *Quiet Music* [for orchestra, 1994] I used another set of constraints. *Quiet Music* came from a sound image, not from an idea. That sound, which I'd heard in my head for years, had high, active woodwinds playing patterned figures, and low brass with beautiful, rich, deep chords. The whole thing was to be very quiet and peaceful but also very complex.

A few years before I had written a piece called *Waves* [for chamber orchestra; 1988] that was very fast, with driving sixteenth-note motion from beginning to end. It's in expanding variation form, and a very strict piece from that point of view. Having sixteenth notes going all the time was a strange constraint. For *Quiet Music* I wanted to do this again, but at a *moderato* tempo. But when I superimposed that same constraint on the sound image of *Quiet Music*, I got a different expressive effect. In my first image of the music, those active patterns that I heard high in the high woodwinds and in what I call my gamelan sound [high piano, harp, high mallet percussion] would be the sixteenth notes and would get the piece moving. Beneath that, I would write expanding variations, the overlaid, tapestry kind. I wanted the whole process to be seamless and smooth, throughout the piece. The constant sixteenth notes would provide a backdrop for expanding variations embodying highly contrasting and even disturbing materials. As it turned out, even the sixteenth notes—that is, every single musical strand—became subject to the expanding variation technique.

But then the oddest constraint of all in *Quiet Music* actually came as I was composing it. I was composing along, and I wanted to start building the piece, make it louder, like any normal composer would do, and every time I tried to get loud, the music told me, "No, I don't want to get loud." Now, it's not uncommon for the music to speak back to me, especially if it's going very well or if it's not going well at all. If I didn't have a fair amount of self-confidence, I would have denied what the music was telling me and made it get loud like a piece should get loud. But I said, "OK, you want to be quiet? I'll go for broke. I'll see if I can make you *pianissimo* from beginning to end." The very thought of doing that terrified me. How could I write a fifteen-minute piece that was always *pianissimo*? It took me about two or three weeks to come to terms with this, but I did it, and I achieved my climaxes through orchestration, texture, and other means. The effect is uncanny.

I like my routines. I'm a morning person. If I'm composing well, I'm usually working by nine. If I don't start in the morning, I'm probably not going to get very much done, unless the piece is already basically written and I'm just working on details. But if I start in the morning I can often go all day and into the evening. If I'm working a lot, I always take a nap after lunch—that seems to give me the energy to create again. One of my main problems in life is finding the time to compose—partly because I do music theory as well as compose, partly because I teach and I have a family. There's just a lot going on. But I always do one thing at a time. I never do theory when I'm composing. Composing is more completely intuitive than theory. The whole body is involved.

I use a piano a fair amount, not necessarily to hear what I'm writing but to *feel* what I'm writing, to get the physical feeling of it. I usually work well under pressure, although I've had a couple of close calls—too close for comfort. I hate that. It's incredibly nerve-wracking.

Composing is very holistic—you can break it apart into this or that dimension if you want, but I always think through the instruments for the lines and the harmonies that I'm imagining. The timbral sound, the tone, is terribly important to me. If I'm writing for a singer, I try to hear that singer. I don't put an orchestra piece into full score immediately, but I know what it's going to sound like, down to the details. Some composers write out all the pitches, beginning to end, and then decide what instruments are going to play and what the rhythms are going to be. I can't imagine composing like that. In fact, I disapprove of it. I think it's a disconnected way to work.

I think that atonality will one day be judged as the oddity. When I say tonality, I don't mean common-practice tonality, necessarily, I just mean a pitch center and degrees of moving away or toward it. I think that the need to have reference points is deep in our makeup as human beings. Lots of research in psychology shows that hierarchies enable us to learn and remember better. I think tonality is basically a psychological operation. A composer doesn't have to take advantage of that, but why not? I'm interested in creating a kind of music that is on some level transparent, even though it can be complex. Almost all the music in the world is tonal, in the sense that I am using the word. Tonality is inevitable, which is not to say that I'm restricting it to what we know. I think there are kinds of music that we've only begun to dream of.

Sometimes I wish I could write within the assumptions of, say, Mozart. He had so many schemas to work with: when he appeared, the musical language was at a very stable point; it was a complex cultural organism. There were so many routines: how to write a melody, or a harmonic progression, a certain phrase type, a certain form, the whole thing. He imbibed all of that and was able to compose very quickly because of it. He could put down the main lines of a piece and then flesh it out. We don't have all of those givens now. I suppose we could regret that, but on the other hand it's exciting to explore things that aren't given. I feel I've developed enough givens for myself, and I don't find it as terrifying as I used to. It would be nice if the musical language today were generalized, if we had some kind of consensus. I don't know if that will happen or not. In fact, so far, it's gone the other way.

In one sense, I envy a composer like Boulez, who matured extremely early because he had a cutthroat view of music history and musical style. He could say, "I reject this, I reject that"—he rejected almost everything. He took Webern for pitch, Stravinsky for rhythm, Debussy for color—a pure, narrowed idea of each. That took strength of character, but it also simplified his sound world, because his idea was narrow. I have come to accept and enjoy the multiplicity of my own tastes and judgments, and therefore of the music that I compose.

I teach composition and encounter all kinds of creativity, or attempts thereof. I have one student who can only work from the beginning, from left to right. He runs into formal problems all the time, because he's always following his nose like a dog on a scent. I have another student who's just the opposite, who's enamored of trying to find what I call a gizmo, some mechanism that will justify the actual notes, the rhythms—a kind of top-down systems approach. In most cases I try to get them to do just the opposite of what they're used to, so they'll learn what it's like from the other side.

I think it's incredibly important to listen to what your music is telling you, because it's really your unconscious responding to what you've already done so far. You have to let yourself acknowledge that, and trust that feeling. That isn't easy, because composers are always trying to *make* things work. It's very hard to stop looking over your own shoulder, even when you think you're a mature composer. It's a matter of being able to trust your boldest ideas.

Fred Lerdahl, Selected Works

SMALL ENSEMBLE

Fantasy Etudes (1985)
chamber ensemble

Imitations (1977; revised 1992)
flute, viola, harp

Marches (1992)
chamber ensemble

Second String Quartet (1980–82)

Wake (1968)
soprano and chamber ensemble
text: James Joyce

Waltzes (1981)
violin, viola, cello, bass

LARGE ENSEMBLE

Chords (1974–83)
orchestra

Cross-Currents (1987)
orchestra

Quiet Music (1994)
orchestra

Waves (1988)
chamber orchestra

Without Fanfare (1994)
winds and percussion

Publisher: Boelke-Bomart; distributed by Jerona, P.O. Box 671, Englewood, NJ 07631. Tel. 201-488-0550, fax 201-569-7023.

Fred Lerdahl, Selected Recordings

Eros; Fantasy Etudes; Wake; Waltzes
Beverly Morgan, mezzo-soprano;
Collage/Lerdahl
Musical Elements/Beaser

Bethany Beardslee, soprano;
Boston Symphony Chamber
Players/Epstein
R. Schulte, violin; S. Nickrenz,
viola; F. Sherry, cello; D. Palma,
double bass
The Music of Fred Lerdahl:
CRI 580

First String Quartet
Juilliard Quartet
CRI 551

Waves
Orpheus Chamber Orchestra
Points of Departure, DG
435389-2GH

SHULAMIT RAN

$$\left(\text{B. } 1949\right)$$

S hulamit Ran was born in Tel Aviv, Israel, and came to the United States at the age of fourteen, having received scholarships from the Mannes College of Music in New York and the America Israel Cultural Foundation. Her composition teachers in Israel and in the United States included A. U. Boskovich, Paul Ben Haim, Norman Dello Joio, and Ralph Shapey.

Ran has been composer-in-residence with the Chicago Symphony Orchestra and the Lyric Opera of Chicago and teaches composition at the University of Chicago. Her works have been performed by the New York Philharmonic, the Cleveland Orchestra, the Chamber Music Society of Lincoln Center, and many others. Her *Symphony*, commissioned by the Philadelphia Orchestra, won the 1991 Pulitzer Prize in music composition.

A number of Ran's works are intense expressions of her Jewish heritage. Her 1997 opera *Between Two Worlds*, an adaptation of S. Ansky's classic 1920 drama *The Dybbuk,* is a recent example. The Ansky drama, inspired by an Eastern European Jewish folk tale of a woman possessed by the spirit of her dead lover, haunted Ran as a child. Her music for the opera often alludes to Eastern European Yiddish song and dance.

Shulamit Ran divides her time between Chicago and Sycamore, Illinois, where she lives with her husband and two sons. This interview took place in Chicago in May 1996.

• • •

There are many wonderful ways to lead a rich, meaningful life, but my life had to be in music. I started to compose when I was very young. It was a very natural thing, as natural as talking and walking. It was a normal activity for me that was very pleasurable and felt absolutely right. When you have something with that kind of power in your life, you don't stop doing it.

I started to make up tunes when I was about seven. I went to school in Israel, and in some of the stories we read, the characters would suddenly stop to sing a song. The lines in the book would suddenly change there—they would become much narrower and would rhyme. That for me was an instant cue—when I got to those lines, I would sing the song. Then I would go home to my mother, and she would ask me, "What did you do in school today?" I would say, "We read this wonderful story." Then I would read it to her, and when I got to that place I would sing. She would say to me, "Where does this melody come from?" And I would point to the written words and say, "Right here! Don't you see?" I was convinced that anybody reading those words would hear the same melody that I heard. I thought the melodies were just part of the words. I was really stunned to discover that my mother didn't hear those same melodies I did, that in fact, *no* one else did!

I started applying that same treatment to every verse that I encountered. As it happened, the Israeli writers of the early period of the Israeli state considered writing for children a very high priority. We had many great poets who spent a portion of their time writing especially for young children. So I set some of these writings to music, and I started studying piano, because it was the most wonderful toy that I had ever encountered.

I played my songs for my piano teacher, who was clearly a very good pedagogue because he wrote the songs down and then, without me knowing about it, sent some of them to Israeli radio. A few months later we got a letter notifying us that a couple of those songs were going to be broadcast over the radio, sung by a children's choir.

I remember that broadcast better than anything. It happened when I was in summer camp, and all the children, at the designated time, sat around this box radio, and my songs were coming out of it, and it was fantastic! The songs were mine, but at the same time they were no longer mine. They had their own independent existence. They had a life of their own. I knew I wanted to replicate this experience again and again and again—that was really the decisive moment.

There have been other things that have interested me a lot, and that I could see making for a very fulfilling life. I always liked to write prose, work with words. That was something very natural. Acting seemed very natural, too—I would play the lead role in the school plays and all those things. I suppose I liked putting myself in fantasy land, in any way that was possible. But none of these activities had the same magnetism for me that music did. There was never any question for me. There was never a moment when I had to think, "All right, let's see, what is my career choice?"

When I begin to compose a new piece, there is always a little element of hysteria. It's always there, because the time I have to make the piece always seems too short.

First, I look for an idea in sound that seems like an appropriate central idea for the piece. I want it to be compelling enough to draw the listener in, to make them want to stay with it. Sometimes that part of the process can take a good while. Several things might be playing in my head for weeks until just the right thing or what seems to be the right thing presents itself. And those right things can come at such odd times. One of my more important ideas arrived while I was waiting at a bus stop, and another came when I was taking the garbage to the chute—that gives you an idea of how odd, how unpredictable, those moments can be.

But they don't "just happen" for me. They don't just suddenly pop into my head. I'm constantly working in my mind. The idea is growing, and when that right moment happens, I could be anywhere. The thing, the idea, could be anything. Very often it is just a very few bars—maybe four notes, a succession of some sort that to my mind is interesting and can be developed.

Coming up with ideas is the most difficult thing, and it's also the easiest. I tell my students again and again that a composer is not just about coming up with great ideas, and a piece is not made up of a succession of great ideas. You need to be able to develop an idea, to take it to maturity.

I don't know how composing happens. It's very, very difficult to pinpoint what exactly goes on. There's some kind of elusive and yet absolutely necessary balance between fantasy and rigor. It's a constant back-and-forth thing. It's magic. You work things out and think about them, and manipulate sounds, sometimes rigorously, sometimes intuitively, and then suddenly there is that incredible moment when you feel that you have made a leap upward.

A lot of composers use images or analogies for what they do. They cite other forms of creativity. For example, "architecture in sound"—Ralph Shapey has used that expression, in particular. Varese talks about the engineer in sound. I've heard Joan Tower talk about being a choreographer in sound. These are all very compelling images. The one I personally like very much is "sculpture in sound." When I describe my music, I use my hands, because I think there is a sense in me, a desire, to impart concrete, physical weight to it. I've never witnessed how a sculptor works—I imagine he or she would constantly go at it from many directions. It's not an ongoing narrative, A to B, but a constant back-and-forth. What you do at one angle affects what you do at the other. You go around it, and to the side of it, shaping and molding. I feel that's how I work most of the time, as well.

I work both at the piano and away from it. The "idea" usually comes to me away from the piano. The piano is useful for concretizing the sound, yet it's often necessary for me to get away from the instrument and think about larger issues, the larger proportions of what I am working on. So I go back and forth—closer to, then more distant from, actual sound.

It's very frustrating to work and work, think a lot, and then write a little bit down, and sometimes throw it in the trash—it doesn't feel good to work a full day and have nothing to show for it. Yet I've finally reconciled myself to the fact that these are essential phases of the process. I'm sifting through the many available options. Maybe I have to go through the obvious options before the right road appears. That's very often the only way to get to that special, right road. This process has been described as the agony and the ecstasy, and there's no question that so much of the time is spent in agony! But you go through that agony because the ecstasy is so special.

Sometimes it happens that I make a wrong decision and for a little while I try to convince myself that it's OK. But I'm really no good at pulling the wool over my eyes. Usually, I come back to the piece the next day and see there's no way I can do this, so I backtrack. Sometimes I go on, encounter some trouble, work something out, and keep going, even though it doesn't feel right. And at the end I have to backtrack more than I want. But that excision, that surgical hand, is absolutely essential if a composer is going to get somewhere, because the point at which things go wrong may be a new area of exploration that you didn't see initially. You have to keep going back to that point, trying to figure out what to do. Often the problem is that you've just refused to bend the right way.

I suppose the ideal life would be to just sit and compose and do nothing else. But I'm not sure it would be *that* ideal—maybe for considerable periods of time, it would! I'm actually quite disciplined. I think that most people who are creative and who have deadlines to meet are. But life presents obstacles, and I have not been able to create a regular daily time to compose. It's a fallacious assumption that the schedule of a composer who teaches is easy, that you have a lot of free time. It doesn't work out that way. I try very hard to teach only half of the day so that I will still have part of the day left to compose. It doesn't matter to me whether that part is in the morning or in the late afternoon. The important thing to be able to strike a balance. Teaching is very exhausting—like everything else, it is a creative endeavor, and it takes a lot out of you if you do it the right way. A full day of it can be so tiring that the next day you're not good for anything much.

I've found that if I compose something, I should not copy it right away because I may very well come back to it the next day and want to change it. In

fact, a small section can take a week, because I'll still be shaping it and changing it. I don't start copying any given section until I've made considerable
progress forward from that point. Even so, I've gone back often after copying
to change things, usually because of some idea that wakes me in the middle of
the night.

I know a lot of composers who have a master plan at the beginning and fill
in the blanks. Others just start writing. I'll give you a specific example of how
I work. My most recent orchestral work is *Legends*, which was commissioned
by the Chicago Symphony. When I began working on it, I was very strongly
considering the idea of a two-movement form. I'd written other large-scale
works that had more movements, and I wanted to do something that would
have fewer separate sections.

Once I came up with a basic idea—the one that came to me while waiting at the bus stop—and started working with it, it seemed as though the
piece would have only one movement. I hadn't found the right way of man-
aging the idea of the two-movement form. And I said, "OK, if that is the way
it is proceeding, then this will be a one-movement composition."

But at a certain point—I must have been about a third of the way through
the entirety of the piece—I had the large-scale vision: what I wanted, how the
whole thing would work out as a valid, two-movement piece. There would be
no other way for it to feel right. There was an inner necessity to it. And so,
having done quite a bit of work already, having struggled to find the way, the
larger scale became evident to me.

Deadlines probably have an enormous impact on the way I work. It's hard to
say with absolute certainty, because it's been close to twenty years since I
worked without a deadline. I have no idea at this point what it would feel like
to say, "I'm going to write this large piece, and just do it." Maybe having no
deadline would give you a special kind of freedom. I'm all for composing the
thing that you want to compose. I would never ever take a commission that
didn't really intrigue me, and I won't take anything that's just an assignment.
I want to do pieces that mean something to me, that feel as though they contain the next step for me to develop.

I was going to write an opera no matter what. I'd been talking about writing one for a long time, and I realized one day that unless I blocked out serious time, I would never write one. So I started saying no to a lot of things—
a lot of very interesting, potentially attractive ideas. An opera wasn't
something I could just do in my leisure time! My publisher asked me, "Don't
you want a big commission to write this opera?" And I said, "Well, sure, I'd
like it, but that's not going to determine my doing it or my not doing it. It's
just the next thing that I'm going to do." And I really did free up time, and
then out of the blue came that invitation from the Lyric [for *Between Two
Worlds*], so it worked out perfectly.

The impact of performers on my work is very pronounced. I can think of all sorts of examples where knowing the performer inspired how I was going to make a piece. Even the way that I perceive the relationships between players in an ensemble determines things. It offers fuel for the fire; it makes the sparks fly. You want to make the best of the special qualities that they have.

I've done several pieces for the Da Capo Chamber Players, and they've become wonderful friends. Laura Flax, the clarinetist, was my point of entry into that group. We knew each other when I first came to the United States. Her mother worked with the America Israel Cultural Foundation, which supported me, both in Israel and in this country. Years later, when her mother died, Laura wrote me a letter reminding me of who she was and asking if I would write a piece in memory of her mother. Through working together we became very special friends. I wrote her a piece and others for Da Capo as I got to know the group.

The last piece I wrote for them, for their twentieth anniversary, is *Mirage*, which uses five players, and because I'd already written for Laura, and for André Emelianoff, the cellist, the voice that carries this piece is the flute [Pat Spencer]. One of the best parts of this business is the special intimacy with the performers who play your work—it's a very powerful and intimate art. You get into their souls and they get into yours, via the piece.

Another important collaboration came when I was commissioned by the Eastman School in 1984 to write a piece for Jan DeGaetani, whom I really, really wanted to write for. I loved her voice and what she did with it, and what she stood for. This piece involved a very unusual ensemble: oboe alternating with English horn [for Philip West, Jan DeGaetani's husband], also viola da gamba and harpsichord for another couple, Martha McGaughey and Arthur Haas. The four of them wanted to celebrate the multiple centennial of Bach, Handel, Scarlatti, and Schütz. They planned a program for this baroque combination, and on it they would play one piece written in 1985.

My first thought was, "Oh my God! What am I going to do with this?" I had never thought about writing for the viola da gamba, and the combination is so unusual. But at the same time I knew that if I'd been asked to write for Jan DeGaetani and a kazoo, or Jan DeGaetani and a typewriter, I would find a way to do it! It was a joyous experience, learning the souls of these instruments, discovering the viola da gamba and the way it interrelated with these other voices, seeing how I could make it my own, in my style.

And so, the presence of a very great performer, whom we all miss so terribly now, was a major influence on this piece. Her voice, which was always so magnificent, was at that point in her life a very rich instrument with a fantastic bottom range, an unbelievable sound. And even though she had that magnificent low range, her vibrato had a leanness, a purity to it that not many low mezzo-sopranos have. I explored and exploited that in *Amichai Songs* (1985), knowing full well that there weren't many other singers for whom this piece would be appropriate.

The human condition is full of pains and agonies and hardships—I don't know very many people who just go through life dancing. If they appear to do so, it's because you don't know them very well. The large majority of human-kind lives in such conditions that creativity is a luxury that cannot be fathomed. I'm lucky to have grown up in a time and in a place where there was encouragement, where the fact that I was a woman was not an issue but helped my progress. It is a privilege just to have been born into this life.

Whatever ability I have to use sound as my medium is probably programmed genetically. Talent is an innate thing, but it's only a foundation. What counts is everything that you put into developing it. In order to write you need to have imagination. You do need to be involved with life, whether it's by doing things or imagining them.

One piece I felt a need, a compulsion, to write, is *O, the Chimneys*, a setting of five poems by Nelly Sachs. I wrote it when I was nineteen, and the subject is the Holocaust. It was my way of saying, "Do not forget." In the last few years I have seen a resurgence in the amount of work on that theme, because we are reaching the point where fewer and fewer people who actually lived through that period are still around. Many people are beginning to realize that unless they make a mark in some way, all will be gone, forgotten. It is essential that we remember it.

When I wrote my piece, there were hardly any works written on the subject. I could take my imagination wherever I wanted. I was born in Israel, a free country that had come through tremendous hardship and is still struggling with basic issues of survival. As a child, I read a lot about the Holocaust—it was part of my growing up, even though I hadn't gone through it myself. Many times after a performance of my piece, people would come up to me, roll up their sleeve, show me a number on their arm, and say, "I was there—how did you know?" One man said to me, "You made me relive this!" That was a profound moment for me.

I'm only saying this to make the point that if there's one thing that is a little bit special about an artist, it is that they are able to put themselves in places where they've not actually been. They can imagine, with empathy, the greatest joy and the greatest suffering.

Some people say to me, "Oh, you're an artist, you must have suffered an awful lot," and others say, "You're an artist—how wonderful it must be to have the muse come visit you, to just sit down and have these things happen!" Well, both are equally fallacious points of view. I think there is a muse, actually, but you have to make it come visit you—you have to find a way to invite it, and then find a way to work with it. Again, it comes down to discipline—the huge amount of work required to persevere and follow a vision.

I say to my students, Don't assume that your first thought is going to be your best thought. Sometimes it is, but just because something quite nice comes out of you doesn't mean you shouldn't push yourself further and further, until something that is *really* special emerges. After all, we are dealing with the one thing that means more than anything else in the world, and that is time. We're also dealing with other people's time—listeners' and performers' time. We're monopolizing it, occupying it in some way. So we have to make their experience very special. Don't assume that you know everything, don't be so conceited to think that what you have will be good enough. Push yourself further.

Shulamit Ran, Selected Works

SMALL ENSEMBLE

Apprehensions (1979)
voice, clarinet, piano
text: Sylvia Plath

Concerto da camera II (1987)
clarinet, string quartet, piano

Excursions (1980)
violin, cello, piano

Mirage (1990)
flute/alto/piccolo, clarinet, violin,
    cello, percussion

O, the Chimneys (1969)
mezzo-soprano, flute,
    clarinet/bass clarinet, cello,
    percussion, tape
text: Nelly Sachs

String Quartet no. 2: "Vistas"
    (1989)

Three Fantasy Pieces (1971)
cello and piano

Verticals (1982)
piano solo

LARGE ENSEMBLE

Concerto for Orchestra (1986)

Legends for Orchestra (1993)

Symphony (1989–90)

STAGE

Between Two Worlds (*The Dybbuk*), (1995–1997)
libretto: Charles Kondek

Publisher: Theodore Presser,
    Presser Place, Bryn Mawr, PA
    19010. Tel. 215-525-3636;
    fax 215-527-7841.

Shulamit Ran, Selected Recordings

Apprehensions; *Concerto da camera II*; *East Wind*
Da Capo Chamber Players
CRI 609

Fantasy Movements for Cello and Chamber Orchestra
Nina Flyer, cello; English
    Chamber Orchestra/Falletta
Koch International Classics KIC
    7269

Hyperbolae
A. Stokman, piano
CRI 609

Inscriptions for Solo Violin; *Mirage*;
    Private Game; *To an Actor: Monologue for Clarinet*
Da Capo Chamber Players
Bridge BRI 9052

Quartet No. 1
Mendelssohn String Quartet
Koch International Classics KIC 7269

CHRISTOPHER ROUSE

(B. 1949)

Christopher Rouse grew up in Baltimore, where he developed an early interest in both classical music and rock and roll. He began composing at age seven and studied the guitar and drums. His composition teachers included Richard Hoffman at Oberlin Conservatory and Karel Husa at Cornell University, where he earned a doctorate in composition. He also worked privately with George Crumb in Philadelphia.

Rouse became known in the 1970s and early 1980s as a composer able to combine formal classical training with the spirit of rock music (he also happened to offer the first accredited course at a major music school on the history of rock and roll). In the past decade, his music has grown increasingly impassioned and introspective.

Christopher Rouse was composer-in-residence of the Baltimore Symphony from 1986 to 1989 and teaches at the Eastman School of Music and the Juilliard School. His music has been commissioned by the Baltimore Symphony, the Houston Symphony, cellist Yo-Yo Ma, and many others. His trombone concerto, commissioned by the New York Philharmonic, won the 1993 Pulitzer Prize for music. Rouse lives in Rochester, New York, with his family. This interview took place in Rochester in March 1996.

•   •   •

I don't know why I compose—it's almost like manifest destiny.

I feel like it's why I'm on the planet. I don't mean to sound pompous, because I don't actually enjoy composing. Most of the good friends to whom

I've spoken about this say the same thing—composing is not an enjoyable process. After the piece is completed and the performance goes well, it seems like it was worth doing. But the actual process of sitting down and trying to find the right notes and getting them correctly onto the page is not fun. I do it because I'm driven to, I suppose. It's just an obsession.

Look at Rossini and Sibelius, composers who said, "OK, I've had my say, and I'm going to pack it in." They spent the last three or four decades of their lives not producing any more music, at least none of great substance. Sometimes I feel that would be an attractive option.

I think I was about six when I decided I wanted to become a composer. That was always my dream. It didn't occur to me then that composing would be anything other than a delight. I imagined myself sitting at the piano, looking heavenward for inspiration, getting the music down without a great deal of work, just hurriedly scribbling à la Mozart or Schubert, with a never-ending stream of ideas.

It was nearly that easy for me when I was younger. In college I wrote piece after piece, just churned it out like there was no tomorrow. Now I work very, very slowly. I think there are a couple of reasons for that. Most of us get more self-critical as we get older. We don't accept the easy solutions we accepted as sophomores in a conservatory. Also, I think the flow of ideas tends to slow down with age. Brahms said that when he was young he had idea after idea, but no concept of what to do with any of them. As an older man, he knew what to do with an idea, how to develop it, put it through its paces—if only he could get one!

When a project comes along that I get sufficiently excited about, I find the process of composing a little less unenjoyable. Then it's not such an onerous burden to generate a piece. What gets me interested in a piece is the person or group requesting it, whether it's somebody I've enjoyed working with in the past, or someone I haven't worked with but hold in high regard. With luck, the piece will get played more than once, or get recorded. That's always very gratifying, because it means more people will have a chance to hear it.

We live in such cynical times that I feel almost embarrassed expressing myself altruistically. But speaking for myself and for other creative artists, I think there is a need to speak to humanity, to say something meaningful about the human experience. We realize, of course, that the vast majority of Americans will never know our work exists. Even the majority of people who hear our pieces will not be struck by what we're writing about. But the connection our work makes with the few people who are affected, moved, or excited by our music validates the effort. To bring to receptive peoples' ears and eyes, hearts and brains a vision of what it is to be a human being is the real purpose for me—that's the reward.

I've never believed in composing or painting or writing as simply a form of masturbation. I've always been a little suspicious of somebody who creates only "so I can express myself." That's part of the equation, but an artist has to realize that he is at that same time expressing himself as part of a community and has an obligation to provide something worthwhile to that community. Sheer entertainment is fine, although a person who devotes his entire life to that and no more has probably missed an opportunity to accomplish something deeper.

I'm reacting in part to composers who have stressed technique over expressivity via systems, trying to control everything mathematically, allowing concepts to drive a whole piece. It's the influence, I think, of certain highly intellectualized types of music theory. It leads people to believe that because Beethoven put together a piece using a certain method, he intended it to be appreciated only on that level, that his whole raison d'être for writing a particular work was to organize his materials in this fashion. In our time, composers do a lot of precompositional organizing of materials, and if everything scans right, if people can find wonderful interrelationships and correlations in graduate analysis class, the piece must be good. Who cares if it attempts to address the emotions or the spirit? Cage had a different concept: total non-control, instead of total control. But both the Cage followers and the serialists were more concerned about polemics than about writing music, it sometimes seems to me.

To me, the great error of certain trends in twentieth-century music was ignoring the emotions or anything that speaks to the spirit. I'm not just referring to Webern and the post-Webern serialists. Stravinsky also was nearly afraid or unwilling to express emotion. His entire life's work, it seems to me, is a commentary on traditions, like a professor lecturing listeners on classicism instead of retranslating the spirit of classicism into his own time. I admire Stravinsky; how can I not? What an incredible musical mind! What invention! What imagination! But I can't think of one measure of Stravinsky that moves me.

Greg Sandow wrote in 1984 that a lot of people equate minimalism with the New Romanticism. In point of fact, minimalism has much more in common with serialism. Its roots are in an objective movement. Steve Reich has worked to simplify, slowing down the process of change while developing his materials. But Reich's music was no more meant to be "expressive" than was Milton Babbitt's. John Adams seems to have changed all of that—he joined the language of minimalism to the big statement, the emotionality, the desire to express something. That is what the New Romanticism was all about, and I think it in turn has come to influence Reich in a very effective way.

On to practical matters. Let's say I've been commissioned to write a twenty-minute orchestra piece, using no more than the basic complement of instruments, no extra players, no organ, no offstage brass. The first thing that occurs to me is what the piece will to try to say, what it's about. Next, I usually decide on the material near the end of the piece, the final point of arrival. Then I decide on various waystations, including the beginning of the piece (which may or may not be the next thing that occurs to me after the ending). Once I have enough waystations, I feel ready to begin writing, even though there are still millions of musical decisions to make. With enough waystations not too far apart from one another, I have an overall sense of the architecture of the piece. Figuring out how to get from A to B and B to C can happen during the process of writing.

On a few occasions I've gotten two or three minutes into a piece and thought, "No, no, no, wait! This is heading into a thicket that it shouldn't head into." So I start all over again. I haven't had to do that in awhile, but it can happen.

I use a little Casio keyboard to check things occasionally, but I really don't work at the keyboard. I'm not a pianist at all—I'm really incapable of playing the instrument. Long ago I was a percussionist, but I'm not trustworthy now. If you gave me a pair of snare drum sticks, I'd make a horrible sound.

I write everything out in full score, from the start. I'm pretty fastidious about my manuscripts. One of the advantages of taking pains is that it keeps the wheels turning, keeps me reevaluating. I work in pencil, but I try to make the score look as close to engraved music as I can. This slow process not only keeps me thinking about the piece, but it prevents me, I hope, from making mistakes I might have made had I worked faster. For me, the quality of the visual presentation has something to do with the quality of the music itself.

I know some people write music on the computer, but I like the tactile sense of holding an implement in my hand and pressing my ideas onto paper. I know there are advantages to a computer in terms of editing, but it seems that there would be a certain loss of connection sitting at a keyboard, moving a mouse around, just watching the notes appear on a computer screen. It's different if you've actually drawn the notehead, the flag, and the flat.

I try to stay a year ahead of my commissioning deadlines. I am somewhat like Mahler in the sense that I'm a summer composer. When Eastman is in session I just ponder a new piece when I have some free time. The actual process of getting the music down on paper begins when classes end, and it's always a race for me to finish up before the beginning of the next academic year.

I do much better work when I smoke cigars, but I can't smoke them indoors, so when I'm planning a piece, I walk around outside with a cigar. I find the creative juices flow in direct proportion to the tobacco juice! Also, I always work better with other sounds going on around me, something that I can give a quarter of an ear to. I've never been able to go to a place like the MacDowell Colony because the silence would kill me. I like to have the TV on when I write. I need a certain kind of chaos, but not chaos that I need to interact with. I can't have music on when I compose, and if the kids are downstairs with me it's hard to get much done. But if CNN or some silly talk show is on TV, that's good, and I always tune in to my soap opera at two in the afternoon. If I'm not here, I tape it. There's only one I watch—Another World.

Even as a student at Oberlin, I composed in the conservatory lounge where the other students were milling about. I didn't do so well if people sat down and started to talk to me, but as long as I could just be there, like a voyeur, and just write with everything going on around me, I got a lot more done than I would alone in my dorm room. I can't really explain it. Maybe distraction jazzes me up a little bit more. Or maybe it actually helps me see things—you know how sometimes you can't find the answer because you're too close to it, and when you back away from it, it becomes clear? Maybe listening to Sally Jesse Raphael ask, "How can you talk that way to your mother?" to a bunch of rude, bad-attitude kids—maybe that level of inane distraction sometimes helps gel ideas that I'm trying to get down on paper. Bizarre! Lord knows I have plenty of friends who go crazy if they can't have absolute silence.

There's no right way to do it. Sam Adler, for example, believes in keeping the machine oiled, the gears running. Every day you get up and write music for two hours. You may not keep any of it, but you do it. Others write when they feel they've got something to write. I fall into this category. I'm perfectly content not writing when school is in session—I don't feel any need to sit down in the middle of the fall semester, the third week of October, and start writing a piece. Sam could never work that way, and I could never work the way Sam does.

I went to visit George Crumb once when he was working on *Star Child*. He had written out the full score, and he had all the pages tacked up on the wall. Well, there was one blank page, page 11. And I said, "What's happening here, George?" And he said, "I don't know. I don't quite know what music's going to go there, but it'll go on that page." I found that fascinating. He had no idea what it was going to be, but it wasn't going to be any longer than a page, or any less. Talk about an interesting creative process! I could never do that, but it worked for him.

Occasionally a piece seems to be enough of a stinker to warrant euthanasia, and I'll just pull it from my catalogue. But I don't usually revise or rework pieces. There may be a little something or other I decide to change, like moving a few notes from the horn to the first trumpet—that's easy to do. But in terms of rewriting, say, five pages of a piece, I just never do it. It's not that I think my music is so perfect; it's just that I want to go on to the next project.

I've pulled virtually everything I wrote before the age of thirty except for a couple of the percussion pieces. It didn't feel particularly good or bad to do that; it just felt necessary. In most cases I had lived with the piece, listened to it on tape over several years. Every time I listened, I felt queasy about certain passages, more and more with each listening, until I reached the point of deciding, "This just isn't good enough. I don't want this piece kicking around." If I felt anything, it was a sense of tacit relief: "OK, this dog is not going to be out there to embarrass me any more." It helped that I'd written five or six pieces in the interim, pieces I felt better about. There are still people who think I made a mistake by pulling my old wind ensemble piece. The best part of it was ripped off from the *Jaws* soundtrack. I had to pull the plug on that piece—it deserved it. The last thing I jettisoned was a fanfare I wrote for the Houston Symphony in 1986. It took me six months to write this two-minute piece—that's always a sign that you're in trouble, when it takes that long to write such a modest work. When I heard it, I thought, "This sounds like Janitor in a Drum—it's turgid, it makes no sense, I don't want people to hear this!"

I don't revise much, but there's a passage in my first symphony that I have reused in two other works, my trombone concerto and a piece called *Jagganath*. In both instances I consciously referred to the first symphony because that passage, which is an enormous orchestral scream of annihilation, means something very specific. It's become a totem for me, and it means the same thing when I use it in other pieces.

In the first symphony the passage comes where the music reaches a point of resignation, as if an enormous earlier struggle is going to lift away, with a sense of reconciliation. But instead, what pops up is this orchestral scream. It destroys the repose and, with it, the imagined human spirit that the symphony is about. The passage represents the idea of destroying a hero, for no purpose whatsoever.

I used that unanticipated scream of agony when I wanted a similar effect in the two other works. Nobody's ever picked up on it, but I intended it to represent the same thing each time.

I certainly believe in a *lingua franca* that many of us understand, ways of instantly expressing certain emotional states. In that vein, the shriek in my first symphony was inspired by the Montagues and Capulets movement of Prokofiev's *Romeo and Juliet*. In the beginning there is just one note at a time, but the music grows into a grindingly dissonant roar. Now, my notes were different and my harmony was totally different, but that basic gesture of the orchestra, the trumpets on top, the high screaming "Agghhhh!" and the trumpets coming down in half-steps—that's from Prokofiev. Prokofiev knew what the effect of that gesture would be, and I've used it for the same purpose.

I don't like to bias people by saying, "This is what my piece means." There are several ways of looking at the composer's role in establishing "meaning." One point of view says the piece already existed and the composer only acted as a channeler to bring it into another dimension—so that what the composer intended in the piece is no more valuable than what anyone else thinks about it. In literary criticism these days, that point of view is all the rage, as if there's no point in asking the artist what he or she intended, because it doesn't matter.

On the other hand, there are people who say the creative artist is the sole arbiter of the meaning of the work, and if you don't get what the composer says is in the piece, there's something wrong with you and your ears. I'm somewhere between those two points of view.

As a student, I felt like something of an outcast because the composers I loved were not the accepted "great ones" of the first half of the century—Schoenberg, Bartók, Stravinsky. I loved Prokofiev, Shostakovich, Sibelius, and Ravel. I also loved that wonderful generation of American composers, like Copland and Piston. All of them were suspect beyond belief in the '60s. I was expected, of course, to worship at the shrine of Webern, and I tried, I paid my dues. I certainly respect the intelligence behind Webern.

But I want to be moved when I experience a work of art. I don't want just to respect one's intellectual accomplishments. That for me has been a problem with so much "great" writing of the twentieth century, too. I've done my duty with Proust and Joyce, and I realize that they're "great" writers. But although I can stand back and admire the vision and novelty of Joyce, I'd rather read Thomas Hardy, thank you. What ever happened to a great story with characters you care about? My favorite writer in our time is Robertson Davies, who is very untrendy in some circles because he is so Dickensian. Some people call him an old fart. Well, I'd rather read about characters I can carry with me for the rest of my life, not about a bunch of dull people whose motivations I can't understand. I'm sure I'm coming off as a terrible philistine. Maybe I totally miss the point. But I just couldn't care less about neurotic, self-absorbed, self-pitying, and ultimately very boring characters.

If there is such a thing as normal, I would say that no one who chooses composing as their vocation, their commitment for life, is normal. That does not mean that the desire to write music manifests itself in overtly neurotic or psychotic ways. Most composers I know are pretty down to earth—they function well in a society. I'm perfectly capable of talking about baseball at a cocktail party. Lord knows there are lots of people who are loonier than we are. After all, how many creative artists have actually committed crimes? We may be unusual, generally, but we're not dangerous to the public. Maybe we're just sociopaths with an outlet, as someone once suggested.

Some of my favorite pieces caused me the least toil, and other favorites caused me the most. The works that other people find more impressive are the ones that gave me more trouble. I'm always thought of as a "doom and gloom" composer, but not all of my music is of that type. The pieces that were composed quickly and comparatively effortlessly are the ones that aren't doomy and gloomy. Maybe I enjoy writing them more because they cheer me up.

If you're a good composer, your music should surprise you, but not too often. Too many surprises and you don't know what you're doing, you're not in control of your materials. But if a composer says there aren't any surprises when he hears a new work for the first time, that it always turns out exactly as he thought it would, I tend to think he's a very unadventurous composer, perfectly willing to stay with the tried and true, cranking out formulaically the same thing, not taking any risks. I would guess that most of my pieces contain about 10 percent surprises for me. Sometimes there are pleasant surprises— "Hey, I wrote that? That's pretty nifty!" And other times—"Jeez, oh well, that didn't work at all!"

Karolju [1990, commissioned by the Baltimore Symphony], a piece for chorus and orchestra, is based on Christmas carols I made up and that don't go beyond Schubert in terms of harmony. I happen to love Christmas carols and the Christmas season, and I wanted to write my own set of carols that sounded like a continuation of that tradition. The piece is not a commentary on Christmas carols or an excuse to do artsy things with the carol tradition. I just wanted to make a kind of Robert Shaw international celebration of carols, but with carols I composed myself.

For the texts, I decided to use several languages, but since I didn't actually speak most of them, I just picked out words for their look and sound. My sources for words were my opera recordings. I'd pull out a libretto, listen to the opera, and select the words I liked, based on their sounds. I didn't look at their translation.

Now, for the Swedish carol I didn't have many choices—there aren't many Swedish operas on disc. The only one I have in my library is *Aniara*, by Blomdahl, a space opera set in 2038 A.D. It's about a spaceship that goes spiraling off course, so that everyone in it will ultimately die. When I'd finished the piece, the choral director of the Baltimore Symphony said, "I know most of these languages, but can you help me pronounce the Swedish?" I said, "There's got to be a Swedish person in Baltimore who can help you."

Well, the choral director called me up later, laughing, because the guy he found to help him practically collapsed on the floor over the text I'd worked out. He couldn't help but translate it. It seems I'd understood the word for Christ, but because of the nature of this particular libretto, most of the other words I'd picked at random were terms like turbo-charger and gyro-stabilizer. Christ's gyro-stabilizer!? So that carol is full of wild scientific jargon. Talk about surprises!

Sometimes I feel a need to write particular music, perhaps a piece that grieves about something or for someone. Yet at the moment I come to compose it, I'm not necessarily in a grieving mode. I don't believe that the details of one's life at a given moment must of necessity influence the nature of what a piece is. Beethoven wrote his D major Symphony when he was thinking about suicide. Stravinsky composed the Symphony in C when everyone close to him was dying. Tchaikovsky's *Pathetique*, Mahler's Sixth, were written at the happiest times of those composers' lives. Berlioz said that hot passages must be set forth in cold blood.

My flute concerto is basically a Celtic piece. The two outer movements are meant to sound like very simple Irish folk songs. Irish folk music is part of my heritage—both sides of my family have been in the States for several centuries, but I have a sense of genetic memory when I hear this music; in a deeper recess within myself I feel like I'm home. The concerto is meant to tap into this. The third movement, the adagio, was written in memory of James Bulger, the two-year-old English boy who was led off several years ago by two ten-year-old boys. That destroyed me. There is some very dark music in that adagio.

It seems that I've written a lot of pieces recently in memory of someone who died. The flute concerto in 1993 was for James Bulger, and Symphony no. 2, in 1994, was for Steve Albert [the composer]. My trombone concerto was written in memory of Leonard Bernstein, and my cello concerto was for William Schuman and Andrzej Panufnik. *Envoi* was composed in response to my mother's death. I have written little pieces like the one for the memory of David Huntley [music editor for Boosey & Hawkes]. I hope I don't have to do any more of those for awhile . . . too many friends have died of late.

We have no control over death, but deaths are potentially the most important events to affect us. How do we say goodbye? Somebody said he felt my music was about saying farewell to a tradition, which it is. I guess I've always thought of my music as saying goodbye in general. Goodbye to people, goodbye to experiences, goodbye to innocence. I feel I may be seeing the end of classical tradition, not just in music, but in all of the arts—it's as if the barbarians are just beyond the gates. There is no longer tacit respect, but outward hostility toward the greatest artifacts human beings are capable of producing. The poetry of Sappho or the architecture of Gaudí—those justify our existence, not Michael Jackson and Madonna.

I remember the wonder, when I was a kid, of hearing the Beethoven Ninth Symphony scherzo for the first time. I can still see where I was sitting in the living room. And the *Peer Gynt Suite*! That was a wonderful favorite of mine. I remember getting that on my ninth birthday, and just playing the grooves off it. Or music from the *Nutcracker*. What a joy that was. I hate to think the experience of music like that could be lost.

People always want me to talk about rock and roll, and I say, no, I'm not going to talk about rock and roll anymore. It doesn't need my help. It's not that I no longer like that music, but I feel the wagons have been circled, and I'm going to stick with my high-falutin', elitist, dead white European male brethren and, if necessary, go down fighting.

Christopher Rouse, Selected Works

SMALL ENSEMBLE

Bonham (1988)
eight percussionists

Compline (1996)
flute, clarinet, harp, string quartet

Mitternachtslieder (1979)
bass-baritone solo and ensemble

Quattro Madrigali (1976)
8 solo voices

String Quartet No. 2 (1988)

LARGE ENSEMBLE

Concerto for Violin and Orchestra
   (1991)
violin and orchestra

Envoi (1995)
orchestra

Iscariot (1989)
chamber orchestra

Jagannath (1987)
orchestra

Phaethon (1986)
orchestra

Publisher: Boosey & Hawkes, 35
   East 21st Street, New York, NY
   10010. Tel. 212-228-330;
   fax 212-473-5730.

Christopher Rouse, Selected Recordings

Concerto for Cello and
   Orchestra
Yo-Yo Ma, cello; Philadelphia
   Orchestra/Zinman
Sony Classical 66299

Concerto for Flute and Orchestra;
   Phaethon; Symphony no. 2
Carol Wincenc, flute; Houston
   Symphony Orchestra/
   Eschenbach
Telarc CD 80452

Concerto for Trombone and
   Orchestra; *Gorgon* for
   Orchestra; *Iscariot* for orchestra
Joseph Alessi, trombone;
   Colorado Symphony Orchestra/
   Alsop
RCA Red Seal 09026-68410-2

Ku-Ka-Ilimoku
Continuum Percussion Quartet
New World 80382

Madrigals for voices and chamber
   ensemble; *Mitternachtslieder*
Leslie Guinn, bass-baritone;
   Eastman Musica Nova/
   Hodkinson
Albany Troy 192

Phantasmata; Symphony no. 1
Baltimore Symphony
   Orchestra/Zinman
Nonesuch 79320

STEVEN STUCKY

(B. 1949)

Steven Stucky grew up in Kansas and Texas and studied at Baylor and Cornell Universities with Richard Willis, Robert Palmer, Karel Husa, and Burrill Phillips. He was composer-in-residence with the Los Angeles Philharmonic from 1988 to 1992 and is Professor of Composition at Cornell University, where he has taught since 1980. Stucky's music has been commissioned by the Los Angeles Philharmonic, the Chicago Symphony, the Baltimore Symphony, Boston Musica Viva, and many other ensembles. In 1989 his Concerto for Orchestra, commissioned by the Philadelphia Orchestra, was named one of two finalists for the Pulitzer Prize in music. The Los Angeles Philharmonic plans to release an all-Stucky CD in 2001.

Steven Stucky is also an active conductor, writer, and lecturer and a well-known expert on the music of the late Polish composer Witold Lutoslawksi. His 1981 book *Lutoslawski and His Music* (Cambridge University Press) won the ASCAP Deems Taylor Prize.

Stucky lives with his family in Ithaca, New York. This interview took place in Austin, Texas, in February 1996.

*   *   *

Composing is something I wanted to do from a very early age. It was an improbable career choice, since I came from a family with very little music in it. But I gravitated to the two records of classical music my mother owned— Dvorak's *New World Symphony* and Prokofiev's *Peter and the Wolf*—and listened to them over and over again, wanting somehow to make the same kind of thing for myself. I tried to make scores even before I could read music, sprinkling sharps and flats all over the page—complete nonsense.

It's not that I knew I had something to say. I *still* don't know if I have anything to say. I find out by listening to a piece after I've finished it if it says anything to me. But I have always been attracted to the sound world of orchestral music, especially, and wanted to create it even before I could play an instrument. I recall that after a lesson about composers in one of my grade school music classes, I made a composer notebook with a page about Wagner and a page about Tchaikovsky and a blank page for myself.

Eventually I played the viola. (I did not take piano lessons until I was required to in college, and learning the piano was a great struggle.) Orchestral playing was wonderful training for me. I wasn't a terribly talented string player, but I kept it up through college and a little bit afterward, so I learned a lot of repertoire and got completely plugged into the orchestra as my home. It's not quite the same now, not being a performer. Conducting, which I do occasionally, is a way of performing, so it's better than nothing. But I miss playing, and I think it's important that I did it. I only stopped because I couldn't do it well enough without lots of practice, and I just didn't have the time to do everything. In the end, composing was more important. But I tell all my students not to stop playing.

I'm not a person who wakes up in the morning and says, "I have a burning need to express myself—I have this wonderful thing I have to get off my chest!" But I must need to compose, because I continue to accept requests for pieces, and I'd be embarrassed and sad if I didn't produce them. Sometimes I think that if I didn't have commissions or other external pressures, I'd probably take years off from composing, because it's a nasty, difficult job!

Have I ever thought of stopping? Absolutely. When I got out of graduate school I wasn't happy with any of my music. I was right, too. My music was pretty bad, and nobody was paying any attention to it, and I felt fairly hopeless. I took a teaching job and I didn't write very much, but eventually I wrote one piece that I sort of liked and somehow parlayed that into another one. In the early 1980s I began to write music that I still like. I was already in my thirties then.

I think I'm just a slow developer. I'm still learning, still getting comfortable with my own music. I've got my own voice, and I'm learning to use it well. As a student I experienced what I think many students undergo, a crisis over the originality problem. When I was an undergraduate in the 1960s, the pressure was strong first of all to write a certain kind of modernist-inspired music, and second, to be absolutely original in every piece—never to seem to be connected to anything that had come before. Well, of course, that's a very unnatural situation. It was hard for me not to admit who my real models were and which music I really loved. It took me awhile to get to the point where I could say, "What I really like is *this*, and what really shaped me as a musician are *these* experiences, and I want them to be in my pieces."

I think success in composition is partly elbow grease and perseverance. If you force yourself not to abandon a problematic piece, you can usually find a way to make it work. It may not be the piece that you hoped for, but it will be something close enough, something you can live with.

As a student and an early professional without many prospects for performances or commissions, I abandoned lots of pieces. I kept trying things that wouldn't work. But none of that work was wasted. I haven't recycled any of that old material, but I have recycled from successful pieces, the way an eighteenth-century composer would. I've actually borrowed chunks from myself for different purposes. I don't keep it a secret, either. There's nothing shameful about it.

For example, I was writing a wind quintet a few years ago and had a lot of trouble with it. For some reason, it was hard for me to get going in each of the individual movements. For one of them, I ended up borrowing a chunk of fifteen or twenty bars from an earlier piece and developing it differently. It turned out to be just the right way to get me started in that movement, so it was a successful tactic. In my wind ensemble piece *Fanfares and Arias*, the point of departure is a fanfare I wrote for the seventy-fifth anniversary of the Los Angeles Philharmonic. That fanfare, reorchestrated, is how the band piece begins. Then that material is developed in a whole different way, as well.

Maybe this is a natural way for me to work—to make something, then reuse it and also transform it several times in the course of a piece. Working from a model and enjoying the distance I create from the model while I'm still modeling is somehow pleasurable for me. I've done that many times in different pieces. The model could be material that already exists or that I create especially for this purpose. I might make a piece in which I complete a first section, then build all the other sections around that chassis. As a listener, you wouldn't recognize all of the transformations.

I try never to start a piece before I know a lot about its character, the kind of sound world it will exist in, what the piece will feel like (although there have been emergencies where I had to start before I was ready). In a way the "personality" of the piece is more important than any of the notes or technical details that I'll eventually work out. If I know enough about the personality and the general layout of the piece, I can sort of fly over it as if in an airplane, see its basic shape, visualize its neighborhoods. I can see a series of problems to be solved in technical ways—a series of questions to be answered. Most of this is in my head, although I might draw the shape of the piece and keep the picture around for a few days or weeks until I know the piece better. But by the time I sit down to write, the picture will be obsolete.

I don't amass bunches of sketches and then sort through them and decide which to use and which to throw away. I imagine passages in my head, then sketch just enough on the side to work out technical details, then go straight into the full score. If the essential layout—length, movement, character, emotional climate—are more or less known, I can start at the beginning and write the piece from beginning to end. Sometimes I get ideas that I will use later in the piece and I save them, but not in an extensive sketch. I just say, "Wouldn't it be neat if this happened at the end?" and I sort of work up to it.

In my music the ways the instruments or voices contribute to the texture are as important as the notes, so I orchestrate as I go. Orchestration can't be a separate phase, because of the specific nature of my music. It's often thickly textured—a lot of different things go on at once, and they have to be worked out at the same time. I'll have a page on which I try things out, and when I've gotten what I want, I'll throw that page away and put what works in the score. There isn't a sketchbook left afterward for somebody to look at—nothing to see except the piece. Besides which, it's such a relief when the piece is over, that I would throw any incriminating evidence away. I don't want a memento of the difficult parts, I just want the finished piece. All sketches go in the waste bin. Maybe I'm protecting myself from dissertation writers.

Right now I'm writing a piece for the Chicago Symphony [*Pinturas de Tamayo*]. It's a set of five short movements based on paintings by the Mexican painter Rufino Tamayo [1899–1992].

In fact, what I had intended to write for Chicago was a symphony, a very serious, substantial piece, because I need to write a piece like that now, just to make sure I can do it. But it doesn't seem like I will get that done while being chairman of the music department at Cornell. A collection of shorter pieces using a different working method than I would use for a symphony is more practical under the circumstances. Anyway, I love the paintings, and I love the idea of using a visual stimulus. I've never done anything like this before. Of course, I want to write a piece that makes perfect sense whether or not one has seen the paintings. So it's fun for me—I'm enjoying the project.

These are two-, three-, four-minute pieces, and by the time I'm ready to write one of them I'll be able to see what the whole thing might look like. Still, it isn't easy. When I try to write one, it might not work the way I envision it, and I'll have to do something else. But I can start by sketching processes or harmonic background or rhythmic material—whatever is going to be needed for the piece—and then try to put it into practice. Sometimes these rather abstract sketches can lead to a different piece than I imagined in my head, but you have to get used to that. It's the difference between imaginary music and real music.

My approach to music has for a long time been sort of painterly, I guess, except that I actually know nothing about painting. The way the coloristic surface of a piece works is really very important to me. That's first of all how one experiences my music. I've been told by some painters that they understand it immediately because it's often in broad, obvious, coloristic blocks. Now in writing pieces inspired by paintings, I'm not translating visual stimuli into aural ones. But a painting can suggest an idea that also makes musical sense, in purely musical terms.

For example, one of the Tamayo paintings is called *Women Reaching For the Moon*. It is from the late 1940s, I think, and it looks like a combination of Diego Rivera and Georges Braque, sort of muralist and sort of cubist. There are two very solid, chunky figures striving upward, and a moon way up high, an irregularly shaped blob. It's a very touching, very active painting. The piece I wrote uses a lot of upward rushing materials, so it turns out to be a piece about striving, not a representation of the painting itself. It's a reaching piece—not Tamayo-esque at all. Tamayo "reaches" in his way, in paint, and I "reach" in my way, in music.

Another of the paintings, *Sunset*, is a wonderful, long, narrow panel, with roiling red stuff that spills from the upper left corner of the painting down into the center. It ends in cubist sunbeams, trumpet shapes coming out of the bottom of the painting. If you heard the piece I wrote, you would not think of a sunset. But something about the way that the eye flows through that painting gave me the impetus to write about something that interests me more than sunsets. It is about motion, arrival, and volume of space.

The movement I'm working on now is called *Friends of the Birds*. For that I'm writing a birdlike piece, not really connected at all to the visual nature of the painting, except that the painting is over-bright, over-intense. The colors are always very bright in Tamayo, which is one thing that attracted me to his work, but I also find a rather human, spiritual element in the paintings that is very moving to me. The painting I'm saving to write last is called *La Grand Galaxia*, the Great Galaxy. It's the first of his paintings I ever saw, in the Tamayo Museum in Mexico City. I walked in, saw the painting, and was rooted to the spot. I couldn't shake it off. It's hard to explain what moves me about that painting. When I show it to people, some get it and some don't. I have no idea how to make a piece of this painting, but it means so much to me that it would be dishonest to leave it out.

Composing is so hard for me that I don't try to do it on airplanes or in hotel rooms. I try to save it for some version of my ideal situation, because that's the only way I can hope to get anything done. Ideally, I get up early and work in the morning for a few hours. I have to stop fairly soon, because once I begin to get mentally tired I can't trust my taste. I'll come back the next morning and evaluate where I left off, see if I've gone too far, determine what's useful and what's not. Getting up early is also a way of avoiding other people and having some privacy. I need to be by myself, completely undistracted. I don't even want to hear anybody else's breathing—never mind a clarinet or a trombone! When I'm on a deadline, I try to get up as early as 5 A.M. or 5:30, although I'm getting a little old to make that work. I work at home because there is no soundproofing in my office at school. Occasionally I borrow somebody else's house, go over there very early every morning. There's the story of how Milhaud's wife would drive to the store with him in the backseat. By the time she came out with the groceries he'd have a new quartet finished. Maybe that kind of facility makes his music superficial, but do I envy anyone's ability to work like that, to shut out the world under all circumstances.

I need to work at the piano. I think it's really important to have some kind of living sound in the room. No matter how good your ear is, how experienced you are, and how strong your imagination is, mental sound and physical sound always turn out to be different from one another. You need to keep going back and forth between imagination and reality.

I have a complicated trajectory where I postpone starting a piece as long as possible because I know that my idea for the beginning is not good enough. Then, when nothing else turns up, I start it anyway, and it turns out that this *is* the piece—I was just unwilling to accept it at first. I hold my nose and work on it for awhile, I begin to get used to it, and eventually I say to myself, "Maybe this is OK." Toward the end I think, "This is actually a pretty good piece."

After the piece is copied I go to the first rehearsal and my reaction is "Oh, God, this is terrible." Or "It's OK, but it's such a pale imitation of what I hoped it would be." Somehow I get through the first performance, and the second or third, and I begin to think, "Well, actually, this is a pretty good piece." It's as if I have to learn the piece twice! I have to learn to tolerate it while composing it, and then as a listener I have to learn to like it when it exists in real sound.

I think I experienced more lightning bolts when I was a kid, but that was before I developed a strong sense of taste. It's easy to be flooded with ideas when your standards are low. In fact, the ideas I get through bolts of lightning are not very good. For me, the Thomas Edison formula—95 percent perspiration and 5 percent inspiration—is right. You have to create the conditions for inspiration by working really hard at ideas that might at first seem unpromising. Maybe you have to prepare the synapses for something to happen. Without work, "it" doesn't just come.

Often it takes a concrete situation for me to get inspired. Thinking about real performers is very helpful to me. Maybe it's because I played in orchestras for a long time, but I'm constantly aware that a new piece will create a relationship between me and 105 other people. If I want it to come out right, the piece has to be rewarding for all of them.

I can remember very clearly the circumstances of writing a piece for the Baltimore Symphony. I knew [the conductor] David Zinman's personality, and what he was good at, everything he would bring to a new piece. But I also knew the program on which the piece would be premiered and I was going up against *Petrouchka*. This presented a very concrete artistic situation to me. My piece [*Son et Lumière*] does have a kind of spiritual relationship to *Petrouchka*, and it's not the only piece of mine one could say that about. Early Stravinsky was very important to my formation, as it is to my work now. I think that influence came out more strongly than usual in the piece for Baltimore, because I was thinking a lot about *Petrouchka*, knowing that I had to occupy the same program. (In between the two pieces was the Brahms violin concerto—there's nothing much one can do about that; it's one of the great pieces of all time!) *Son et Lumière* has the busy textures and some of the bright, attractive surfaces of the Stravinsky. My language is different, but there are many points of connection.

The Baltimore commission also came along at a moment when I wanted to capture for myself some elements of minimalist music. I'm not a lover of minimalism, but there is something in the music of Steve Reich and especially John Adams (which is not so minimalist, anyway) that's very attractive to me. *Son et Lumière* gave me an opportunity to write a piece made of ostinati and repetitive rhythmic patterns in ways that are mine, not anybody else's. It's not Adams, it's not any of those guys—they wouldn't recognize what my project had been if they heard it. But I made a conscious attempt to co-opt the rhythmic vitality of minimalism without the brain-dead harmonic structure. Maybe that's a little harsh, but for me, minimalism's harmonic movement isn't interesting. Adams is different—he was never brain-dead, and his recent pieces are sort of maximal, not minimal. They have an incredibly engaging surface, which I wanted to learn from in some way.

Here's another concrete situation. I was commissioned by the Los Angeles Philharmonic and Carnegie Hall as part of a project to celebrate their centennial season. I believe my piece was the first commission performed. It came right at the beginning of the season, just by a fluke of scheduling. I imagined various ways of connecting the piece to the occasion, finding a hook, a way into the piece. For example, I thought about taking the first program played in Carnegie and somehow making a piece about that. I gave that up very quickly, but it was worth thinking about. Then I began thinking about Carnegie's space, the kinds of events that have happened there, what it's like to be in the hall, what it sounds like, and I designed a piece intended to set that space ringing in a particular kind of celebratory and beautiful way. I don't think *Angelus* is my most successful piece, but I like what I tried to do. It's full of bells, not only literal bells like chimes and hand bells, but instruments like the piano and the trumpets making bell-like sounds. The piece turned out the way it did purely because I was thinking of the volume of the space, and what the walls have heard. I wanted to bring it all to life.

There are many difficulties in being a composer. First of all, it's hard to accept day to day, even though you know it very well, that you're only one person, that you have a limited repertoire of tricks. Some of the tricks you're good at, others you're only sort of good at. It's a challenge to accept this and make the most of it.

Every time you sit down to write, you feel like a student again. You say to yourself, "I can't write the same junk as yesterday, I have to do something *really* good this time!" Well, it's still *you*, you know. You're going to still write *your* music, and not some better, ideal music that you can't quite imagine. Trusting yourself is very hard. You get something that's sort of OK, and you leave it until the next day to see if you can still stand it. Tomorrow it may not be as bad as you thought, although sometimes it's worse.

Sometimes it feels as if I've never written music in my life, and I wonder whether it's too late to get my real estate license! I feel like I'm constantly learning how to work, always inventing from scratch. And then I look back and see that I do it the same way every time. There's a story I like about [the Japanese composer] Toru Takemitsu. I don't know if it's true, but the story goes that whenever Takemitsu writes a new piece, he takes it to his wife and says to her, "I've written something completely new, completely different." Then he plays it for her, and she says, "No, it's the same." That story feels very true to me. You try, always, to make something completely new, and it turns out you've made more or less the same thing you made the last time. That can be comforting, because it means you exist as an artist, that there is something in there that turns out to be you. But it's important to try not to repeat yourself, because you're going to, anyway. The only way to stretch is to pretend, at least, that you're going to write a piece that's completely different from the last one.

In a way composing is like being a playwright. When a piece has enough of its own existence, it begins to talk to you instead of you having always to talk to it. Its characters begin to lead lives; its settings begin to seem more real, and you get used to them. You begin to trust the piece a little more. I nearly always write endings pretty quickly and easily because by that time, I trust the piece enough to finish it with confidence. I know where it's going, and I know how it should end.

Composers also feel an incredible sense of responsibility. You've joined a profession with Beethoven, Haydn, all the heavies, and you have the gall to pretend to be extending, contributing to this tradition! There's a lot of pressure to make something worth people's attention, worth your *own* attention. It's a very old-fashioned notion—maybe I'm an old-fashioned composer in that way. I'm just not interested in pieces that one uses and throws away.

I'm encouraged by the extreme modesty of some of the composers I love the most. Lutoslawski, who was a great influence on me, used to say that his reason for writing each piece was to do better than the last one. I think that's part of what keeps me going. If I ever felt truly satisfied with a piece, I'd probably stop composing for fear of not being able to do it again.

Steven Stucky, Selected Works

SMALL ENSEMBLE

Ad Parnassum (1998)
chamber ensemble

Boston Fancies (1985)
flute/alto, clarinet/bass,
    percussion, piano, violin,
    viola, cello

Serenade (1990)
wind quintet

LARGE ENSEMBLE

Concerto for Orchestra (1986–87)

Concerto for Two Flutes and
    Orchestra (1994)

Concerto Mediterraneo (1998)
guitar and orchestra

Double Concerto (1982–85)
solo violin, solo oboe, chamber
    orchestra

Fanfares and Arias (1994)
wind ensemble

Impromptus (1991)
orchestra

Pinturas de Tamayo (1995)
orchestra

Son et Lumière (1988)
orchestra

Publisher: Theodore Presser,
    Presser Place, Bryn Mawr, PA
    19010. Tel. 215-525-3636;
    fax 215-527-7841.

Steven Stucky, Selected Recordings

Double Concerto for violin,
    oboe, and chamber orchestra
Igor Szwec, violin; Dorothy
    Freeman, oboe; Orchestra
    2001/Freeman
CRI

*Fanfares and Arias; Music for the
    Funeral of Queen Mary; Threnos;
    Voyages* for cello and wind
    ensemble
Guy Hardie, cello; Baylor Univer-
    sity Wind Ensemble/Haithcock
Albany, Troy 257

Serenade for Winds
Pennsylvania Wind Quintet
Centaur, CRC 2225

LIBBY LARSEN

$$\left(\text{B. } 1950\right)$$

*L*ibby Larsen grew up in Minneapolis and was educated at the University of Minnesota, where she studied composition with Dominick Argento, Paul Fetler, and Eric Stokes. She is a prolific composer who has written for orchestra, dance, opera, chorus, theater, and chamber and solo instruments. Much of her music makes use of American folk and popular idioms, and it is often inspired by historic and literary figures.

Libby Larsen is also a well-known crusader for new music and music in education. In 1973 she cofounded, with the composer Stephen Paulus, the Minnesota Composers Forum (now the American Composers Forum), a composers' cooperative that became the model for similar organizations.

From 1983 to 1987 Larsen was resident composer with the Minnesota Orchestra. Her music has been commissioned by the St. Louis Symphony, the Cleveland Lyric Opera, the Ohio Ballet, the Los Angeles Chamber Orchestra, the Cleveland Quartet, the flutist Eugenia Zukerman, and many more.

Libby Larsen lives in Minneapolis with her husband and daughter. This interview took place in Dallas in November 1996.

     •   •   •

I started composing out of a need, and that need was to communicate things that I was not able to express through any other venue. I had no idea of how deep the need was. I started composing in grade school, putting sound in order, attempting to communicate a sense of being. I didn't recognize it as a valuable or even successful activity until college.

Everyone in the Catholic grade school I attended learned to read music in the first grade, but only so that we could sing Gregorian chant in the church services: daily mass, funerals, and so on. I instinctively wanted more, so I organized my friends into pieces. Some pieces were songs—we'd make them up in front of the teachers. But other pieces went on for a long time—I had one that evolved over three years, starting in the fourth grade. It was sort of an opera, a performance art piece that had to do with the elements. Each one of my friends chose an element—earth, fire, air, or water. This was not contrived, it was just an instinctual thing. We created a performance piece that had role-playing and allowed us to move about in unconventional ways. We kept adding to it, changing it, according to what our needs were. The teachers knew about it. They didn't encourage it, and they didn't discourage it, which can be, I know now, good teaching. The piece wasn't formally performed. It went on during recess, so it was performed as it was being composed. The performance of the piece was also the composition of the piece.

I think I know why this happened. We'd all started singing Gregorian chant in the first grade, in a language we didn't know, in a conductorless situation, in a flexible, wet space. Those conditions created a very intuitive, sensitive kind of musicianship. They must have been what fueled the ability of that piece to not only grow but to keep on moving. There was no director. Nobody was saying, "You do this, you do that." I started the piece, but it grew on its own. I took piano lessons, too, but I can't say that that's where the impetus to compose came from—it didn't come from any formal experience.

I had some terrific teachers along the way who supported what for me was a very natural urge. My seventh grade teacher was very unconventional. She was a nun, and she taught through the arts all year long. Whenever I felt like it, she'd let me go up to the blackboard on my own, while everybody was off doing other things, and write music all over the board. Nobody taught me how; I just picked it up from playing the piano.

By decision, I left the Catholic faith in fifth grade and went through the motions until I could move out of the Catholic school. The faith is particularly repressive to creative personalities, I think. That's a shame, but never mind, you're forced to make a choice. Composing was very natural to me, and maybe it was the natural consequence of not wanting to live in a repressive atmosphere. Maybe I chose music because it's abstract—with music, the nuns don't know what you're thinking about, and more importantly, the priests don't know. I'm a gregarious communicator, and since I had to sit in rows and be quiet and go to confession and follow all the rules, it actually turned out to be an enormously fertile atmosphere for abstract artistic thinking. Besides, there's no commandment against it! Nobody said, "Thou shalt not create music!"

I'll tell you what keeps me composing. It uses all of my brain, at least all the brain that I can get in touch with, to try to understand how to communicate. The techniques for composing are changing as rapidly as the philosophy of the culture, the society, the musical instruments themselves—it's exploding, there's so much excitement, so the culture keeps the energy going to fuel the need to compose.

I could also become very depressed with that need. I could need to compose but not be able to. I've had a couple of what I think are composing blocks, and both times they manifested themselves in hate for every note I was writing. I continued to write, but I hated what I was writing. And I hated the fact that I hated what I was writing.

I work under deadline by design, and under commission, also by design. I need that pressure. I deal with infinity, so I need the pressure to help me put some kind of structure into infinity! But the blocks I had were about something different—they were about an untruth. Both times I had gone into a fundamental part of the process that I had called true and accepted it as a fundamental building block for the work. And, in fact, I didn't really believe in it.

So the blocks were about becoming angry with the falseness of the situation I'd set up for myself. I got out of the blocks by facing them down, facing the fear. The fear is not that I'll never write music again, because that's not true—I'll always write music. The question is, will I always write *true* music, music that is as true as I can make it? I don't want to tell a lie.

One of the blocks happened when I was in residence with the Minnesota Orchestra. I wrote a symphony, and it was very well received, but I really hated that piece. I used every technique of orchestration I could to evoke a particular image that I know a lot about. What I didn't do was to say what I felt about it. So while the piece does everything that I've been told a successful piece should do—invites listeners in, works on many levels, masters time and space, uses the instruments well—I hid behind my technique. From that experience I learned to always ask myself, "How do you *feel* about this?" If whatever I have on my mind is too frightening to put into the music, I don't write the piece, or I wait until I'm ready to write it.

I think the concert world has missed an important part of the creative process, and that is the ability to wait until the music is ready. It misses it in an effort to produce. So often, at a premiere, the performers aren't ready, the conductor isn't ready, the audience isn't ready, and the composer needs more time with the ensemble.

When I first started working with large ensembles, I was totally unprepared for the lack of access to the performers, who are the most important elements in transferring the music from the page to the ear. It's as if the composer is out of the picture! What *is* in the picture is the amount of time allotted, and this score and these parts. It's a manufacturing line model, and it's unfair to the music. In another era, the composer and the conductor would collaborate on bringing a piece to life. I look for those opportunities now. I pay my way to fly in and work over the score—whatever it takes. Yet that's still not enough. The conductor doesn't have sufficient time to study the score, to give feedback to the composer, and vice versa.

Preparation and communication with performers is very different in chamber music—discussion is part of the process from the beginning. I usually listen to what a group is doing after one or two rehearsals, so the ensemble can first find its own personality with my piece. After that, we all engage in more of a sculpting process.

For instance, I wrote a piece for the Cleveland Quartet and then went to work with them. We spent the entire time as if we were in a painting studio, coloring the phrases this way and that. We all got to explore a lot—it was marvelous! In a sense we were all composing. The quartet members were part of the process, as they should have been. The piece itself was still being made, even though it was fully realized on paper. It's like rehearsing a play: how many ways can you say a particular line? Chamber music gives everyone the opportunity to explore what they know how to do and apply it to a piece of music. It also allows a piece of music to show players what *they* can do.

It would be tempting to write a piece that completely played into a group's unique strengths, but I've never quite done that. I study the commissioning ensemble, understand why they're considered excellent in their field, and write to those strengths—strengths that other people in the field are aspiring to. If I'm successful I produce a work that is artistic and has the potential to attract other people who are aspiring to that level of excellence. It becomes a vehicle for aspiration.

Here's an example. Right now I'm working on a piece commissioned by The King's Singers. They come about as close to being a string quartet in their rehearsal technique as any choral group can. When they contacted me, they said they wanted a piece they could sing with a chorus, so when they travel to a city they can plug into the local choral society. They also wanted a piece they could perform internationally.

Now I could write a piece that only The King's Singers could perform, and they would perform it and record it. But the piece itself will want to live beyond that—it will demand its own independence.

My pieces always stem from an idea, and in the case of The King's Singers piece, I'm trying to understand the double standard about violence in America. Outside of our national boundaries, our culture is often defined by its commercialism and its violence. That's a frightening thought to me. So I'm writing a piece about Billy the Kid, a person we hold up as both a hero and a villain. The legend of Billy the Kid is one of our fundamental frontier models. He represents our fascination with violence as a means of gaining power and maintaining territory. He symbolizes the way Americans reinterpreted basic laws from British rule to accommodate violence.

The idea of personality as cultural muse has existed in me for years and years. It's a question of letting a particular personality find its way into a piece, according to the commissioning and performance opportunity. It's not that I've always desperately wanted to write about Billy the Kid, but that particular figure really came to the surface because of The King's Singers. A voice inside me said, "This is the one, now." I don't think I would have written a Billy the Kid piece for an American ensemble, because the doublestandard exists *here*, you know. I'm interested in a different perspective, a different vehicle for delivery.

I'm blessed with being prolific once the music starts going—that's just great good fortune. But I think for a long time before I put pen to paper. I think about the idea, how it's going to structure itself, and I begin to come to grips with the more mystical questions of proportion, tempo, tessitura, and texture. Those are much more mystical than pitch or rhythm.

Once I actually put the notes on paper, I have a very good idea of the proportions, how it's going to fill out. I can't tell you what it's going to fill out *with*, necessarily, but I know how it should feel. And then I work toward that, with the specifics of pitch and organization.

My intended plan is to write from 9 A.M. to 2 P.M. each day. The reality is that it doesn't happen. I will write for maybe an hour, an hour and a half, take a break, write for another hour, take a break.

Lately, a frightening thing has been happening. I'm not quite sure what it's about. I'll write well and consistently, but about three weeks before the piece is due, I'll throw everything out and start over. It's not that the piece changes that much the second time around. The colors are there, the proportions are there, the musical language is there. But what I've first written turns out to be a warmup for what I *really* want to write. That's new. It's not the way that I have worked in the past.

When it first started to happen, it was very scary. It wasn't writer's block, and it wasn't that I was dissatisfied with what I was writing. It just turns out that I wasn't writing it down. I wasn't writing *the piece* down.

I wonder if it has anything to do with working on a computer.

I don't compose on a computer, but I write a lot of prose on one. On the computer, to just *go* is so much part of the process. Later you use the instrument to rearrange and finalize. Maybe that's what I'm doing, in a way.

I don't like it, because it puts a lot of stress on my body, and there's no chance to think about anything else. It can upset the domestic life, too, particularly when you have children. But I am always much happier with this second version. There's something that seems stronger and truer. The first draft might be very acceptable, but it's just not good enough, you know? That's nothing new—most artists say that. But I don't think I ever allowed myself to say that before. Maybe, before this, I wasn't allowing myself that part of the process, which is to go back and say, "That's fine, but it's not good enough."

This change in my composing process is nerve-wracking for the marketing departments who have to talk to the public and the press about the new piece. Maybe they have heard the original draft and think they know what the piece is? The second draft, to me, is the same piece, and to the performers and the conductor it's the same piece, too, only stronger, better. But people who don't get at music via the structure only see exterior features, and to them, a second draft seems drastically different from the first one. Maybe something that originally centered in the woodwinds becomes centered in a combination of percussion and muted brass. Well, that makes perfect sense to those of us who live inside the music. But to those who live outside music, it doesn't.

After a premiere I make little revisions, usually in dynamics, and almost always one change in meter, usually at a point of transition. It's almost always in a place where I've held a note one beat too long. There are rarely large proportional changes, because I think so hard about that before I begin. A lot of composers find the proportion through the process.

Sometimes it happens that I think I know what I'm doing, yet afterward I see the piece isn't good. That means I throw it out, but once in awhile someone else keeps a copy. This year I did a residency at a college, and they had prepared a piece that I had thrown out. It was a real shock. Part of me cringed—just cringed! But they had prepared it with such care that I wondered if I'd been too judgmental. Once a piece is out there, serious questions of ownership arise. Maybe that's contributing to this new stage in my process: Not Good Enough. Because once a piece is out there, you can't take it back, like you can't take back the air.

I have one piece I've recycled four times! It's a piece called *Tambourines*, and it's based on the rhythms of a Langston Hughes poem.

The poem is printed in the program at a performance, but it's just the impulse for the piece. The rhythms that govern the piece come from the rhythm of the words of the poem.

Tambourines started out as a harp solo, turned into an orchestra piece, then became a concert band piece, and finally wound up as an organ piece. That's where it really belongs—on a three-rank organ. I wasn't trying to economize on time with commissions. It's just that the piece needed to go through that process to find its home.

The harp version is not performed often because it is the least successful. The orchestra piece is performed, and it works well because the poem is so strong. The concert band piece works probably *too* well, because the rhythms of the poetry are quarter-note and eighth-note rhythms, with changing meters. In the concert band world, that's considered a successful cliché—so the piece works too well because it doesn't do anything new—it negates the search for an idea.

You know what's really interesting? The full title of the Langston Hughes poem is *Tambourines to the Glory of God*. I had put it into three secular ensembles, first. Curious! Now here we are—back to the church! The poem talks about the tambourine as a humble instrument, dedicated to the glory of God, just as, in another tradition, the organ is to the glory of God. So maybe I didn't think hard enough about the piece at the outset.

And maybe I was trying to get as close to human breath as possible, to mirror the spoken word. The harp is the furthest, and then strings, and then the breath of the band instruments, and finally, the breath of those pipes. The organ has the most breath, but the sound of the organ is also the most ambiguous. It's one of the most abstract instruments we have.

Every time I begin to doubt my work, I'm challenging my own ego—the enormous ego that any creative personality needs. Ego is a good thing, but it's not good without doubt. I used to have contempt for doubt, because I *knew* I knew what I was doing. I had a love for debate, but contempt for doubt. Now, I'm very frightened if I don't have it—I seek it, and I am uncomfortable without it. It's a part of my own maturing process, to become entirely comfortable with imperfection. Beauty lies in the ability to trust the unresolved. I want to explore that. In order to do so, I have to have both doubt and ego on my team, in equal amounts.

I was taught to believe that to doubt was to be weak—to forge ahead in spite of everything was to be strong. That's definitely an American thing, and it's part of other cultures, too. It's linked with the American notion of progress: progress is good, progress is everything, so forge ahead without considering the consequences. As if forging is the only way to define progress.

The ideal composing situation for me is a studio that has a fine piano and is protected from interruption. The space has to be resonant too, because part of my process is to try things out on the piano and then collect them out of the air. I finally have this! I got enough money together to buy a good Steinway, and it's in my living room, which is a resonant space. And I can structure my days so that they're uninterrupted.

But I also need the opportunity to interact with people. My definition of people is not an artist's colony—I don't want to talk to other artists on my time off. I'm notorious for not answering the telephone. When I go out to see other people (which I have to force myself to do), I do it partly to remind myself that I am working in real time, that the eight hours that felt like one were really eight. Hardly any of my friends are musicians. I have running partners, I go down to the store and talk to the storekeepers. I see people who live their lives in other ways. Plus, I read lots and lots of books. I don't usually listen to music in my free time, but when I do, I'm very careful about that I choose. I listen to a *lot* of blues. It helps balance me out.

Libby Larsen, Selected Works

Beloved, Thou Hast Brought Me Many Flowers (1994)
mezzo-soprano, cello, piano
texts: Elizabeth Barrett Browning, H.D., Rainer Maria Rilke, Percy Bysshe Shelley

Slang (1994)
clarinet, violin, piano

Songs from Letters (1989)
soprano, piano
text: letters from Calamity Jane to her daughter, 1880–1902

Ulloa's Ring (1987)
flute and piano

LARGE ENSEMBLE

The Atmosphere as a Fluid System (1992)
flute, string orchestra, percussion

Blue Fiddler (1996)
orchestra

Marimba Concerto: *After Hampton* (1992)
marimba, orchestra

Piano Concerto: *Since Armstrong* (1992)
piano, orchestra

Symphony no. 3: *Lyric* (1992)
orchestra

STAGE

Frankenstein: The Modern Prometheus (1990)
music drama

Mrs. Dalloway (1993)
two-act music drama
libretto: Bonnie Grice

Publishers: Oxford University Press, 198 Madison Avenue, New York, NY 10016. Tel. 212-726-6000. ECS Publishing, 138 Ipswich Street, Boston, MA 02215-3534. Tel. 617-236-1935; fax 617-236-0261.

Libby Larsen, Selected Recordings

How It Thrills Us
Kings College Choir/Cleobury
EMI Classics CDC 54188

Missa Gaia (Mass for the Earth)
Oregon Repertory Singers
Koch International Classics KIC 7279

Parachute Dancing, overture for orchestra; *Ring of Fire*; Symphony for Orchestra: *Water Music*; Symphony no. 3: *Lyric*
London Symphony Orchestra/Revsen
Koch International KIC 7370

The Settling Years
Dale Warland Singers/Dale Warland
Innova Recordings ACF 002

Sonnets from the Portuguese
Members of the St. Paul Chamber Orchestra and Minnesota Orchestra; Arleen Auger, soprano/Revzen
Koch International KIC CD 7248

Ulloa's Ring
Eugenia Zuckerman, flute; Lisa Emenheiser, piano
Pro Arte PAC 1086

What the Monster Saw
Cleveland Chamber Orchestra/London
GM 2039

LOIS V VIERK

$$\left(\text{B. } 1951\right)$$

ois V Vierk was born in Hammond, Indiana, and grew up in Lansing, Illinois, and Jenkintown, Pennsylvania. She attended Valparaiso University and studied composition at the California Institute of the Arts with Mel Powell, Leonard Stein, and Morton Subotnick. For twelve years she studied gagaku (Japanese court music) with Suenobu Togi in the United States and with Sukeyasu Shiba in Tokyo.

Vierk has been commissioned by leading contemporary music performers, including the Kronos Quartet, pianists Ursula Oppens and Frederic Rzewski, Ensemble Modern, accordionist Guy Klucevsek, and the Bang on a Can Festival. In 1996 her new work for the Reigakusha ensemble of Tokyo was premiered at the Lincoln Center Festival. Her cocreations with tap choreographer Anita Feldman have been commissioned by the American Dance Festival, Mary Flagler Cary Charitable Trust, and Meet the Composer, among others. Some of Lois V Vierk's pieces utilize principles she has developed of "Exponential Structure," in which, depending on the emotional content of the music, exponential factors are applied mathematically to such elements as time, rates of change, and pitch movement.

Lois V Vierk lives in West New York, New Jersey. This interview took place in West New York in October 1995.

•   •   •

I've always felt I had something to say. That's why I started composing, and that's why I continue. And I love it. I love the sounds. I love working with sounds to put pieces together. After I write a piece I love to hear the sounds that I had been imagining and hearing in my head, played for real. The sounds of instruments, even after all these years I've spent composing, always take me delightfully by surprise—how beautiful they are, how rich and full. These are the things that keep me going.

When writing a new piece, I need to start from the sensuous, visceral sound itself. I need to hear and feel what the instruments can do—things like how loud and powerful they can be, or how soft and delicate, how high, how low, how fast, how slow, how lyrical, how accented and agitated, how smooth and languid, and so on. I like to get together with players face to face and improvise sounds. For example, even though I've written two string quartets, I know that when I write my third I'll schedule a session with players so that I can hear and feel the string sounds afresh. Fine players often show me qualities of the instrument and playing techniques that I couldn't come up with on my own, because they work with the instruments and live with them, day in, day out.

After that, when I take pencil and paper, the physical sounds will still be ringing through me. I'll sketch maybe 100 pages or so, depending on the piece. I try not to censor anything I write. I look at what I've put down on paper and let myself feel how the sounds flow—their energy and their direction. When I feel the sounds in this way I want to work on them to make them more beautiful, or clearer or stronger or more dynamic or dramatic—in other words, I want them to flow as much as possible. It's incredibly fun to do this.

At some point as I'm hearing and feeling the sounds, I start to think about the piece as a whole. I don't care to work on just sound or just structure, independently. They're always together in my mind. I'll consider things like which sounds work together, how do they fit, what do I want to say with these sounds? What order should they be heard in, and what kind of structure suits them? How does a certain sound have to change to create a stronger or clearer structure? Or how should the structure be modified to better show off certain sounds? And what doesn't fit here at all? Gradually I discover a form for the piece. Based on the sounds and the emerging form, I decide how one sound will develop into another, and I get a sense of the relative durations that each kind of sound will have in the piece.

I've always felt equally drawn to the West and to the East, in terms of my analytical training in Western music and the musical principles I learned during twelve years of actively studying and performing *gagaku*, ancient Japanese court music. *Gagaku* is a slowly unfolding music that is at once massive and loud, as well as sensuous and refined. The word *gagaku* literally means "elegant music."

Many of my early pieces written in the 1980s were for multiples of the same instrument—an ensemble of eighteen trombones or eight cellos or five electric guitars, for example. I think that this multiples idea first came to me from certain pieces in the *gagaku* repertoire, where three bamboo *ryuteki* flutes or *hichiriki* double reeds play canons in free rhythm. The transparency of timbre allows small nuances of dynamics, articulations, pitch slides, et cetera, to be clearly heard. I began thinking of two or three instruments within my ensemble acting together to form one voice, or what I call a "sound shape." One sound shape interacts with another sound shape, which is likewise made up of several instruments. In effect, I have a "counterpoint of counterpoints." The sound to me is at once complex because of its many parts, but also clear and direct, because of the transparent timbre.

One of the sounds I find myself writing over and over is the glissando, or sliding tone. I don't know why I always write glissandos—maybe it also started with *gagaku*, which has a lot of sliding tones—but it is just such a beautiful and also natural sound to me. For example, there's a sweep in the sound of water flowing, the wind blowing, in the cry of the loon. I hear glissandos everywhere.

I've written music for all kinds of musical forces, from solo instrument to chamber ensemble to orchestra to Japanese *gagaku* orchestra. But I have to say that I always get very excited when I work with tap dance, and specifically with Anita Feldman Tap, a company of tap dancers and musicians. Since 1987 the tap choreographer Anita Feldman [known in dance and music circles for her extensive work with composers] and I have been collaborating on "new music/tap dance" pieces, where we try as much as possible to eliminate the distinction between music and tap dance. The tap dance sounds are part of the total orchestration of the piece and are notated along with the other instruments. The fact that Anita studied percussion and reads music really facilitates this process. We've done pieces for tap dance with percussion instruments, with strings, with singers, and with electronics. Some of our pieces use Anita's gorgeous Tap Dance Instrument. She and the instrument builder Daniel Schmidt designed this patented instrument for tap dancers to play with their feet. Its six modules consist of the "tap marimba" (with seven keys of different pitches), two brass floor segments of different sizes that ring when struck by a tap shoe, and three wooden modules with different kinds of resonances.

Typically, Anita and I collaborate in all stages of creating a piece. We gradually develop the basic sound and movement materials together in sessions with dancers and musicians. Then we continually work and rework the raw materials, eventually creating phrases and sections and the work as a whole. I really like the physicality of using the body and the foot to play music. I find it's easy to get all wrapped up in the combination of movement, bodies, and sound. It's so satisfying to me and completely compelling.

I don't come from an artistic family, although my mother did have an old piano in our house. She taught me the basics of music. To start, we took a pencil and wrote C, D, E, et cetera, on the piano keys. My mom played for fun, out of hymnals and folk music books. She wasn't a pianist in any way, shape, or form, but she taught me how to read notes, and she gave me some little notebooks to write in. I wrote notes all over them—I was three years old or so—she still has those notebooks with my scribblings in them. Did they make any sense? No, I don't think so. But my mom always says those were my first compositions.

I took some ballet and tap lessons at the neighborhood dancing school, but I didn't begin piano lessons until I was about twelve years old. My home town was Lansing, Illinois—quite close to Chicago, but we really didn't go into the city very often. As a child going to a Lutheran school, I was also very interested in sports. We played softball every day for eight years through grade school. Besides that, I loved mathematics and was coached and encouraged by my father in this. When it was time for me to go to college, I didn't know what I was going to do, music or math. I also loved visual art a lot, but I didn't have a portfolio, and I had never taken drawing lessons.

All of this time I had been playing piano, but I wasn't composing. I ended up studying music at Valparaiso University, a Lutheran school in Valparaiso, Indiana. Not too surprisingly, the emphasis in the music department was on church music, especially on playing the organ and on choral conducting. At first I didn't really know what I wanted to do in my musical life, but after a couple of years at Valparaiso, I found that I really wanted to study non-Western music, wherever that might take me. This desire came about partly because I had African American friends who said to me, "You're studying all of this Western music, but there's a lot you just don't know about." I started to think about what they said, and it propelled me on an odyssey that has affected the rest of my life. I transferred to UCLA, because at that time they had an excellent ethnomusicology department with top-rate performing musicians from all over the world.

UCLA in the early '70s was a cornucopia of musical riches. When I first arrived in 1971, besides continuing my study of piano, I went from one ethno class to another, learning a little music from Japan, China, Ghana, Bali—along with some dance from Yugoslavia and Japan. The Japanese dance I studied is called *bugaku*, which is performed to *gagaku* music. After about a year I decided I loved *gagaku* and *bugaku* the best, and that's what I stuck with. Even after leaving UCLA, I continued for ten years to work with my *gagaku* teacher, Mr. Suenobu Togi. Eventually I went to Tokyo for two years and studied with Mr. Sukeyasu Shiba, lead *ryuteki* flutist of the emperor's Imperial Court Orchestra and a colleague and friend of Mr. Togi's. Both of these exquisite musicians come from families of *gagaku* musicians who trace their ancestry back to about the eighth century A.D., when the first artists and scholars were brought to Japan from China.

By the time I graduated from UCLA, I knew I wanted to compose, and I also felt I needed to study more of the basics. So between undergraduate and graduate school, when I was making my living playing piano for dance classes at the Los Angeles Ballet, I asked my piano teacher, Aube Tzerko, what to do. He recommended that I study with Leonard Stein, who had been a student of Arnold Schoenberg's (and eventually founded the Schoenberg Institute at USC). I called up Leonard Stein and explained who I was and who had told me to call, and he said, "Where do you live?" And I told him where I lived, and he said, "Do you have a car?" And I said, "No, I don't have a car," and he said, "Well, there are no buses here, so you can't come." His point was that he really wanted me to study with one of his students first before I came to him. He gave me the name of Dean Drummond—Dean was my very first composition teacher. (Dean Drummond is known these days for his gorgeous compositions on the Harry Partch instruments, and on "regular" instruments as well. With Stefani Starin, he directs the well-known performing ensemble Newband.) I worked with Dean for about a year and then he sent me back to Leonard.

I took private lessons from Leonard for two years. He's one of those rare people who can lead you to discover just what it is that is important to you musically. He does this without making you do something in particular, without limiting you to a particular method or style. Leonard would never tell me what to do—he'd say, "Let's look at the way Composer X solved a similar sort of problem." We analyzed a lot of pieces by composers like Schoenberg, Webern, and Berg, and Leonard also introduced me to Xenakis and Ligeti and Berio and Stockhausen, and to LaMonte Young, who had been one of his students, too. Leonard was always interested in my study of *gagaku*. He knew a few of the best players of other types of traditional music in Japan, and on occasion they would give concerts at his home.

After a couple of years Leonard suggested that California Institute of the Arts, where he himself taught several classes, would be a good place for me to do graduate work. I entered Cal Arts in 1976. While there I studied composition with Mel Powell and Morton Subotnick. Mort would look at my scores and say, "OK, I see what you're doing, but now, push it! Push it, take it to the extremes. Do more of it, find the end point." That was exactly what I needed to hear then. I learned how to make strong statements even stronger. Mort also taught his students, by example, what it could mean to be a professional composer. He had concerts and performances all over the place. He showed us that there was an exciting world outside academia and that we could take part in it.

Mel Powell told me so many important things. Even today when I sit down to compose, some of his succinct, profound words come to mind. Mel would often use the term "multiplicity." To me this meant that a piece could be doing more than one thing at a time. Or that a sound could be complex, even though its shape or flow were very clear. The word also made me consider how a piece exists on different levels at the same time. As I thought about it more and more, I realized that for me, a piece has to make sense in many different ways at once. I want it to flow sensuously, intellectually, emotionally.

Mel would say, "Here's a beautiful sound—now what's the destiny of this sound? Think of the whole piece, and ask yourself, where does that go, what becomes of it?" I realized that one sound might undergo a certain rhythmic development or get louder and louder or become more and more ornamented, while another might gradually fade out and disappear, because that was what was called for to strengthen the piece as a whole. Mel made me aware, in a conscious way, of many aspects of composition. I figure he cut about ten years off my learning process.

At the point I worked with Mel, I was still doing Japanese music. If I had been learning it in the traditional way, I would have been a boy, of course, in one of the hereditary *gagaku* families connected to the emperor's court. I would have started off at age eight or nine, learning the dances that had been handed down through the centuries to my family members. Well, I did start out learning the dances, but I was in my twenties by then. First, I learned to move my body and to breathe with the movements. The next thing was to learn to sing the vocal parts to pieces. These vocal parts are sort of like solfège, but it's more a solfège of gestures than of pitches. When I got to Japan, my teacher there very kindly recorded the vocal parts to a large portion of the *gagaku* repertoire on cassette tape. I would play these tapes and memorize pieces by rote, phrase by phrase, singing them back without using notation.

The next step in the traditional process would be to finally pick up an instrument. At UCLA Mr. Togi had to let us begin with the instruments right away, since university students usually don't spend many years learning the art form. Also, university regulations dictated that students receive course credit for only two or three quarters of class—hardly enough to scratch the surface! But traditionally with *gagaku*, before you touch a bamboo flute, double reed, or mouth organ, you have already been learning with your ears for a long time. If you ask your *gagaku* teacher how to do something, he might say, "Just do it." Or you might not get an answer at all. It's a very, very deep way to learn.

Since the 1980s I've been developing my own principles of sound organization, which I call Exponential Structure. This came to me from my knowledge of math and physics. All sensory phenomena in the body are measured in exponential terms, not in linear terms. The one exception is the length of a line—if you look at two lines, you can judge pretty much if one is, say, twice as long as another. You perceive it as twice as long, and it is, in fact, twice as long. But other examples are not so straightforward. A sound that subjectively sounds "twice as loud" as another does not have twice the amount of energy. A light that looks "twice as bright" as another doesn't have twice the amount of energy. The same applies to touch stimulation and perception of pain. There have been many studies by acousticians and psychoacousticians of sensory perception versus amount of actual stimulus present. After lots of experiments, researchers have shown that every kind of stimulus yields a different equation, a different curve. The relationship between perceived and actual amounts of stimuli is an exponential relationship, not a simple arithmetic one. What sounds, looks, or feels like "twice as much," "three times as much," "four times as much" as the first stimulus is not two or three or four times the first stimulus. It is actually some number squared, cubed, to the fourth power, et cetera, times the first stimulus. It's fascinating. So I wondered, what would happen if I applied this idea to time, to rates of development and rates of change in a composition?

That started me on another lifelong path, which at the beginning I followed in a very simple and direct way. The first section of the piece, which might be based on a certain pitch, would be x number of seconds long. The second section would be, say, .9 times x, the next section would be .9 squared (or .81) times x, the next would be .9 cubed (or .73) times x, the next .9 to the fourth power (or .66), and so on. In this scenario the sections of the piece are always getting shorter and shorter, and the pitch centers are changing faster and faster.

Then within that macrostructure I would develop rhythmic changes, say, from a slower to a quicker rhythm. Maybe in the first section of the piece I would have only half notes, and by the last section I would have mainly sixteenths. I might make another structure for timbral changes, following a totally different equation. In other words, I would nest several structures for different aspects of the music within the overall structure. Changes of different aspects of the sound would take place at different rates.

This mathematical process is integrated with and dependent on the emotional thrust of the piece. For instance, in my piece *Simoom* for eight cellos, I felt that the piece should end dramatically, on the lowest pitch on all the instruments with energetic accents and tremolos. I knew that the glissandos were going to occur over a wide range and be loud at that point and that I wanted the music to end with a lot of strength. I knew I should use a gradually contracting set of numbers, gradually shortening time segments, to get to this point. Little by little, excitement and drama would build up, both in the sounds and in the structure.

Different sets of numbers will produce different kinds of results, and I can use these results to get at different kinds of emotional qualities. I think of Exponential Structure as a sort of meshing of emotional impulses with a system that expresses them. And the more I write, the more freely I use it. Sometimes I won't use it at all, or maybe I'll use it for a certain part of the piece. It's not an abstraction, it's a tool.

I've come to be able to work in almost any situation, as long as it's quiet. If it's noisy, I have to turn on a white noise machine. When I first began to compose, I always needed to write first thing in the morning. Now I can be dead tired, and if I have to, I'll stay up all night and work. I don't like to, it's not great for my body, but I can do it when I need to. When I'm working on something every day, day after day, it seems to become both a conscious and an unconscious expression at the same time. When I'm in that mode of working, it's just terrific. I am in the piece, the piece is in me. I can write without thinking about it and then go back later and see if it's what I wanted. If I'm really in the right working mode, it still makes sense when I go back to it. Sometimes I'll go back later and see that I've got the right general idea but it's got to be more developed, or longer, or more embellished, or more emphatic, or something.

I've also found that the way I feel emotionally has nothing to do with the way the music comes out. Sometimes I feel very good when I'm writing—it all seems to be flowing along—but when I go back later I have to make a lot of changes. Other times I'm feeling awful about what I'm writing and I put the work down and come back the next day and it's all fine. I think the music comes from a place other than where my immediate emotions originate. I think the best thing to do if you're creating something is just to keep doing it, no matter what. Just continue.

I need to be renewed by nature. I love hiking, and I've done a fair amount of backpacking. Just last week my husband and I went up to Vermont because the leaves are turning from green to brilliant reds and oranges and yellows. I need that. I need to hear the water falling and the surf crashing. I need to feel the wind. I need that motion, that movement. I need to see the clouds in the sky. I also like to have animals around, and I love to garden.

I read a study about people recovering from illnesses in hospitals, and those who had a tree outside their window recovered in 40 per cent less time than the ones who did not have a tree to look at. I think there's something so deep in that, some kind of resonance that exists between the growing tree and the human observer.

I think it's important to constantly be reaching. Some people say each composer does the same piece over and over. I think there is some truth in that, because music comes out of the person, music is of the person. When the person changes, the work changes.

A piece is an expression of a certain time in a composer's life. If I write a brass quintet next year, it will be different from the one I wrote last year just because it's a different time in my life. If I write a phrase today, it will be different from the one I'll write tomorrow. I don't believe that each particular note is precious. A note is just part of a piece. But some principles carry through an entire piece—that's what you have to hold onto. I don't really worry about making little mistakes—I go for the whole thing.

Lois V Vierk, Selected Works

SMALL ENSEMBLE

五 Guitars, "Go Guitars" (1981)
five electric guitars

Hexa (1988)
with tap choreographer Anita
    Feldman
percussion, three tap dancers on
    Tap Dance Instrument
    (patented), live electronics

Jagged Mesa (1990)
two brass choirs—two trumpets,
    two trombones, two bass
    trombones
(parts may be doubled)

Manhattan Cascade (1985)
four accordions

River beneath the River (1993)
string quartet

Silversword (1996)
gagaku orchestra (Japanese court
    music orchestra)

Simoom (1986)
eight cellos

Spin 2 (1995)
two pianos

Timberline (1991)
flute, clarinet, bassoon, viola,
    contrabass, piano/synthesizer,
    percussion

LARGE ENSEMBLE

Devil's Punchbowl (1993)
orchestra

Publisher: Lois V Vierk, Times
    Square Station, P.O. Box 2652,
    New York, NY 10108. E-mail:
    LVVVV@aol.com.

Lois V Vierk, Selected Recordings

Attack Cat Polka
Guy Klucevsek, accordion, with
    voice and ensemble
Who Stole the Polka? Wave-Eva
    WWCX 3027

Cirrus for six trumpets; Go
    Guitars; Simoom
Gary Trosclair, trumpets; David
    Seidel, electric guitars;
Ted Mook, cellos
Simoom, XI Compact Discs 102

Go Guitars
Seth Josel, guitar
Go Guitars, oodiscs OO #36

Manhattan Cascade
Guy Klucevsek, accordions
Manhattan Cascade, CRI 626

Red Shift for cello, electric
    guitar, synthesizer,
    percussion
Bang on a Can All-Stars
Cheating, Lying, Stealing, Sony
    Classical SK 62254

Red Shift for cello, electric
    guitar, synthesizer,
    percussion
Ted Mook, cello; David Seidel,
    electric guitar; James Pugliese,
    percussion; Lois V Vierk,
    synthesizer
Real Estate: New Music from
    New York, Ear-Rational
    Records
ECD 1015

Red Shift 4 for trumpet, electric
    guitar, piano/synthesizer,
    percussion
A Cloud Nine Consort
Bang on a Can Live, vol. 2, CRI 646

Timberline
Relache Ensemble
Outcome Inevitable,
   oodiscs OO #17

Yeah, Yeah, Yeah
Aki Takahashi, piano
Norwegian Wood,
   Toshiba-
     EMI TOCE 7345

JOHN ZORN

$\left(\text{B. } 1953\right)$

rawing on his experience in a variety of genres, including jazz, rock, hard-core punk, classical, klezmer, film, cartoon, popular, and improvised music, John Zorn is creating a body of work that defies academic categories. Zorn says he feels most connected to the tradition of the avant-garde; he most admires the maverick musicians, theoreticians, filmmakers, painters, and writers of the past and present who have consistently questioned given boundaries, "creating a universe all their own."

As a student, Zorn acquired formal musical training as well as exposure to jazz, but the bulk of his education and development as a creative artist came through close working relationships with fellow jazz performers. For many years he spent significant amounts of time in Japan, working with musicians there and drawing on the influence of Japanese culture. Most of his written music to date has been notated in a manner suited to virtuoso improvisers who work intimately with Zorn to realize new pieces for definitive recordings, of which there are many. (Jazz fans know well the dozens of discs by Zorn's groups Naked City and Masada.) But as his work has been increasingly sought by more traditional concert ensembles, Zorn has produced scores on commission for such groups as the New York Philharmonic, the American Composers Orchestra, the Kronos Quartet, the Bayerische Staatsoper, and the WDR Orchestra Köln.

John Zorn lives in New York City. This interview took place in New York in May 1998.

•   •   •

I've always been interested in two things, film and music, and when I graduated from high school, I had to decide to do one or the other. That's what it takes to do something really well, to take it to a place beyond yourself, to get beyond what the thing itself *is*.

I went into music because to do film you need a lot of money and have to spend a lot of time schmoozing and fund-raising. I have friends who make films. They come to me and say, "We want you to do the music," and I say, "Great, where's the tape?" And they say, "Oh no, we're fund-raising now. It's going to be three years before . . ." This is what it's like! I'm not good at going to parties. Music was something that I could do with a pencil and a piece of paper. But film is still an important influence on what I do, and a constant companion. I can't write music unless a movie is on in the background.

I'm writing music because I'm compelled to do it. There's something inside me that isn't comfortable unless I am doing it. I'm always working on some kind of piece. Why is that? I'm sure it's part of my psychology—maybe it gives me the sense of worth my parents weren't able to give me because of their background. So enough of that. But there's something there that I've found attractive since I was small.

I didn't really pick up the sax until I was twenty. At first I played guitar, piano, bass, trombone—a lot of different things, and nothing really well. My parents wouldn't get me a piano, but my aunt and my grandmother had pianos, so I'd go over to their places. I'd improvise, play around, pretend what I did were compositions. It really fulfilled me in some strange way. I had friends who were composers, and that was encouraging. I grew up in the United Nations School here in New York, where Leonardo Balada was the music teacher. Stephen Hartke was a close friend of mine—he was a year older, and I looked up to him. We compared scores, organized concerts. I found my support group outside my family, kind of reparented myself.

When I went to Webster College [St. Louis] for a year and a half, I discovered the music of the Association for the Advancement of Creative Musicians in Chicago—Anthony Braxton, Leo Smith—and in St. Louis the work of a black arts group with Oliver Lake and Julius Hemphill. That music touched me directly because of its energy, its spontaneity. It also brought a lot of things together for me. I'd been improvising, but without knowing it was improvising. I'd been thinking, "What I'm doing is not *really* music because it's not composed." But when I heard this music that used improvisation and composition, real music by respected people, it made me feel that what I was doing made sense.

A lot of things I've done since then have involved mixing the kind of thing that can only happen once, and cannot be written down, with things that *are* written down, that can be repeated in some way. I think I've been lucky. The reason I'm still composing is that I've met so many great musicians and have been able to collaborate with them. I learn from them, and they learn from me. It's a community. I think that's what I need.

Composers don't think in terms of boxes and genres. They just do what they do, and they love good music, whatever hits them. It doesn't matter where it comes from, who's doing it, or what it's trying to say. Maybe you won't compose a piece for gamelan, but something about the Balinese music you've heard—the hocketing in *kecak* [a type of choral chant], the orchestration, or the long form—touches you and you think, "There's something here that I can use." Then you translate it into your own language. The sensibility of the generation that I belong to, which is interested in world music, jazz, funk, hard-core punk, classical music, every possible kind of music, is the same one Mozart had. He made use of everything around him.

There are various methods and processes that go into different areas of my work. I'm involved in a lot of things simultaneously, and there's a lot of overlap. I don't think my work can be divided into periods. Maybe once I'm dead people will look back and figure out what the hell I was doing. I personally would rather not know! There are a lot of things about being creative that you need to keep mysterious. You need to *not* know. To constantly think and talk about your work is deadly. It takes a lot of the fun out of intuitive exploring.

You know, I used to practice the saxophone ten hours a day. I did that for years. I was so obsessed, I'd bring the saxophone into the bathroom with me because I didn't want to waste time. I even counted the breaths I took, and wouldn't count them as practice time. I'd think, "Well, I practiced six hours, but with the breaths that's really only about three and a half." Wow—this was sick. Then one day I woke up and said, "I have had it. I am not going to do this any more. From this day on, *everything* I do is practicing." I have not practiced a day since then, and that was back in 1982. Now I go to the movies, watch TV, have a meal with friends, take a walk in the park—whatever I do, I'm going to get an idea from something, because I'm open to it.

I'll talk about my game pieces, like *Cobra*, which is played all over the world, now. I look at it as a later *In C* [Terry Riley's seminal minimalist work]: something that is fun to play, relatively easy, written on one sheet of paper. Game pieces came about through improvising with other people, seeing that things I wanted to have happen *weren't* happening. I'd wonder, "Why aren't people leaving more silences?" So I'd write a piece for improvisers that inherently had a lot of silences. Or, "Why doesn't everybody, all of a sudden, change at one time?" So then I'd create a little system and write a piece involving that.

There are about twenty-five of the game pieces. Ten initial pieces explored different improvisational problems, very specifically. There was a piece about putting different genres of music on top of one another in an Ivesian way, and a piece about concentrating improvisations into short statements, so that each player thinks very hard about every note. All of the pieces involved the performer in the compositional process, either in the structural elements or in the details. All of the early game pieces exist on timelines.

The game pieces worked because I was collaborating with improvisers who had developed very personal languages, and I could harness those languages in ways that made the players feel they were creating and participating. In these pieces, they were not being told what to *do*. You don't tell a great improviser what to *do*—they're going to get bored right away

For me, composition is problem solving. I try to go new places by setting myself parameters and trying to solve the problems they present. How can I create a piece that has only three sounds in it? Or a piece where every bar is a different genre of music? With improvisers, I can say, "Improvise a piece that only uses three sounds." It's a very simple idea I can incorporate into a more complicated structure. I'll put that idea with thirty other ideas, and *that* will be one piece. When another composer looks at this piece, he won't know what to make of it. He'll say, "This is just a piece of paper—they're just making this up." But an improviser can look at it and say, "Wow. There's a lot going on here. We could play this forever, it would never be the same."

Eventually in the game pieces I created sets of rules, like the rules for baseball or football, and the players would interact using those rules. If they followed the rules properly, they could create certain structures and tactics, do whatever they wanted at any time. "You don't want to play? You don't have to play. If you want to play, here's the way you go. You want to play with this person? You can do this." Some pieces are meant to be ten or fifteen minutes long; some can last a full evening or go on forever. There's no set beginning, middle, or end, but there are ending cues—you can call them at any time. Some pieces can be for any number of players, some are for three players, some are for any instrumentation, some for a specific instrumentation. Each game piece is like a series of toggle switches—on and off, on and off—with a very complex series of rules that make it challenging. I'll never be one of those composers who says, "OK, everybody, let's do a little piece that says 'Water.'"

After awhile I didn't need to write game pieces anymore, and I started writing a very different set of pieces that I call file card pieces. I think there was a natural growth, a reason why my writing went in that direction. I had begun to hear sections of music created in the game pieces in very specific combinations and wanted to orchestrate them in a more controlled way. There's a system that I used a lot in the game pieces where a prompter, a kind of conductor who relays information, gives a downbeat cued by one of the players to indicate a sharp change of some sort. Using that system, I was able to create in performance a series of blocks of very different music, played one right after the other. I learned it from Stravinsky and from cartoon music. So a file card piece is a series of file cards on which I jotted down ideas. I'd order the cards and go into a studio and record them, one after the other.

For notation, I used everything. Sometimes a card would have a set of chords, which I would orchestrate in the studio by saying, "OK, I want the harp to arpeggiate them, I want the keyboard to hold one chord, and I want the guitar to solo on top." Sometimes a card would read "car crash," and I'd give it to a percussionist, a guitar player, or a pianist and I'd say, "Do a car crash," and they'd do it, and I'd say, "That ain't no car crash!" and then I'd mold it. Again, I was working with creative improvisers, not Juilliard-schooled musicians who want every note written. Sometimes I'd give them a book to read, then I'd say, "OK, do your version of this book in this six-second slot." So the notations on these file cards would vary from written instructions, to music written out on a traditional staff, to chord names, to a suggested melody, to visual ideas, to sounds I was hearing that you can't write down but I'd heard an improviser do. ("You know that thing you do with the slide when you go way up high? Let's use that sound!")

At the time I began the file card pieces, I was fascinated with the early works of Schoenberg, where he wasn't quite sure what he was doing. He needed something that grounded his work, so he used text or a dramatic subject. When the text ran out, the piece was over. In the file card pieces, I needed something to tie all the different genres of music together, so I used dramatic subjects, like Mickey Spillane or Jean-Luc Godard. Each moment of music related to the dramatic subject in some way. Take *Spillane* [*Spillane: A Tribute to Mickey Spillane*, for eleven performers; 1987]. I read books about Spillane, I saw the movies, bought the records, whatever kind of cheesy thing I could find. Then I culled ideas from those sources and put them on file cards. I picked the best ones and ordered them and ended up with maybe sixty moments of music that I then fleshed out in more detail. When I could see the whole arc of the piece, I would go to a bunch of improvisers and say, "Look, I've done my homework—now let's go in and create a piece."

Then we'd go into the studio and put it on tape. We'd record section one, do it over and over in the studio. I'd say to the band, "OK, it starts with a scream, then you come in with a swinging beat and the bass comes in, and the piano, then we do this melody, we bring it to a crescendo, and then I'll cut you off." That was twenty seconds, or forty seconds, or whatever. We'd rehearse it until it was perfect, do a couple of takes, move on to the next card, and then punch that in where it needed to go. If it wasn't right, we'd stop, do it again. Stop, do it again. Sometimes we'd do fifty takes of one moment of music that lasted only six seconds.

I don't believe that a composer envisions all the music in his head. Even while I'm writing something straight, like for the Kronos Quartet, I'm not exactly sure what the next section will be. Part of the fun is in exploration. There's always interaction, a give-and-take with the sounds that you're dealing with. But what I was doing in those file card years was sculpting sound with musicians, describing what I needed, having them do it. We were constantly trying to get something special.

I also knew the players very intimately, interacted with them in a very special way. You can't go to Gidon Kremer and say, "Give me a car crash." But with players I've improvised with over the years, I can sculpt with sound, using musicians' personal languages to create a composition that could never exist in any other situation. They're fulfilling my vision. I remember the electricity in the studio, creating three minutes of music over the course of an entire day, coming back seven days in a row to create a twenty-minute piece, working ten hours a day. A *lot* of work, but an exciting time, everybody just knowing that *something* was being broken there.

The file card pieces took a long time to generate. I have this blackboard where I chart long-range pieces, and the file card pieces were up there sometimes for over a year. It was a very natural process of study, research, and then slowly getting the ideas together and coming to the point where I felt ready to go into the studio. The written scores came from the file cards and were put down on two or three sheets of white paper. I'd write out the chords or describe in words what goes on. It's kind of a shorthand. You can't put everything down, and lots of times I prefer *not* to put everything down. It's nice to leave a few things up to performers. The final score for a file card piece is the tape, because I've molded the music in such a way that it's exactly the way I envision it. Without my explanation or the tape itself, the paper scores aren't going to mean much to anybody.

Sending a piece like *Spillane* to a college new music group won't work. These pieces are meant for musicians with special skills. The guitar part needs to be played by someone who can read their ass off, blow jazz over changes, play hard-core at the drop of a hat, play country music, rockabilly, make noises. I think we're getting more musicians like that, but it's never going to be a standard in the academic world. There's always a no-man's land, where players in academic scenes think they *can* do those things, but the last thing I want is for them to butcher the guitar part on *Spillane*.

Different ideas are always floating around in my head, and sometimes ideas from one piece get incorporated into another. One idea gets dropped completely, another gets put aside and later returns. With the long file card pieces I got frustrated waiting so long for a new piece to be born, so I started the band Naked City. Again, I wanted to create a problem, challenge myself. What could I do with just guitar, sax, keyboard, bass, drums? Naked City was a compositional workshop for pieces I could write in a day. I'd be walking down the street, get an idea, jot some notes down, and the piece would be done. Some pieces were born in a couple of minutes.

One of the parameters I limit at the beginning of a project is the music paper. I decide what kind of paper I want to work with, and it will determine things about the piece. All the Naked City pieces were written on one particular kind of paper, and when I got to the end of one sheet, that was the end of the piece! I'm also lazy—I don't like copying parts. Like in the Mozart movie—what did he say? "I've got the piece finished in my head, and all the rest is just scribbling." There's a lot of truth to that. Once you've finished something in your head, you want to move on. So I would create a piece completely on one sheet, hand it out to all the players, and explain the arrangement to them. Again, there was a shorthand involved.

Still, with Naked City pieces we're talking about timelines, and getting closer to traditional musical notation with melodies and chords. There are sections of improv, noise, and other things, all written for a specific group. Naked City started with rhythm and blues/*Spillane* kinds of things, then went into this hard-core period. That came about, I think, because I was living in Japan and experiencing a lot of alienation and rejection. I had a lot of anger in me, and that came out in this hard-core music. In the ten years I went back and forth between here and Japan, I soaked up a lot of information, new ideas from the people, from the music. I still have great relationships with musicians there, but for me it was information overload. My interest in hard-core also spurred the urge to write shorter and shorter pieces. How can you create a ten-second piece that has integrity? That's not so easy.

I'm not a minimalist. I can't take a small idea and work it into something wonderful over twenty or thirty minutes. Some of those early minimal pieces are hours long, and they're fantastic! I guess one of the reasons I try to pack so much information into my longer pieces is that I'm reacting against the minimal movement. I loved that stuff, but I knew at the time that this was the best it was going to be. Riley, Glass, Reich—those are the cats; there's no point in following them. So I took this maximalist idea of packing as much information as I possibly can into a piece.

Toward the end of Naked City I realized I had taken that band about as far as I could, compositionally. We made seven or eight albums' worth of material, and there are still a lot of pieces that we haven't recorded. But when I started hearing classical music in my head again, I said to the players, "I think this band is over." And they said, "What do you mean it's over? After all this work?" But when Joey Baron saw *Elegy* [a twenty-eight-minute piece for flutes, viola, guitar, turntables, sound effects, percussion, voice], he said, "Wow, if I could write a piece like this, I wouldn't be traveling with Naked City. Forget it. I totally understand what's going on." And Naked City was over.

It made total organic sense, so there was no regret. It wasn't difficult at all; it would have been more difficult to continue. I canceled the last tour and had to pay all the business expenses, but I didn't have a choice. I said, "This is it. I don't want do this anymore."

Cat o' Nine Tails (1988) was the first piece that the Kronos Quartet commissioned from me. It was actually a notated file card piece. I ordered the cards and, one card at a time, wrote out the piece. The time for this change was right: I had put in my homework and was ready to sit down and write a string quartet. I fell very naturally into that mold and was really excited about breaking it. The following year was the chamber symphony. There were no commissions in my life before those pieces. Then slowly other things started coming in. Steve Drury [Boston pianist] commissioned *Carny* [1989; a thirteen-minute work for solo piano]. *Angelus Novus* [1993] was commissioned by the Netherlands Wind Ensemble. Now, even though that creaked the door open and I stuck my foot in, I'm not getting commissions all over the place. But I'm doing good. This kind of music seemed the perfect thing to do after Naked City.

When I quit Naked City to do the classical pieces I thought I was never going to play the sax again, I was fed up with it. Of course, six months later I started Masada so I could play! Go figure. Masada came about because I'd always wanted to write a book of melodies. Again, it was a challenge—I had never done this before. Ornette Coleman's compositions—wow—what a book of tunes—incredible! I wanted to contribute something like that. My idea was to write a hundred compositions in a year. That was my goal. The second year, I wrote fifty, the third year, twenty-five.

For the Masada paper, I restricted myself to five lines. The idea of a head in jazz—you play it at the beginning, improvise on the form inherent in the head, and then play it again at the end—always intrigued me. To create a melody that people can improvise on for ten minutes—that's a trick! So Masada's music was five lines, and when I ran out of five lines, it was over. I used repeat signs in very weird, creative ways. Sometimes the road maps got very complicated.

All the Masada pieces used Hebrew scales, and mainly two: what I call the matzo ball scale, the Mizza berach, and Avaraba—the Havah Nagilah scale. (Basically minor with a sharp four, and major with a flat two.) I had a kind of Jewish revival, a reawakening, and then I created *Kristallnacht* [a forty-three-minute, seven-movement work for violin, guitar, keyboards, bass, percussion, clarinet/bass clarinet, trumpet; 1992]. You know, being Jewish isn't just being angry about the Holocaust and being pissed about this, that, and the other—it's also a celebration. I'm proud of who I am. Critics sometimes completely miss the point—they haven't got a clue. They simplify; they say, "This is Ornette Coleman meets klezmer." That kind of thing gives me a headache. All of my projects draw upon a wide variety of musical influences. Everything I've learned has gone into everything I've written. I don't say, "OK, now I'm not going to pay any attention to the influences of surf music and world music, and I'm just going to do jazz and klezmer." You can't think that way.

The classical piece I'm working on now will be performed in the middle of July [1998] in Munich. It's for voice and nine instruments, and they need the score sometime in June. I started at the beginning of March. For the most part, I set my own deadlines. I'm a real workaholic; I push myself to write, because it's fun! My life is so great. Every day is a vacation, and every day is work. They're the same. When people say, "Do you take two weeks off and go on a vacation?" the answer is no. It's just all one lifestyle. To go and sit on the beach for two weeks would drive me crazy. I don't understand that at all.

With the classical pieces, sometimes the title comes first. It's like the dramatic subject that helps to define the direction or the content.

But with *Eporious*, the name was put on at the very end, after reading this book by Derrida. *Eporoius* is a set of requia for a variety of people who died over the year and a half I was working on it. Each piece was a tribute to these people. Marlene Dietrich, Francis Bacon the painter, John Cassavetes the filmmaker, and Cage died that year, and others.

One of the things that I do to give each classical piece structural integrity is use another composer's work from which to derive pitch information. With *Eporious*, I used the *Requiem Canticles* by Stravinsky. I mirrored the basic structure (several movements with a prelude and a postlude) in a certain way, and then I took certain phrases and chords and wrote out the pitches, just in letters. Sometimes it would be as many as twenty-five pitches, all the pitches in one large chord. I'd write them out and create melodies out of them. Or I'd take a melody and create a chord out of it. Or I'd copy out an actual viola part and compose other parts on top of it. Using someone else's work as source material gives a piece a kind of unity. Everything's coming from one place.

The piece I'm finishing for Munich is a twenty-five-minute work in four or five movements. For source material I'm using Stockhausen's *Kontrapunkt*, because it's for nine instruments, a similar instrumentation. I'm taking thirty pitches from *Kontrapunkt* and repeating them, over and over, in that order, throughout my piece. Right now I'm dealing with orchestration, distributing those pitches around the group. I'll start at one point in the row, give it to one player, start a little bit later in the row, give it someone else. I'll skip pitches, play around. If there's something I want, like a B-flat major chord, I can find it somewhere in my row. I'll say, "OK, if I skip three pitches and then skip four pitches, I'll get my B-flat major chord." So I'll do that for awhile. Skip three, skip four, skip three, skip four. I do what I want with this information. I do this to amuse myself, and if it amuses someone else, that's an added pleasure. Maybe nobody will be amused; maybe nobody will know! Maybe nobody will care even if they *do* know! But it makes me feel stronger about the piece.

Also in the Munich piece, there's no text. I'm using the voice just "vocalise." I told them I want someone who can sing with no vibrato, and use a little bit, and use a lot. I'm getting down to detailed suggestions of when vibrato is used, and just shading, so it's not there all the time. My God, the operatic vibrato is an unusable sound, I don't care whose it is! It drives me crazy. I'm also using two wind machines in this piece. Percussion is one of my favorite things—you know, metal balls rolling in a bowl, or someone slamming a door, like on an old radio show.

I've never been interested in development. I work on one moment at a time. Cohesion comes eventually, and I don't see it right away. Once in awhile I have to go back through the piece in my mind, in time, and catch up to where I am so I don't lose the sense of line and narrative. I'll say, "OK, I've got to calm down a little bit here, or it's time to really pick it up, or change the orchestration." It's a challenge to keep the piece unified.

Every piece I've written is like a little frame. There are things that belong in the frame and things that don't belong at all. At the beginning of a piece I can sometimes lose sight of that frame. The challenge for me with this new piece is drawing the frame as I write. It tries to push out, and I keep pulling it back. I say, "But that's not this piece. It shouldn't go there. That doesn't belong." In the end, I'm the only one who knows what belongs, and if I don't know that, I'm bullshitting.

John Zorn, Selected Works

SOLO/SMALL ENSEMBLE

Angelus Novus (1993)
two oboes, two clarinets, two
  bassoons, two horns

The Book of Heads (1978)
thirty-five etudes for solo
  guitar

Carny (1992)
piano solo

Cat o' Nine Tails (1988)
string quartet

Cobra (1984)
ten–twelve players

Dark River (1995)
four bass drums

For Your Eyes Only (1989)
eighteen players

Rituals (1998)
mezzo-soprano, ten
  instruments

LARGE ENSEMBLE

Aporias (1995)
requia for piano, orchestra, six boy
  sopranos

Orchestra Variations (1996)
orchestra

Publisher:
Carl Fischer, LLC
65 Bleeker Street
New York, NY 10012
212-777-0900

John Zorn, Selected Recordings

Absinthe: Naked City
John Zorn, alto sax, vocals; Bill
  Frisell, guitar; Wayne Horvitz,
  keyboards; Fred Frith, bass; Joey
  Baron, drums
Avant Avan 004

The Classic Guide to Strategy
John Zorn, alto sax, soprano sax,
  clarinets, game calls
Tzadik TZA 7305

Duras (two violins, piano, organ, two percussion); *Étant Donnés: sixty-nine paroxysms for Marcel Duchamp* (violin, cello, percussion)
Tzadik TZA 7023

Elegy
Barbara Chaffe, alto and bass flutes; David Abel, viola; Scummy, guitar; David Shea, turntables; David Slusser, sound effects; William Winant, percussion; Mike Patton, voice
Tzadik TZA 7302

Filmworks, VII: Cynical Hysterie Hour
music for four shorts by Japanese cartoonist Kiriko Kubo
Tzadik TZA 7315

Kristallnacht
David Krakauer, clarinet/bass clarinet; Frank London, trumpet; Mark Feldman, violin; Marc Ribot, guitar; Mark Dresser, electric bass; Anthony

Coleman, keyboard; William Winant, percussion
Tzadik TZA 7301

John Zorn: Parachute Years
game pieces, 1978–1981
Tzadik TZA 7316-2

Live at the Knitting Factory: John Zorn's Cobra
Knitting Factory Works KFW 124

Naked City: Black Box
Torture Garden (1991); *Leng Tch'e* (1992)
John Zorn, alto sax, vocals; Fred Frith, bass; Bill Frissell, guitar; Wayne Horvitz, keyboard; Joey Baron, drums; Yamantaka Eye, vocals
Tzadik TZA 7312-2

New Traditions in East Asian Bar Bands
works for pairs of instruments (guitars, drums, keyboards) with spoken texts in Chinese, Korean, and Vietnamese
Tzadik TZA 7311

MICHAEL DAUGHERTY

(B. 1954)

*M*ichael Daugherty finds much of his inspiration in American pop culture; one has only to glance at the titles in his catalogue to see the connections. *Metropolis Symphony* (based on Superman) and *Elvis Everywhere* (for string quartet and tape) are prime examples, as is Daugherty's opera *Jackie O*, commissioned by the Houston Grand Opera and described at its 1997 premiere as "a window on American celebrity culture of the 1960s, '70s, and '80s."

Daugherty was born in Cedar Rapids, Iowa. As a boy he studied classical piano, played percussion in a drum and bugle corps, and formed a funk band with his four younger brothers. He attended North Texas State University and the Manhattan School of Music and spent a year in Paris studying at IRCAM (Institut de Recherche et de Coordination Acoustique/Musique, France's institute for musical research). He also studied with jazz arranger and composer Gil Evans, with György Ligeti, and with Earle Brown, Jacob Druckman, Bernard Rands, and Roger Reynolds at Yale, where he earned a doctorate.

Daugherty's music has been performed in the United States and abroad by such ensembles as the New York Philharmonic, the Tonhalle-Orchester Zürich, the Baltimore Symphony, the St. Louis Symphony, the Kronos Quartet, and the Netherlands Wind Ensemble. He teaches composition at the University of Michigan and lives in Ann Arbor with his wife and daughter. This interview took place in Ann Arbor in May 1996.

• • •

My creative outlet has always been music, and I've never been able to play it straight. I've always liked making things up. When I was in junior high school, I played percussion in the orchestra and got in trouble with the conductor because I added my own music to the part. When I was in high school, I played cocktail piano in restaurants and nightclubs and always deviated tremendously from the melody and came up with all sorts of bizarre chord progressions. I've always liked to do things different, offbeat, and I've always enjoyed performing in front of people. For me, composition is a form of performance. As I write, I think of how the audience and performers might react.

Two composers who really shaped the way I think were Gil Evans and György Ligeti. It was an extraordinary experience to work with Gil Evans [in New York, 1980–82]. Gil said that I was one of the few people who had ever asked to study with him, and I actually ended up helping him get his music organized and published. He was a very kind and sensitive soul and extremely poor, too. I was with him once when he received an honorary jazz award in the mail for lifetime achievement. He said, "I don't need awards; I need some money." He was still friends with Miles Davis at the time, but Miles had bought the copyrights to Gil's arrangements for *Miles Ahead*, *Porgy and Bess*, and other tunes and made a lot of money from those recordings, which Gil didn't share in. Gil was incredibly disorganized in his personal and financial life. All of his music sketches and arrangements were thrown into various cardboard boxes in a closet in his Manhattan loft. He had no desire to catalogue or preserve his music for future generations. This was the complete opposite of, say, a Stockhausen, who is very careful to document every aspect of his life and music. I realized from Gil that it isn't enough to be a genius in music; one has to be practical as well. Musically, I learned much from Gil about timbre. The sounds of chords were very important to him: he would play a "Gil Evans" chord on the piano and say, "Man, listen to that sound." He loved music of all sorts. He was a big fan of György Ligeti, for example.

In the early 1980s I was dissatisfied with the music being written by many composers my age. Much of it was heavily influenced by Elliott Carter and Boulez. It was abstract, based on scientific, arithmetic, or philosophical formulas, and pieces would be simply the result of a system. That didn't appeal to me, because I was used to playing popular music, interacting with other musicians. In jazz you create the music on the spot with other players, so it's not abstract. I wanted to combine my interest in American pop culture and classical music in a serious and sophisticated way, but that approach was very unfashionable at the time.

Then I read an interview with Ligeti in which he stated that he loved American jazz and rock music. I thought that perhaps he could help me find my way, so I went to Hamburg, found his apartment, and said, "I want to study with you." He asked me, "Do you like Milton Babbitt?" and I said no. Then he asked me, "Do you like Thelonious Monk?" I said yes, and he said, "Then you can study with me."

Ligeti's class was very small—only about six students. I was the only American. Ligeti thought most music he heard was "academic" and "not original." For Ligeti, "originality" was everything. All of us in the class were afraid to bring in our music because we feared the inevitable verdict of Ligeti: "not original." I found the atmosphere to be interesting, but much too intense, so I decided instead to follow Ligeti around Europe and hear his music performed. It was in Graz, Austria, at a Ligeti performance that I met Conlon Nancarrow, who was at that time Ligeti's great discovery—he was introducing him to European audiences in 1982. I really took to Nancarrow because as a kid I had learned to play on an old player piano like the one Nancarrow used.

Ligeti was a great inspiration to me, and I enjoyed my time in Europe. But after two years I was ready to return to home and compose my own music.

When MIDI first came out in 1980, I was ready to jump into it because I knew the possibilities, the potential for me. I can't imagine things in the abstract— I'm like the painter who has to put the red on the canvas, the blue and the green, then look at it, physically touch it. This new technology allowed me to try out ideas and have them played back to me, just like the player piano back in Cedar Rapids. I started working with synthesizers, samplers, Macintosh computers. Today I have a large studio in my home in Ann Arbor with two Macintosh computers, two laser printers, a rack of Proteus samplers, two DAT machines, a Yamaha Disklavier, and a Kurzweil PC 88 MIDI keyboard. For software I use the Digital Performer sequencing program for composing, and Finale to print out my music. I never really read the manuals, I just dove in and came up with my own sort of idiosyncratic ways of dealing with technology. The idea of being tainted or influenced by any sort of commercial aspect of technology never bothered me. I found that I could use the tools that were readily available to anybody and be creative within the supposed constraints of technology.

Snap! [for winds, strings, percussion, and synthesizer; 1987] is the first piece I wrote working with MIDI, and I think it's the first piece that was really in my own style. It was a big breakthrough for me. The idea for it came from watching an old Hollywood movie where James Cagney tap-dances on a large piano keyboard. In the movie, there are two bands on either side of Cagney, and he dances back and forth, interacting with the two bands. There are also two drummers, one on each side of the stage.

I used to tap-dance as a kid, and I also liked the idea of physical separation, which I used as a metaphor in *Snap!*. On the left and right of the ensemble there are two cymbal players, working off the idea of stereo—the sounds of the cymbals move antiphonally. As I wrote, I thought of film techniques—

like a camera panning back and forth on the sound stage. That was a personal way to write, and it allowed me to mix together a lot of experiences and instincts.

I compose by multitracking (writing one line at a time), which is also how I wrote for my rock band in the late '60s. For *Desi* [for symphonic wind ensemble; 1991], I composed the bongo part first, then the bass line, then the woodwinds, then the brass, etc. I have always used polyrhythms in my music, which goes back to playing funk music as a kid. I tend to work late at night — it's a habit from those years as a nightclub entertainer. Sometimes I even compose with a television in my studio — the picture is on, but the sound is off. Visual images help me write — I especially like watching old Warner Brothers movies from the 1940s. Everyone has to find her or his own way to become musically inspired. Brahms composed with a cigar, Bernstein with a cigarette, Bartók with a seashell, Stravinsky with a piano . . .

In fact, before I can write a note of music, I have to have a visual image — an American icon like Elvis, a pink plastic flamingo, or Jackie Kennedy. Just like an actor, I like to research my "role" before I compose. For example, I watched videos of Liberace and read his autobiography before I composed *Le Tombeau de Liberace.* Before I composed *Elvis Everywhere,* I attended the International Elvis Impersonators Convention in Las Vegas and heard more than 200 Elvi perform. I can only write music about an experience I have lived myself. It would be difficult for me to set the poetry of Sappho, for example. But I could be inspired by *Star Trek,* because I have seen every episode. I use icons like Superman, Liberace, Jackie O, and Elvis in composing because they allow me to play with "public" vs. "private" emotion, "external" vs. "internal" feeling, "fake" vs. "authentic" representation.

In starting a piece, I usually write one line of music, then begin to multitrack, start adding lines. Then I'll experiment with the sounds of different instruments playing those lines. What would happen if a triangle played this or a trumpet played that? I have always admired the way Stravinsky orchestrated, and I like to come up with unusual orchestrations, too.

I have a sequencing program that plays back everything I write, like a player piano. After I have composed some music I like, I hire instrumentalists to come to my studio, and have them play through the parts that I've written. I usually rewrite them again, based on the possibilities of the instruments. Working with the live instruments inspires me to take each line to another level.

Sometimes I have performers improvise. I'll give them ideas to start with, we'll tape the session, and then I'll select the different aspects that I like, put them onto a hard drive, and edit the material using a program called Sound Tools. I might cut something into as many as 100 different sound bytes. Then I'll dump it over to the sequencer and start pasting the ideas together, listening to the instruments doing various things.

For my piece *Dead Elvis* [solo bassoon, clarinet, trumpet, trombone, violin, double bass, percussion; 1993], I got a group of musicians together and had them improvise all sorts of ideas and textures. I spliced up the session and then structured the piece, decided how I wanted it to go. Of course, that was just the first step. After that there was layer upon layer of work.

It's not dissimilar to how a film is made. You'll have some dialogue written—it might be sketchy—and the performers might improvise to a certain degree. You'll have three or four cameras shooting simultaneously from different angles. Then in the editing room the piece will be reconfigured again, reconstructed in different ways.

For *Elvis Everywhere* [for three taped Elvis impersonators and string quartet; 1993] I wrote out a text, then found three Elvis impersonators in Chicago and had them improvise off of the text. We produced four hours of raw material. Then I came back to my studio, selected parts I liked, put them into the hard drive, and constructed a tape part of Elvis impersonators. The result is nothing like the session, because it was reconstructed, reconfigured in various ways. After that I composed the quartet part.

To get exactly what I want, to really fine-tune the piece, I'll sit back and let the sequencer run, say, a section of thirty measures at a time, over and over and over. I'll listen to it hundreds of times. Maybe I'll shift a layer of counterpoint ahead two beats, or shift another one back and add a different layer to harmonize it. I'll listen to everything I do so many times that by the time the performance group has the piece, I know exactly what it will sound like. There are no surprises.

In the end, the choices come out of my musical judgment. It's the same sort of intuition I use if I'm playing cocktail piano in front of an audience. Instincts are based on a lifetime of being a musician, a performer, and a listener.

To get ideas for pieces I sometimes drive in the country to small towns. It goes back to being a kid—I always liked driving outside of Cedar Rapids, out to the cornfields and rolling hills, the kinds of landscapes that Grant Wood (who lived in Cedar Rapids) painted. There'd be the land, and a farm—a self-sufficient community.

I like eating in a small-town mom-and-pop restaurant, the family dining place. The cuisine might not be great, but it's where the townies go. I also check out the thrift stores, antiques malls, the stores that are not part of a chain—where you can sense the individual who runs the place. I like going to state fairs and county fairs, where there are large groups of people. I like looking at old books and magazines from the '40s, '50s, and '60s. I like collecting old books about twentieth-century music that are out of print. I want to make connections between things past and present.

After a long drive I'll come back to my studio with everything I've seen sinking in, and some idea will hit me and I'll start writing.

The myth of the soloist is fascinating to me—the convention of being a soloist, the whole mystique around it. Liberace is an interesting character because he represents the idea of show business, of Las Vegas, one of the ultimate, bizarre American constructs. My grandmother liked his playing, and I liked him, too. He had a hidden identity, like Clark Kent's Superman. Dressed in outrageous furs and rings, he was definitely an eccentric, but also a great pianist who made a conscious decision to be commercial, to reach a mass audience. He even wrote a book that describes how he did it. For me, that was a fascinating subtext for a piece of music. Taking it as a point of departure, it allowed me to write a very strange piano concertino, *Le Tombeau de Liberace*.

The first movement is called "Rhinestone Quick-Step." The orchestra is very Vegas-like, but the material is a difficult canon with all sorts of interesting rhythmic possibilities. In the second movement, "How Do I Love Thee," I use a theme that sounds like it's from a Catholic mass. At the same time, there's a tango, a kind of dance of death. Liberace would recite Elizabeth Barrett Browning's poem at almost every concert, and there's also a famous picture of Liberace kissing the Pope's hand that inspired this. For the last movement, "Candleabra Rumba," I was thinking of a big swimming pool shaped like a grand piano with all sorts of flamboyant people and celebrities sitting around—a kind of cocktail party.

Those are just the ideas, the images that were in the back of my head when I wrote the piece. But musically the piece had to work on its own.

I revise my pieces quite a bit. It's not uncommon for me to cut out whole sections, reduce a piece, if I feel it needs it. I try to avoid fat, or unnecessary music, in my pieces—I want them to be very lean and to the point. It took me five years to write *Metropolis Symphony*. I revised each movement many times. I tinkered with the individual movements and listened to the symphony played in various configurations before I finally came up with the piece as it now stands.

Revisions are based on experience, on audience reaction, on timing, and on letting the piece sink in. It's not unlike the way the Marx Brothers would try out their material on the road before making a movie.

I'm always trying to make each piece better than the last one. I try to refine an aspect of music I've been working on or do something in a more interesting way than I did in the previous piece. I suppose I'm always striving for the perfect piece, which I'll never realize.

As a student I was told, "Don't write clichés—write what the instruments *can't* do." Well, as I got older, it became obvious to me that *everything* is a cliché. In other words, a nineteenth-century gesture is just as much a cliché as a twentieth-century one. To me, extended instrumental techniques offer no more surprises than baroque ornamentation, at this point. So if one takes all gestures as equal, it means that the individual gesture is meaningless. What has meaning is how the gestures are put together.

Everything is fashionable for awhile. A very famous twelve-tone composer in the '70s told me that all that non-twelve-tone music was just "fashionable music." It would be here today and gone tomorrow. Well, the same thing happened to twelve-tone music. It came and went.

Each composer finds his own rhythm. It's important to find your own and go with that. Ten years ago I would check out Ravel or Boulez or Sibelius and see how they would address a particular aspect of composing. I don't do that anymore. Now when I write a piece, I'm within in my own world. Maybe you have to go through other people's worlds before you can get to your own.

Michael Daugherty, Selected Works

SMALL ENSEMBLE

Dead Elvis (1993)
solo bassoon, clarinet, trumpet, trombone, percussion, violin, double bass

Firecracker (1991)
solo oboe, flute/piccolo, bass clarinet, violin, cello, percussion, piano

Shaken, Not Stirred (1995)
three percussion, electric bass

Sing Sing: J. Edgar Hoover (1992)
string quartet and tape

LARGE ENSEMBLE

Bizarro (1993)
symphonic wind ensemble

Metropolis Symphony (1988–1993)
movements may be performed separately: "Lex," "Krypton," "Oh, Lois!," "Mxyzptlk," "Red Cape Tango"
orchestra

Motown Metal (1994)
four horns, four trumpets, three trombones, tuba, two percussion

Niagara Falls (1998)
symphonic wind ensemble

Le Tombeau de Liberace (1996)
solo piano, flute/piccolo, oboe clarinet, bassoon, two horns, trumpet, trombone, tuba, two percussion, violin, viola, cello, double bass

STAGE

Jackie O (1997)
chamber opera in two acts
libretto: Wayne Koestenbaum

Publisher: Peermusic, distributed by Theodore Presser Company, 1 Presser Place, Bryn Mawr, PA 19010-3490. Tel. 610-525-3636; fax 610-527-7841.

Michael Daugherty, Selected Recordings

Dead Elvis; Snap!; What's That Spell?; Jackie's Song; Le Tombeau de Liberace; Motown Metal; Flamingo
London Sinfonietta/Zinman
Argo 458-145-2

Desi
Baltimore Symphony/Zinman
Argo 444-454-2

Elvis Everywhere
Kronos Quartet
Nonesuch 7559-79394-2

Metropolis Symphony; *Bizarro*
Baltimore Symphony/Zinman
Argo 454-103-2

Paul Robeson Told Me
Smith Quartet
Smith Quartet Records 4001CD

Shaken Not Stirred
Ensemble Bash
Sony Classical SK 69246

Sing Sing: J. Edgar Hoover
Kronos Quartet
Nonesuch 7559-79372-2

Snap!; *Mxyzptlk*
Oberlin Contemporary
    Music Ensemble/
    Rachleff
Opus One CD138

JAMES MOBBERLEY

$(\text{B. }1954)$

J ames Mobberley grew up in central Pennsylvania and spent his high school and college years in North Carolina. He credits his elementary school music teacher with instilling in him a great love of music. As a child he took up the clarinet, then taught himself the guitar at age fourteen and, as he puts it, "hooked up with some other novice rockers in high school and college and nursed a band for seven years—all original stuff, mostly wacky songs about aliens and fast food and the Ayatollah Khomeini." Mobberley earned a bachelor's degree in guitar and a master's degree in composition at the University of North Carolina at Chapel Hill, and a doctorate at the Cleveland Institute. His teachers were Roger Hannay, Donald Erb, and Eugene O'Brien. His work, which often combines electronic and computer elements with live performance, spans many media, including film, video, theater, and dance. He has been commissioned by the St. Louis Symphony Chamber Series, the Nelson-Atkins Museum of Art, and the Cleveland Museum of Art, as well as individual performers. A CD of his orchestra music is in preparation for release in 2001.

James Mobberley teaches at the Conservatory of Music of the University of Missouri–Kansas City, where he directs the conservatory's Music Production and Computer Technology Center. He was Kansas City Symphony's composer-in-residence from 1991 to 1997. He lives in Kansas City with his wife and sons. This interview took place in Kansas City in November 1996.

·   ·   ·

Most of us get into things because of encouragement from a teacher or somebody in the field, and with composition, it happened at just the right time for me. I'd been searching through various college majors for a number of years, and music composition was my fifth major at the University of North Carolina. The others were math, biology — each of those lasted a few weeks — then philosophy for two years, guitar performance, and finally composition.

I had entered the second semester of freshman theory without having taken the first semester, which was a mistake on the registrar's part, and the teacher said, "Well, I'll let you stay, but if you get to the middle of semester and you're floundering, I'll let you withdraw with a passing grade." I did well enough in the course, and at the end of that semester, he said, "I'm teaching a composition class. If you have some free time I'll let you take it." Off I went.

I didn't suspect that I had any aptitude for this, so the education process was critical for me. I'm sure some people come out of the womb with a quill pen in their hands, but I wasn't one of them.

Part of the reason I compose is that I have a lot of control over what happens on the page, or at the computer. Anybody who teaches or works with other people knows that the minute your project involves others, it doesn't go as well because their investment is often is not as high as yours. With composition, the notes give me less trouble than people do.

The advantages of electronic means are *control! control!* and an endless, endless palette. Control comes in two ways. First you have control over absolutely every element of every note. I'm one of those really ridiculous people who works in a programming language that requires a lot of code to describe each note. It's a language called C-Sound — there are very few of us around using it. With it, every single note, every sound, can be sculpted from beginning to end. I'll construct pieces that consist of 250,000 lines of code, each one identifying the placement, length, and the universe of every sound. The trade-off is the tedium involved in making that happen. Sometimes it isn't worth the effort. But that level of control is an extraordinary challenge, and an extraordinary delight.

The drawback to electronics is that the medium is inherently static, although getting dynamic results out of static materials is easier than it used to be. Another drawback is that, bearing in mind what live performers bring to melodic lines, to phrasing, you can spend 98 percent of your time tweaking, trying to make the electronic medium sound as sensitive as a human performer. Most electronic composers aren't trained in such nuances as well as performers are, so often the output is a little bit rough, to put it kindly.

To balance that, the other reason I love to compose is that I'm often surrounded by gifted players who enjoy playing and talking about new music, even dreaming it up together. Composers and certain kinds of performers are capable of a strange sort of creative symbiosis. I seem to have found a place where there are a lot of those performers, so there's no reason to quit.

The most satisfying situation is when there's a lot of give-and-take with the performers during the composition process. I've been writing a piece for trumpet and tape for the trumpeter on our faculty. Our modus operandi was to get into the studio and record various trumpet sounds, which I would then manipulate to make the tape part. He's a very imaginative, quick, creative person with an extraordinary sense of humor, and nearly 50 percent of the sounds that went onto the tape had something to do with odd parts of the trumpet, even the trumpet stand. There were also twenty-five individual laughs from this recording session that found their way into the piece. I had no clue it was going to be like this when we went in there. I just knew he was a funny guy, and I was expecting that this would be a fun session, so this piece turned out to be my perception of his personality. It's not the first time that's happened. Spending that kind of time around players, using their raw material, makes quite a difference in how a tape and instrument piece comes out. I enjoy being involved with other people at that level of the creative process, tremendously.

When it comes time for the piece to be performed, there's a lot of ownership of the piece, because the player actually hears himself or herself. In the trumpeter's case, it wasn't just his instrument, but his laughter, and expletives, and all sorts of things.

I have a clarinet and tape piece that requires the clarinetist to play into a bowl of water, and I heard about a performance that was done in England using dry ice and fog. The clarinet player came out wearing fins! Wonderful! Anything a performer can bring to one of my pieces is fair game.

How composing happens is always rather mysterious, even in retrospect. Where did all this music come from? I don't remember! You might have six or eight ideas, and one of them just seems like the right thing to work on. I used to do the exercise [the composer] Sam Adler talks about: when you're starting a piece, you sit down, shut your eyes, and imagine the stage, the performers, and the applause. Then you imagine the conductor's stick going up and coming down and—what do you hear? That's what you write.

I like that. It really is helpful to imagine the whole thing. So I don't do a lot of precompositional activity, unless there's a program, explicit or implicit. I might know that I want to do three movements or that I want to involve the soloist more here, and less there, but I have no grand plans. It's more of an organic thing. I used to try making blueprints, but I always ended up tearing them up. For me, they were a complete waste of time.

I get pretty fixated on whatever is working itself out at the moment. I spend probably 98 percent of my time tweaking the original idea and reworking it, extending it, adding the next thing. It's funny how some ideas can take a minute to come up with, then six months to execute.

These days I almost always involve computer or MIDI simulations of music I'm writing for live instruments. That enhances my ability to work beginning to end, because I can get a very clear idea, not of anything purely musical (MIDI simulations of timbre and phrasing are fairly abysmal) but of the shapes of sections within the lengths of time I'm dealing with. It's very easy to lose track of the shape of a piece by the tenth minute. What you think you're writing and what is actually happening over time can be under- or over-estimated much more easily than whether or not you're writing the right harmonies or melodies. So my process has evolved not only through the particular situation I find myself in but also by the fact that I'm using the computer in different ways and becoming much more adept at getting a reasonable idea of what people are going to hear.

The process of making prototypes [electronic tape representations of music that will eventually be performed by live players on acoustic instruments] requires a lot of tweaking because if you use standard electronic sounds or even samples, most of the notation programs available for them give you a brute force reproduction method of sound. So I have to make two versions of the score: one that I listen to, and the other that is appropriate to look at and has the right notation for conductors to follow. Not only am I tweaking the way it looks, I'm tweaking the way it sounds.

I really got into this when I wrote a ballet this year. The choreographer and the dancers had to use my prototype for the rehearsals because the orchestra wasn't available until just before the performance. I spent a huge amount of time trying to make the tape sound as close as possible to an orchestra, and of course it failed miserably in important musical respects. In another respect it was dangerous, because the precision and clarity that you can get with electronics can never be matched in live performance, especially in a resonant space.

So in the prototype we gained precision and lost musicality. With the orchestra, we gained a lot of musical intensity and passion but lost precision because of the sight lines in the pit, and because it is the nature of a real orchestra in real space to be less precise than sequencers.

There's always the question of whether or not to write "for yourself" first. But it doesn't hurt to be aware of the limitations of a particular situation. Writing music for orchestras requires that you know how well they play. Also, you can't overdo it in the way that you can for your faculty colleagues who give two recitals a year and have months to prepare. Orchestra players give the equivalent of two recitals a week. It's no wonder that they get bent out of shape when you ask them to do things the circumstances don't allow. I'm trying to be more sensitive not only to players' abilities but also to the amount of woodshedding and rehearsal time they're going to have.

I think composers who spend a lot of time in electronic studios can be less understanding about the process of putting pieces together for a performance —what the resources are, what the players can do, especially in terms of time.

Being a composer-in-residence has given me some insight into what life is like in the pit and on the stage. I'm not a concert guitarist, and I've never set foot in an orchestra situation as a player, so it took me awhile to understand the situation.

I don't discard very much material, because if something's relatively stupid when it first comes out, I usually don't hang onto it. If I have something that is at least workable, I usually try to figure out how to deal with it. I do take ideas from other pieces of mine that were underexplored or explored only in a certain direction, and I'll work them out in a different way. Occasionally I do that unconsciously, and my wife usually points it out. "That sounds a lot like that piece that you wrote two years ago," she'll say. I don't enjoy discovering that I'm doing that. I suppose in heaven we will be able to write each piece as a completely self-contained unit, but I'm not there yet, so I do recycle ideas. Sometimes it's out of necessity, but most of the time I'm working with these ideas in a new way.

Maybe you keep doing something until you get it right. I think there are a number of composers, Mozart among them, who take the sort of ceramist's approach. You throw lots and lots of pieces out. Half a dozen out of fifty are really extraordinary, and the others, in Mozart's case, are just wonderful. Some composers write one piece every year and a half, and each one is unrelated to the previous work. I tend to work more slowly, and my pieces are relatively self-contained. Each environment is different—it's like I'm exploring another planet.

I tell my students, "If you don't like something you've written, bring it in and let's talk about it." Usually they say that what's wrong is very general, very vague—the work is "just dorky," or "it's not good enough." My job at that point is to help them pin it down, to understand what is really bothering them. Sometimes it's a matter of the difference between what students hear and the technique they have to realize that. Most of the dorkiness stems from rhythm. Students tend to have a lot more control over pitch than anything else. Also, it's particularly difficult to write slow music that is rhythmically interesting when you don't understand ornamentation yet. The exercise of writing down jazz solos is terrific for that, because nearly all of the notes are ornaments, and you have to develop your own shorthand to approximate rhythmic weight.

Figuring out why you dislike something is probably more important than writing something you're happy with. If all you do is write pieces that you like, you're probably not doing a lot of growing, especially as a young composer. You're not getting used to that really creepy feeling of being off into a new lagoon and having no idea what's in it. Or putting on shoes that don't fit—sometimes you have to change yourself to fit the shoes.

When people experience creative block, it seems they're at a point of style change, where the old style has become uncomfortable. It's gotten stale. I rec-

ognize it by my dissatisfaction. "This sucks!" I say, or, "I've done this before."
Yet anytime you try something new you're going to be uncomfortable with it.
It feels like you can't possibly write anything that's as good as the older, more
comfortable stuff. I keep telling my students to try new things now, because
as hard as it is to try something without knowing what you're doing, it's ten
times harder when you're a pro, and you're under more pressure to get everything right.

It's all right to not know what you're doing—to try to discover *what* you're
doing. And you can't really fully know what you're doing as you're doing it.
There's a sort of a Zen about just having it happen, about letting what you are
writing be a natural expression of yourself at the moment. Getting to that
point where you trust yourself is a function of experience. When you come to
grips with the main body of a discipline over a period of time, then there are
an infinite number of chutes that you can go into, creatively.

Ideal situation? I think "sabbatical" would be the right word. "*Retirement*"
would be a good word. I would prefer to write three or four hours a day, every
day, six days a week. I wouldn't want to work more than four or five hours
every day because when I'm really working intensely, I'd collapse if I tried to
do more. If I took more than five, all I'd do is take five hours' worth of work
and expand it. The work expands to fill the time allotted.

I used to have the luxury of taking a week or a weekend, staying up all
night, whatever was needed, to get a real intense result. In six weeks a piece
could be done, start to finish, while I put a lot of other responsibilities off
until later. That was B.C.—Before Children. Now I get in an hour here, three
hours there, forty-five minutes, sometimes even less. If I have just fifteen minutes to myself, I'll review what I'm working on just to keep it in my head. I
don't have the luxury of staying up all night any more, because then I would
have to take days away from the children.

So things external to music have a great impact on how I work. It took me
a year to get used to having one child, and then we had another one eighteen
months later, so I ran into it all over again—a complete reorganization of life.
Four and a half years later, it's finally working. Not every piece has to be written in a white heat, but I'm trying to figure out how to maintain intensity
under these new circumstances. I used to be a late morning–early afternoon
composer, and then I could go again from 9 P.M. to 1 A.M. Again, children required adjustment. Now I'm primarily a morning and afternoon person.
Evenings are no longer productive, because I'm fried. If I had a month at an
artists' colony, I'd probably sleep the entire time.

I think it's important to have fallow periods. I haven't had one for about
five years. I really need a year off to listen to other peoples' music, to know
more of what's going on out there and to go back and fix all the mistakes in
the pieces I've had no time to clean up. (I make corrections in pieces, but I

don't revise. I think it's rather pointless to revise when you're in graduate school or even in the first few years afterward because by midcareer, most of that stuff isn't interesting anymore.) If I go without a fallow period, I begin to feel like I'm cranking it out. Right now I feel more in danger of repeating myself than I ever have. If I really take the time to go back and look at what I've done in the last couple of years, I might find I've done it all before! Not all, but some of it.

I'm really on a crusade for the emotional involvement of the composer in the writing process. I think we went through a tremendous denial phase in the first half of this century, for various reasons. Psychologically it was difficult for composers to deal with the reaction to the overblown romantics of the late nineteenth and very early twentieth century. It became very unfashionable to be so exposed. All of the major "-isms" in the century—neoclassicism, aleatoricism, serialism, minimalism, and others—were cool or completely detached movements. I don't mean to say that all serious composers were disconnected. Some of them wrote coolly on purpose. John Cage used to make a manifesto out of disconnecting the ego and, therefore, the personality. But not everybody can do that. When I talk to symphony audiences, I tell them that in the last twenty-five years, composers have begun to risk being themselves on paper. The entire person is able to come out into the musical score, and what we're seeing now is a huge eclecticism because we're all different. Some of us are melodramatic, some of us are staunch atonalists, others are delving into specific cultural materials. This has to do with wanting to create work that satisfies ourselves emotionally. And audiences respond more to music that has emotional shape or content.

Certain experiences in my personal life have had a tremendous impact on me, emotionally: a divorce, the deaths of very important friends, having children—the most incredible emotional experience I could ever hope to have. All of these things give me musical strength to be myself on paper, and I hope that anyone who listens to one of my pieces will get an idea of what I'm like. Of course it's different with each piece—I have different moods. But I'm not interested in hiding anything. I don't see how we can help being influenced by our environment, both internal and external.

The most recent event of significant impact was a near-death experience I had with necrotizing fasciitis, better known as "flesh-eating strep." In thirty-six hours I went from healthy to very nearly deceased. Surgery and antibiotics kept me alive, but what really brought me back was the constant presence of my family and the wider circle of compassion provided by my friends and colleagues. Though I have not purposely produced music about this experience, I have had some reasonably profound shifts in personal and musical priorities. I have rethought my orientation toward my career and am less interested in success as defined by anybody else, or by the external appearances of success. I try to stick with what feels good internally. I spend less time going after things, and more time enjoying the process of composing. After all, even if you get what you want from the outside world, it only lasts a microsecond. I've also become more eclectic, musically, more interested in a lot of different sides of myself, and less monolithic. More of my music is full of laughter, is nearly silly in spots. I don't think I would have done those kinds of things before. Mexican marimba music, even—that's a new direction for me. Not every piece has to be a metaphor of the late twentieth century. There are pieces that are the culmination of a search, and others that are about the beginning of one.

Having been involved with Meet the Composer for several years, I'm also on a soapbox for the composer who is involved in the community. I think we're all going to be better off if we make efforts to connect with other people. Most of us have survived—as symphony orchestras have survived—by having people come to us. But that security blanket has been unraveling. An orchestra has to meet the community halfway, and composers would benefit tremendously by doing that, too. I think it's possible to be a composer who struggles passionately on a daily basis with the purity of the art and is also willing to write a piece for the handbell choir at church, or a piece stylistically managed for the opening of a convention center. That's very much a Meet the Composer point of view. We've got to try to be Bachs out there, if we can, although I realize that some of us might not be good at it. The point is, there's room for everybody.

James Mobberley, Selected Works

SOLO, SMALL ENSEMBLE

Caution to the Winds (1987)
piano and tape

Icarus Wept (1995–97)
trumpet (or trumpet and organ)
   and tape

Lullaby (1989)
SATB chorus and piano

Soggiorno (1989)
violin and tape

Toccatas and Interludes (1992)
flute, clarinet, violin, cello, piano,
   percussion

TNT [Turetzky 'n' tape] (1994)
contrabass and tape

LARGE ENSEMBLE

Arena (1996)
ballet for orchestra

Ascension (1988)
wind ensemble and electronic
   tape

Concerto for Marimba (Eight
Hands) and Orchestra (1996)

Concerto for Piano and
Orchestra (1994)

Five and Two (1997)
eighteen-piece jazz band

Publisher: MMB Music,
3526 Washington Avenue,
St. Louis, MO 63103-1019.
Tel. 314-531-9635. Cautious
Music, Box 32493, Kansas City,
MO 64171.

James Mobberley, Selected
Recordings

Alleluia
(for SSA chorus)
ACS Records ACS S277

Caution to the Winds
Richard Cass, piano
EAM-9401

Icarus Wept
Keith Benjamin, trumpet
EAM-9701

Spontaneous Combustion
John Sampen, saxophones
Capstone Records CPS-8636

BRUCE ADOLPHE

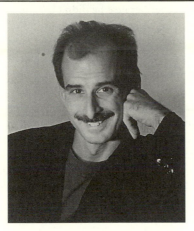

$\left(\text{B. }1955\right)$

ruce Adolphe enjoys a triple career as composer, author, and educator. Since 1992 he has been education director of the Chamber Music Society of Lincoln Center, a position that draws on his talent to communicate in a lively, authoritative way with music lovers. He has composed pieces for Itzhak Perlman, the Beaux Arts Trio, and the National Symphony Orchestra, among others, and has been composer-in-residence at Chamber Music Northwest, the Santa Fe Chamber Music Festival, and Music from Angel Fire.

Adolphe is a native of West Hempstead, Long Island. A number of his pieces have been inspired by memories of his parents, who both died before Adolphe finished college. Indeed, memory is one of Adolphe's passions. As a "fanatic reader" of cognitive neuroscience, he often discovers ideas for pieces in descriptions of the ways the brain works.

Bruce Adolphe has written many works for young listeners and is the author of two books: *The Mind's Ear: Exercises for Improving the Musical Imagination* (MMB, St. Louis) and *What to Listen for in the World* (Limelight Editions, 1996). He lives in New York City with his wife, the pianist Marija Stroke. This interview took place in New York in October 1995.

*   *   *

I started wanting to play the piano when I was about three or four, and my parents thought it was cute, but they didn't give in to it. So I was banging silent music on the dinner table, and things like that. By the time I was seven, they bought a piano, and I started taking piano lessons.

I hated my first teacher, because when I was first learning to read music he played examples for me, but not what was on the page. The reason was, this guy was sort of a jazz player. He didn't read music all that well. So he would play a simple melody, not quite the way it was printed, and add chords that weren't written. He was a very bad teacher because he didn't tell me he was doing this. Then I would imitate what he was playing and he would tell me, "*That's* not what it says—play what it *says!*" So he sent me mixed messages. He told my parents I would never amount to anything because I had no discipline. He should have said I'd amount to something because I could make things up!

My second piano teacher was very straight, and very good, and very classical, and after a year, she had me perform at a musicale with her other students. I had this very strong internal feeling then, a very powerful message, that I didn't want to play a piece that anyone else had ever played. So I went home and wrote my first piece. I wanted to be sure that I came in with something that none of the other kids had practiced, or tried, a piece that would be very special.

I probably wanted to be the most special one on the concert. That's not too unusual for an eight-year-old. But I didn't have any idea that making up my own piece would be a strange thing to do. My piece was in A minor, and very simple and folksy, occasionally modal, almost like Jewish folk music, which I heard a lot of because my parents were into folk dancing, seriously. At the concert, the program listed the composer's name as just "Adolphe," so after I played my piece and people applauded, my father stood up and took a bow as the composer. He thought it was very funny, had a big smile on his face. Afterward I went up to him and said, "But they didn't know that I wrote it!" And he said, "Don't you see that the piece is so good they think your father wrote it? They think an adult wrote this piece!" So I thought that was really cool. We laughed about it all the way home. After that, I started writing other things, and my father would bring me to the junior high school where he taught and put me on the stage, and I would make up pieces in front of all of the kids—overtures to Broadway musicals, things like that.

So the original reason I started composing was that I didn't think it was hard. And secondly, because it seemed like the most direct way to be special. I was surprised when some adults told me composing was a separate thing from playing the piano. They were wrong. It's not a separate thing from playing the piano, and as a teacher I would never say that to anyone. But they didn't know, they thought it was strange, so I was hauled off to all sorts of special teachers, and by the time I was ten years old, I had my identity as a composer.

It didn't occur to me until much later that I had other professional options. When I first realized that, I suddenly panicked—Oh, God, I could have done something else, couldn't I? But I really love composing. It's second nature to me, and I also do a lot of other things. I've been writing prose and some poetry. I've also written some scripts. I don't think writing words is any different from writing music—I mean, the process doesn't feel that much different. Either way, I like to think about what's important to me and put it in a language that I understand, to make it as clear as possible. And I want to make sure that I like it enough to want to show it to someone.

Part of the reason I keep going is that I got so much recognition so early, and it never stopped. I have never had a bad year, professionally—it's really true. But I've had other kinds of bad years. I had a horrible accident that stopped me from playing the piano for a long time and permanently limited the use of my right-hand fingers. Both of my parents died before I was twenty. I've been married several times. So my life has had many ups and downs. I've managed this balancing act between some very terrifying events in my real life and an easy ride as a composer. And I've been able to write about very serious things because they happened to me.

My father died when I was twelve, and I tried to write about that as a composer. I don't know how successful I was, but it was therapeutic. And I knew then that I was writing seriously. When my mother died, I was nineteen. She was very sick with cancer for a long time, and I made sure that I wrote things that she would love to listen to. I also got her out to concerts. There was one special evening before she died. She was in a wheelchair and very weak, and we got her into New York, to the first performance of a student piece of mine in Alice Tully Hall, which is practically my home now. She was up in the box, and I was downstairs because I had to sit with my friends, which I wouldn't have done had I been older. But she loved it and was incredibly thrilled to be there. She died not long after that. In a sense, I've been writing for my parents ever since.

I've written very few sad or funereal things. I write about what I remember. A lot of my pieces are about the humor that my father had, and about dancing, because he and my mother were professional folk dancers. I have a piece called *Dreams of My Parents Dancing*, and another piece called *Troika*, which is a dance I did with them. I have a piece called *Dream Dance*, which is also about a dream of them dancing.

More recently I have used composing as a way of thinking about less tangible things. For example, I have been trying to remember more about my childhood, realizing that I don't have an adult perspective on those memories, and wondering how accurate they are, and if it matters. So I wrote a piece about that, called *In Memories Of*. There are no specific incidents in the piece. It's just about the feeling of the struggle to remember. In trying to write that, I didn't go to any clichés or obvious devices for mystery. Sometimes instead of writing music I would just spend hours playing with my brain, not worrying about the musical part of it. I tried to experience how I think. I tried to figure out what it feels like to be in a dream state, what it feels like to try to re-member. When I did that, memories came back.

I'm reading a lot about how the brain works and have become good friends with a rather important neuroscientist and brain specialist, Antonio Damasio. I've discovered through talking to Antonio that our brains don't store memories intact. Memories are continuously reconstructed from lots of bits and pieces within what are called convergence zones, which is why mem-ories come out differently, sometimes. You're always reconstructing. Damasio says that if all of our received sensory information was stored in little com-partments, our brains would have to be gigantic, much bigger than *we* are. What the brain *does* have is the most efficient storage system ever known. It's almost like a digital situation—lots of separate bits converge on impulses that are like signals. It's very complex—I can't really explain it well—but that much is enough to influence my writing of some music.

So with *In Memories Of* I tried to convey the feeling of convergence zones, of bits and pieces coming together to form ideas which then re-form. They keep changing, and become very clear, and then get reorganized. When you retell a dream, it's not important if you change it, because the new version is just as revealing as the original.

Body Loops, my new piano concerto, was also inspired by a term of Anto-nio Damasio's. A body loop is the kind of memory experience that makes us sweat or cry—it brings about a physical response, as opposed to a memory that remains an image in the mind. These loops are real. They're neurological paths. *Body Loops* is a piece about thoughts that recur with this kind of emo-tional intensity.

For a number of years I've consciously written pieces about external things. Most composers I know go in and out of doing that. But I also do it in a way that is far less complex than what I just described. For example, I wrote a se-ries of solo violin pieces for Itzhak Perlman about food. It was his idea. He said, "Food's a great subject, we all love it, and it'll be entertaining." So I called the writer Louise Gikow and asked her to collaborate with me and write some Ogden Nash–esque poems about food to go along with the music. Itzhak would recite each poem and follow it with a piece. Now, I did-n't want to overly illustrate these food poems, because that would demean the music. So Louise and I made a pact that sometimes she would write the poem first, and other times I'd write the music first and she'd have to figure out what food was suggested by it. That would make the process more ab-stract and interesting.

I'll tell you how we arrived at some of these—*Mixed Nuts* is one of the best ones. Louise wrote a poem called *Mixed Nuts* because I suggested to her that the image of mixed nuts would be fun for writing patterns. The fact is, I wrote the piece before she wrote the poem, but we were both absolutely sure it was mixed nuts. My piece was sort of a musical representation of what mixed nuts look like in a jar from the side. Her description was very funny. In that case both parts fit together, and Itzhak thought they were wonderful.

But we had trouble with another one. I wrote one piece not knowing what it was going to be about. It was very smooth, and Louise said it sounded like brandy, or cognac. So she wrote a brandy poem. But when Itzhak played through the music, he said, "You know, I don't think this is brandy. This is chocolate cake." And he played it again, and it was so much more like chocolate cake—it was very sticky and chocolatey and rich, and it was all in the way he was playing it. It was the way he felt the music should go. It really mattered to him which food it was, in terms of how he used his bow and his fingers, so I said, "OK, it's chocolate cake. That's great." We threw out the brandy poem and Louise wrote one about chocolate cake. Itzhak's infectious sense of humor and astounding technique were really inspiring to me.

Some of my musical materials come from my environment, an actual rhythmic experience. I've done a lot of writing about traffic, which I think is a perfectly natural New York phenomenon. Just try walking down the street with people moving in all directions, cars honking! I've written a piece for children that has a traffic movement. Also, some of the rhythms in my pieces are based on my awareness of the rhythm of walking down a crowded street in a rush. I've translated those rhythms almost exactly into some pieces. In a way this relates to my use of brain ideas, too, because in those cases I'm translating a thought rhythm into a pitched rhythm, into an actual musical phrase.

When I write humorous music I'm extremely conscious of every second of it. I think in terms of setting up jokes, delivering punch lines—I do it with a lot of delight, and it works. I'm very comfortable writing funny music very quickly. I struggle more over serious movements, and in those, I'm more likely to allow things to occur to me that I haven't thought about before. I try to find more time to write them.

Doubt is a waste of energy when you're trying to be creative, but it's useful when you're editing the piece. I've been lucky enough to not have doubts while I'm writing, but later, when I go through a finished piece, I might throw out whole sections. I've thrown out entire movements. For *In Memories Of* I composed an hour of music and cut it down to fifteen minutes. The other stuff I just tossed out. This doesn't bother me, because I accept it as part of writing. You have to question certain things and then edit them away. I think it's natural.

Each time I sit down to compose, I make a deliberate choice whether or not I'm going to work with the piano. I can write without it, in complete confidence that I'm hearing everything, but sometimes I hate what that feels like. I love to improvise at the piano—sometimes I improvise for hours, find one thing that I want to keep, and take it to the desk and start writing with it.

Often the ideas come faster at a keyboard, but I find that when I sit at a desk, the writing is more sophisticated—that is, it's more intricate and more appealing to me, more compelling. So in order to get the best of both, I often sit at a keyboard to write, even if I don't play. Or I might play for a couple of hours, and the writing that follows might have very little to do with most of what I've played. Or I might play for a few minutes, then write for a couple of hours. Whichever way I do it, it feels like I am continuing the improvisation process without needing the piano. I am improvising in my head.

I always write by hand. I like the process of writing on paper very much. Sometimes I write in all different directions on the paper, and I often write in ink, even if I wind up crossing it out. I like the visual aspect of it; I like how a great pen feels on paper much better than pencil, although I've written in pencil too. Basically, the whole process feels like continual improvisation.

If all I have to start a new piece with is a phrase, I get going by writing different versions of it. I might write the same thing fifteen different ways, then look for another phrase to work with. The second phrase should be in some way a continuation or the exact opposite of what I just did. So I write many versions of the second phrase, and by the time I've done that I might have a whole, possible piece, or enough music for it.

I like to have enough ideas in a piece to make it rich, but not so many that it feels scattered and mindless. Sometimes I add things or take them out, but I decide that later. I'd much rather have too much so that I can edit. I love that situation—I can't stand forcing myself to stretch material thin by exploring every detail of it.

On the other hand, sometimes I write a whole piece from beginning to end and I don't change anything. I've done that a number of times, but it would be weird if I could always do it. My most serious piece is my fourth string quartet, and the second movement was written that way. [There are five movements.] I was in Switzerland with my wife, and we were staying in a place that had no privacy and no piano and no desk. So I went to compose in an elementary school that had a piano. I was in a very dark mood because a very young cousin of my wife's had cancer. I improvised for awhile, and then I just wrote out the best movement in the quartet from beginning to end, in score. It's complex in structure, but all the ideas are very clear and very simple. The reason I could do it was that I knew what the movement was about. There would be a pulse that was the tick of time, indicating possible death. There was going to be a solo violin that kept interrupting it in complete outrage over this disease, and also a very peaceful passage that tried to convey acceptance and the feeling of eternity and something spiritual. I improvised with those three ideas, and then I just kept putting them together in patterns that seemed to be right to me. When it was over, the movement was done. It ended with rage, because that's what I felt at the time. It was the truth for me, at the moment. Everyone who's heard that piece says it's the best movement in the quartet. They say the structure is so complicated. I say, well, this is the only one I didn't struggle over.

The other movements of the fourth quartet were put together like mosaics, where I wrote a lot of material and sketched and juxtaposed things various ways and did more cutting. In the fifth movement, though, I went back to the second movement, the one that I wrote straight through, and took that peaceful spiritual theme and turned it into a double canon for string quartet. Why write a double canon in 1995? Why write a fugue, or any of those things? For me, the only reason to do it would be to fulfill a symbolic purpose. The purpose of a double canon here is to say that there are forces beyond our control. If the theme is like a human being, then the double canon is very much like fate—it has its own path, and the notes just have to follow, which is like accepting fate. That's just what it sounds like. I've seen people cry during this piece. I've had a hard time since then, trying to match it.

I played it for Nicholas Maw, who's a wonderful composer and a close friend, and he said, "Bruce, now that you've done this, it's going to be much harder to write anything as good. You've entered a plane that's going to make creative work more difficult." And I know what he means. The way the message of the piece and the technique of the piece and the materials of the piece are inseparable from each other is something I know how to do, now.

My favorite pieces in the world all do that. Everything is absolutely cohesive and integrated and cannot be separated. To do that on purpose is not so easy—it has to sort of happen. I think the way that comes is to be in touch with your feelings all of the time, and to write when you have very powerful feelings. That's the opposite of the way I've been most of my life, which is to write all the time. I still write all the time, but I try to be aware when something really special is present. It's not just an emotional state, but an awareness. It's a state that brings together everything I know about music and about my real life, so that music seems like the perfect language for saying what I'm experiencing.

One way of describing it is the feeling of the conscious and the subconscious both being present, with no line dividing them. It feels like a completely elevated state when you're like this, because everything's there. Everything's available. Memories and dreams and thoughts and musical things are all completely available, without interfering with each other at all.

If I were to write two pieces a year of the quality of that second movement in the fourth quartet, I'd be on top of the world as a composer. But instead, I write one of those every God knows how long, and a whole lot of other things. Has anyone ever written such integrated music, every time? Maybe not. But the people we think of as the greatest composers did it on a regular basis. All of Beethoven's middle and late string quartets are like that, also his middle and late piano sonatas. With Bach, *everything* is like that—every single piece is a complete integration of every aspect of musical expression and self-understanding.

I don't know how one reaches this state, but I have some guesses. One would be that after one has written a long time, it becomes natural to experience something like that. I had two years of psychotherapy, which was very helpful. It made me conscious of states of awareness, of how artificial the splits between conscious and unconscious behavior are. I probably did this at the right moment in my life, after my first marriage ended, so that I was able then to experience this blending in my work.

I think that inspiration is a lifestyle, not a phenomenon. I think that you can cultivate it. The most extraordinary things happen to everybody. Everyone falls in love for the first time, and everyone sees a flower that is beautiful and reminds them of something—it's just endless! I don't think that any of the things that inspire works of art are unique. They are specific, but they're not unique. It's the person who receives the inspiration who makes it happen, not the outside object or condition. Inspiration is an awareness and a readiness to respond. Some people have a propensity for that and some don't. I think a lot of it has to do with your childhood. If you're in a very fun, spontaneous household, you're probably open to inspiration. I did have a very fun house-hold. There was a lot of dancing, there was a lot of humor, and if I have to write a piece, I can be inspired just by that.

Some composers would say their inspiration is the commission money, and that is also true. Actually, inspiration has everything to do with the money, the players, the hall, the fact of somebody asking you to write something. If you've been asked to write a piece, you are suddenly much more ready to be inspired by things you might never have noticed.

You can cultivate inspiration by creating a window for it. I tell my students to practice being inspired in various ways. For example, to look out the window as a composer. To look out the window as a painter. To look out the window as a writer, a novelist, and ask, What are the things that you notice from these various perspectives? They're states of mind. If you look out the window as a novelist, you might think of stories about people on the street. If you look out the window as a poet, you might try to capture a particular moment. As a composer it might be the rhythm or the patterns that inspire you. I do that exercise myself.

I used to tell people I could only write at home, but it's not true anymore. I wrote that quartet movement in Switzerland, in a school, and I also wrote a violin and cello duo in a practice room in a school in Florida where I was vis-iting somebody. I had a short amount of time, and I knew I had to write this piece, and I was irritated that I didn't have a good pen or good paper. Yet I took this crummy ballpoint pen that didn't have good ink flow and some hor-rible oversized music paper stuck in a spiral binding to a rotten piano that was completely out of tune, and I wrote a really good movement from start to finish with no changes. I don't know how that happened, because it was against what I thought were all my preconditions for good work. That's how I learned there are no preconditions.

I love deadlines. I write fast when there are deadlines approaching. They push me to think about the piece more intensely so when it comes time to write it I know what I want to do. Often I don't know how much I've been thinking about a piece until I sit down and start working on it. Then I realize that I've done a lot of—either unconscious or subconscious or superconscious or semiconscious, whatever the expression is—thinking! We all know that the stuff we don't know we're thinking about is much more interesting than what we're consciously talking about or doing. So when we finally bring the unconscious material to the surface, we're surprised by how rich and worked-out it already is.

Once in awhile I write a piece that for some reason doesn't work out. For example, a long time ago I was commissioned to write a piece about a Soviet prisoner. I wasn't that well known and I wasn't that good, either. I forget how it happened—it was a Jewish connection, and someone thought I could do it. So I wrote an entire oratorio for violin, tenor, chorus, and orchestra, and then all the politics changed, and the guy got out, and they never played the concert. I just took the piece and tossed it. I decided the text and the music were too specific to the circumstances, and I didn't like it anymore.

In cases where a piece doesn't come to life, I save the music for another piece. That is, if I love the music, I recycle it, rework it. I can easily turn music for a chamber orchestra into a completely different kind of piece. Not different musically, but different instrumentally. It could be a string quartet, it could be lots of things.

It's a survivalist thing, you know. It's like having a stash. If you have a lot of work to do, and not a lot of time, you might as well have drawers full of ideas. Writers do that—everybody does that! Even my aunt keeps everything she ever cooked frozen, waiting in the refrigerator for future use!

Often, the most inspiring thing to me is another musician. The violinist Ida Kafavian is a great example—just her confidence that I would write something wonderful made me want to write for her. She'd rather play a new piece that somebody wrote for her than Beethoven. That shouldn't be a surprising thing, but a lot of musicians don't feel that way. David Golub, the pianist, has been very inspiring. I wrote a concerto for him with no commission, no money, no guarantees of performance, because his musicianship is so special to me. Yet the piece wasn't about him, it was about the ending of a relationship that was full of torment, and I called it *After the End*. It's a piece full of missed connections. The piano is the protagonist, and the orchestra is basically resonance. But it helped knowing David would play it, because he has a certain kind of seriousness of purpose and a poetic quality that I kept thinking about. Hearing him play made me write things I would not have written otherwise, and certainly if I'd pictured myself playing it—which I would never do—the piece would have turned out differently.

Mark Steinberg, the first violinist of the Brentano String Quartet, is another inspiring performer. I wrote a violin and piano piece for Mark and my wife, Marija Stroke, and it's one of the most daring pieces I've ever written, because Mark is a very daring violinist, somebody who has scary energy. I wouldn't have written this piece for Ida or Itzhak. It's Mark's piece, and Marija's. There are players and pieces that go together.

Mark's piece is called *And All Is Always Now* (it's T. S. Eliot) which is about what we've been talking about—the idea that all your memories are happening, and you either notice them or you don't. Your past only exists because you can remember it. That doesn't mean you only live in the moment, but it means that if you want to live well, you engage your memory. Memory is vital. It may not be accurate, but you can't live without it. If you lose your memory, you lose your identity.

To invoke, provoke memory through the structure of a composition is important to me. We composers have many received forms that might function as memory guides, but these historical forms are mostly too conventional to be meaningful now. Certainly they are too familiar to be exciting to work with. And so the challenge is to create provocative internal references in a composition that parallel memory in life. These references may be as small as a single, unique chord in an exact position and instrumentation, which serves as a signpost or catalyst, like the Proustian cup of tea. Or the reference may be as large as a structural pattern that is perceived subliminally, one that takes many listenings to emerge clearly. For me, the most interesting way to involve the listener's memory is to build a work that is "fractal" in its conception—a work in which the details are refractions of a whole, like a pinecone or an intricate Indian rug. The improvisational approach to composing that I have been describing is only the beginning. After that comes the work of balancing the intuitive and the intellectual, the mysterious and the technical, memory and imagination.

Bruce Adolphe, Selected Works

SMALL ENSEMBLE

And All Is Always Now (1992)
violin and piano

At the still point, there the dance is
   (1990)
clarinet and string quartet

The Bitter, Sour, Salt Suite (1995)
solo violin and narrator
text: Louise Gikow

Grace Notes (1996)
soprano and five players
text: Rita Dove

In Memories Of (1994)
piano and string quartet

Marita and Her Heart's Desire
   (1994)
narrator and twelve players
libretto: Louise Gikow

Night Journey (1986)
wind quintet

Turning, Returning (1992)
String Quartet no. 2

Whispers of Mortality (1994)
String Quartet no. 4

LARGE ENSEMBLE

After the End (1992)
piano and orchestra

Body Loops (1995)
piano and chamber orchestra

Songs of Radical Innocence (1997)
clarinet and orchestra

Publisher: MMB Music, 3526
Washington Avenue, St. Louis, MO
63103-1019. Tel. 314-531-9635.

Bruce Adolphe, Selected
Discography

And All is Always Now; *By a grace
of sense surrounded* (String
Quartet no. 1); *In Memories of*

Turning, Returning (String
Quartet no. 2)
Brentano String Quartet; Mark
Steinberg, violin; Marija Stroke,
piano
CRI 761

At the still point, there the dance is
Chamber Music Society of Lincoln
Center
DELOS DE 3183

Marita and Her Heart's Desire
Michele Mariana, actress; Bruce
Adolphe, conductor
TELARC CD-80460

Night Journey
Dorian Wind Quintet
Summit Records DCD 117

Soliloquy
Curtis Macomber, violin
Koch International 3-7145-2 H1

Triskelion
American Brass Quintet
Summit Records DCD 133

BRIGHT SHENG

$(B. 1955)$

right Sheng was born in Shanghai, China, and started piano studies
with his mother at the age of four. His adolescence coincided with
the Chinese Cultural Revolution (1966–76), during which he was
sent to the country for a rural education. After the fall of Mao Tse-Tung's
regime, Sheng earned a degree in composition at Shanghai Conservatory of
Music, and in 1982 he moved to New York, where he attended Queens College, CUNY, and Columbia University. Among his teachers were Leonard
Bernstein, Chou Wen-chung, Mario Davidovsky, George Perle, and Hugo
Weisgall.

Sheng was artistic director of the San Francisco Symphony's Wet Ink '93
Festival and has been composer-in-residence with the Santa Fe Chamber
Music Festival, the Seattle Symphony, and the Lyric Opera of Chicago, where
his opera, *The Song of Majnun*, with a libretto by Andrew Porter, was premiered in 1992. Bright Sheng often draws on his Chinese heritage for musical
materials and inspiration. *H'un (Lacerations): In Memoriam 1966–76*, his dramatic orchestral portrait of the Chinese Cultural Revolution, has been performed by major orchestras in the United States and Europe. He teaches at
the University of Michigan. This interview took place in Brunswick, Maine, in
August 1995.

.   .   .

Why do I compose? Music is a way for me to express feelings as well as concrete thoughts—it's like telling a story with sound. One part is spontaneous, while the other requires more logical, organizational skills. One helps the other to achieve the maximum result. When they meet, the outcome is wonderful. Writing music is a very straightforward impulse for me, and I cannot resist it.

I get excited when I write, although it's a constant struggle—one keeps looking for a way to write better and hopes it will get easier. I suspect that when Stravinsky went neoclassical, he found a new way to write. If he had pursued the same route as *The Rite of Spring*, a truly original masterpiece, he probably would not have produced so many works. Unfortunately, in my case, composing only gets harder, so it's very frustrating. But I'm also happy that I can compose and make a living.

My normal composing process is this: I think about a new piece first while taking walks. I start to hear sounds and I process them. I pick the music that excites me. It could be an interesting beginning for a piece, or a middle section, or an ending. As I take more walks, I hear more. Each time, I hear more details. Finally I figure everything out at the piano, note by note. I usually have a general shape for the piece before I do this. That doesn't mean I won't change anything or make a detour. But I feel that having a map at least gives me a sense of where the work is going. However, I have also done it the other way around, with no premeditated route at all.

Sometimes I dream of the music. I don't think that's unusual—a lot of composers do. Sometimes dreams help, but sometimes they don't. It often happens that if I have a block and I'm struggling, I go to bed and dream of the solution. I get excited, wake up, and write it down. But when I look at it the next day, it is *not* usable! This has happened to me many times.

But dreaming *can* be helpful, as it was with *China Dreams*, a four-movement work I just finished for the Seattle Symphony. I had written the first three movements and had an idea for the last movement, which is always the most difficult one, since it has to "gel" the rest of the movements structurally. I wasn't intensely thinking about it—I was sort of relaxed. Then one night I had a dream in which I was at the first orchestral reading of this work. I didn't recognize the conductor or the orchestra, but for some reason I knew that I was following the score of the fourth movement, in which all the materials that I had used in the previous movements were put together nicely. "A great idea," I thought. After about five minutes in the dream, the orchestra had to stop because there were too many mistakes in the reading. I woke up and remembered how the music looked on the score—an amazing experience! I wrote down on a pad what I had heard, in words and in notes—whatever happened to come out. I went back to sleep thinking, "Tomorrow it's going to be like those other times, when nothing I took from the dream will be good." But when I looked at my notes the first thing in the morning, what I had was still exciting. The first five minutes of the last movement of *China Dreams* as I wrote it are more or less what I heard in the dream.

Haydn prayed every day to get inspiration, and I do, too. I often think writing music is like having, for example, an antiques shop. You have to keep the shop open everyday. Some days nobody comes, but you still have to be there. Once in a while somebody comes in and purchases a precious object for a large amount of money. If you are not there that day, you will not make the sale. It's very important to be mentally ready to receive when the inspiration comes. Shostakovich said once that you have to write every day, not so much to finish the piece, or to get to the end of the section, but to know where you are. Then when you come back to it the next day, you can pick up easily.

How I came to be a composer and musician is a very odd story. It came out of the political circumstances in China, where I grew up during the Cultural Revolution. During that time there was no high school or college, because one of Mao's missions was to demolish the education system. He believed that people knew more than he wanted them to, so he just cut down the education level. The highest education during the Cultural Revolution, on the surface, was junior high, but Mao further devalued it to the fourth grade.

A problem arose when all these young people graduated from junior high at age fifteen and had nothing to do, a potential social problem. Moreover, in communist theory, the government in a socialist country is supposed to provide jobs so nobody will be unemployed. But there was no further education in China, and the economy was poor because nobody was producing anything. To solve the problem, Mao sent all young students out to be farmers, to be "reeducated" by the peasants. So we all went to the countryside.

Everybody had to go—it was mandatory. The only people who could get out of farming were those who had some talent in performing arts, because Madame Mao, who wanted some credit for herself, was suddenly running the show. She gave more state funding to arts companies and encouraged them to bring in young people. Fortunately, I could play the piano, and I thought, "This beats being a farmer!" I came from a traditional intellectual family that would normally oppose the idea of being in the music business—they viewed music as part of "the show-biz." But under these special circumstances my father conceded. I was sent to a remote province called Qing Hai on the Tibetan border, and I was mostly a performer there. I started as a pianist and percussionist and later conducted. After a while I began to arrange music. In retrospect, there were two elements from that period which became very helpful to my later development.

Shortly after I arrived in Qing Hai, I realized that I could not obtain an adequate music education as an instrumentalist there. I was the best pianist in the province, and I was only fifteen. There was no one to teach me. So I became very used to being self-taught. I would watch and listen to other people when I visited other cities, and learned to grasp quickly whatever they were doing that might help me as a musician. This became a very good habit. One is always one's own best teacher.

The other wonderful experience was with folk music. Qing Hai province was in a very remote area with a special and beautiful type of music. I started studying it on the side without knowing why, and without realizing that one day it would be a great resource for inspiration. I was not thinking about being a composer, although I was sort of playing with the idea all the time.

I was in Qing Hai for seven years, almost to the age I was supposed to be graduating from college. Then the government changed and I took the admissions test offered by the Shanghai Conservatory of Music, the oldest music school in China. I auditioned for the composition department because I was tempted, as every instrumentalist is, at one time or other, to try either composing or conducting.

When I left China in 1982 after graduating from the Shanghai Conservatory, I thought I had a pretty good education in Western classical music and that all I needed was twentieth-century technique to be well off. In my first two years in New York, I learned the basics of many techniques of the twentieth century. I also realized that I could write in any style. But for awhile I got stuck. I could not express freely with the styles I was writing in—I was not writing the way I wanted.

During those first two years in New York I went to a great number of new music concerts, and many times I found myself walking out unsatisfied. I soon realized I would learn a lot more from a performance of Brahms or Beethoven. After meeting Bernstein at Tanglewood in 1985, I attended all of his rehearsals I could. At the time he was recording the second cycle of Mahler symphonies, and I was so fortunate that he was rehearsing a great deal in New York City!

My breakthrough in composition happened gradually, as I started to understand more deeply the masterpieces of tonal music. Compositional styles may change through time, but most human feelings remain unchanged. So whether it is tonal or atonal, Asian or Western, the most important purpose of music, to freely express human emotions, continues to be the same.

Compositionally, all the great composers from Bach to Bartók are my models. I study with them by analyzing their works, and when I write I am conscious of how they thought of music. Sometimes the weight of their achievements makes me feel inferior and miserable! It's a lot easier to think that we should forget about tradition. But you can't erase the history of music, which is one of the greatest human treasures.

I tell my students to study Beethoven, Brahms, Mahler. These great composers often have answers to our questions in their scores—we just need to find them. My students can study with the masters through my introduction. Every time I get stuck with a work, I put on a Mahler symphony—any

Mahler—and I usually get an answer, somehow. Of course, taking a walk is very useful, too.

I enjoy working with great musicians because I learn endlessly from them. For me, going to rehearsals of masterworks is like going to the kitchen to see how the chef makes the dish I am fond of, whereas going to a concert is like tasting the dish.

I like to say that when the performance is great, you forget about the performer and you get into the music. When the performance is very good but is not at the highest level, you hear the performance, not the music. And then, when the performance is not so great, you hear the music again!

An important part of what I understand about composing comes from studying with Leonard Bernstein for five years. He had a special way of approaching things as a teacher. He made things easier to understand. He made you believe that everything he was doing, you could do, too. You realize, "Yeah, I can do it," and you do! When you keep working like that, you don't realize how much you improve. I regret that I didn't know him earlier. But he set me up with a way of thinking in music composition that benefits every minute of my life.

As I mentioned earlier, in music composition you can't rely completely on your intuitive spontaneity, and you can't rely only on logic, either. You need to keep a balance. Bernstein kept a very good balance between the extreme levels of both. He was also a well-rounded musician—pianist, composer, conductor—and it didn't make any difference whether he was playing or conducting or writing music. His musicianship was the same for all.

When he passed away, the *New York Times* asked me, "What part of Bernstein is the biggest loss for us—the conductor?" I believe the biggest loss for the music world is that we lost a great composer and a great conductor in one person. There are few of them around. The last one we had was Mahler. As a matter of fact, Bernstein said to me once that the reason he was a good conductor was because he was first a good composer. Now he is gone, and the world appreciates him as a composer more and more.

Talent becomes something *only* when you work very hard. Individual voice is important, and so is technique. Many young composers ignore the need for technique. They think an individual voice is all you need to be a great composer. I've seen people who have both talent and an individual voice but have never gone beyond that.

I realized this when I started teaching. Sometimes a student will ignore technique, thinking it's irrelevant. He will see examples of composers who became famous even though they avoided these aspects and think he can do that, too. But any interesting musical composition always has a great many surprises, and you must have good technique to create those. Also, we have a great repertoire that was built before us, which we can't ignore. The Chinese have a saying, "To know which one is better, you have only to compare." It's a bad translation, but I think there is something meaningful here.

I used to doubt whether I have any talent, or whether I'm in the right profession. I still have doubt, but it's different. At least now, if a work is good, I know it in myself. Doubt can be good if you use it positively, especially for a work in progress.

It helps when people tell you they like your music and they play your music beautifully. But success is really more within yourself. If a performance of my work is adequate and I like the work, then I'm really happy and could care less what a review says. However, if the work is not that good but I receive a good reception, I'm not quite content. The constant question is, "Did I do my best?"

I revise constantly. Mahler used to say that ideally, he would like all of his symphonies to be republished every five years. That means he was revising all the time. Bernstein at the end of his life was still revising early works like *West Side Story*. I have learned to more often let it go after a certain point.

I have three categories for my works. The first category is, How Could I Have Written This Piece? The second is, This Piece Is Not Bad—it has some good ideas in it, but because of a shortage of talent I didn't pull it off so well. And then there are Pieces I Truly, Passionately Love. I try to abandon the pieces in the first category. But if I only kept the pieces in the third one, there would be just a few works left.

I still get a lot of inspiration by going to concerts, but I also like to be isolated, at the time I choose. Again, to be productive, the shop needs to be open twenty-four hours. I like to have the freedom to work whenever I like. I also need access to ways of listening to music. If I'm isolated in the woods for three months, I need a lot of CDs and a piano. But when I'm actually writing, I need completely quiet surroundings to work effectively. My perfect day would be to get up early in the morning, work the whole day, and go to a concert in the evening. Of course, it doesn't always work out that way.

A stable mood is good for work, but sometimes a very sad or happy condition of the mind helps to bring about the music. One summer when I was in Maine I was misdiagnosed with lymphoma. For a few days I thought I had only a few months to live. Before this, I had read stories about writers or composers who were terminally ill and worked desperately to finish their last works before they died. And I thought, "If that were me, I'd travel all over with the time I had left."

But as I waited for my correct diagnosis (it turned out I was OK), I suddenly realized that maybe it is not so much that dying people want to finish their work, but that working helps them forget that they are dying, a very powerful and overwhelming thought that you can't set aside easily. I worked very well for those few days.

Presently my biggest challenge in writing is the direction I am taking in fusing Asian and Western cultures—a very old problem of cultural identity but also always very new.

Over the years I have grappled with this question: What defines cultural identity—the land you grew up in? The musical language you speak? Your current nationality? Deep inside, I have never felt anything but Chinese, and no matter what I do, people consider me Chinese because of my cultural background and the fact that my music has a very strong Asian influence. Half of me—maybe the whole of me—truly appreciates the Western culture. I have lived in the United States since my midtwenties. The other "whole" of me is an authentic, idiomatic Chinese who grew up in China and whose outlook was formed there, in school and while working in Qing Hai Province and in Tibet. I understand how the Chinese mind thinks. So I am a mixture —why shouldn't my music reflect that? People acknowledge "artistic license"; I embrace "cultural license"—the right to reflect my appreciation and understanding of both cultures in my work.

Of course, the easiest way is to sacrifice a bit of both sides and come up with a "Chinoiserie." But that is like mixing the best beer with the best wine. I am not sure about the result.

I mentioned Bartók as one of my models, especially the way he fuses East European folk music with the high cultured Germanic musical traditions. Using folk or secular elements in a composition started at the beginning of Western history. But what makes Bartók's music great is that he managed to keep the primitiveness and savageness of these folk elements as well as the refined quality in the classical tradition. The result enriches both. That is not easy to do. A composer must understand both sides in great profundity. Then when these two seemingly opposites meet at their most original end, a true transformation occurs.

This is the very goal I am striving to achieve. But I think less and less about whether some element I am using is Chinese or Western. I write whatever excites me while continuing to study both cultures, hoping that Western audiences don't feel they need to understand Chinese music in order to appreciate me, or that Chinese audiences feel that they need to understand Western music.

When I was small, I was told a story about a garden of treasure with a secret entrance. Everyone searched and searched for this garden until, after a very long time, the door finally opened itself and there was no treasure in the garden! But the experience of searching taught people lessons about life. I like this story because writing music is like searching for the garden of treasure. In the end, maybe the purpose of the search is the search itself, through which we learn about composing.

Bright Sheng, Selected Works

Publisher: G. Schirmer, 257
    Park Avenue South, 20th floor,
    New York, NY 10010.
    Tel. 212-254-2100;
    fax 212-254-2013.

Bright Sheng, Selected Recordings

RICHARD DANIELPOUR

(B. 1956)

Richard Danielpour was born in New York City and grew up in New York and West Palm Beach, Florida. He received his professional training at Oberlin College, the New England Conservatory of Music, and the Juilliard School. His composition teachers included Vincent Persichetti and Peter Mennin, and he studied piano with Lorin Hollander, Theodore Lettvin, and Gabriel Chodos. Danielpour also acknowledges the influence of Leonard Bernstein on his music and his outlook on musical life.

In his 1994 String Quartet no. 3: *Psalms of Sorrow*, Danielpour found a particularly dark voice to commemorate the liberation of Auschwitz. "This piece came after seeing my grandfather, who was close to ninety years old," he explained. "Here was a man who essentially took his family across the desert in Iran to escape the Nazis. It was all I heard about as a child, and I finally had to come to terms with it."

Danielpour was composer-in-residence with the Seattle Symphony and the Santa Fe Chamber Music Festival and has been commissioned by the Baltimore Symphony, the Chamber Music Society of Lincoln Center, the New York Philharmonic, and others. He lives in New York City and teaches at the Manhattan School of Music. This interview took place in October 1995 in New York.

*   *   *

There are two basic reasons I compose. One is that composing is what I do best, and the other is that I can't possibly conceive of wanting to do anything else. Life is hard enough without having to do something one dislikes. And to some extent, writing has got to be a natural process. It has to be the thing you do better than anything else.

I started musical life as a pianist and I was fairly good, very capable. But I grew up around some great pianists—in the practice room next to me at New England Conservatory was Christopher O'Riley playing *Petrouchka* so loudly that I couldn't hear myself. Here was someone with a big sound and a big technique, and eventually I realized the thing to do was to ask him to play my music, which I did.

I performed quite a lot until the age of twenty-four, when I realized it was too difficult to do both. Writing was very natural for me, while playing the piano was hard work. But giving up the piano was excruciating; it was like a death, partly because I'd been told that playing concerts was the only practical way to earn a living as a musician. Who makes money writing music? I remember a fellow student at Oberlin asked me what I wanted to do with my life, and I said, "I want to write music and have my music recorded." And he said, "You can't do that. No composer makes records."

On a certain level, composing for me has evolved from something I idealized as a kid to just being my work, like a bricklayer's. This is what I do. That's not to say I've lost my love and respect for it. I sometimes still listen to Mozart like a kid with wide-eyed wonder—I still have the sense of being in the presence of a miracle in time. I also have moments in my own life and work that bring me down to earth. For example, I remember feeling very high and mighty after having finished my cello concerto. I hadn't been to a performance in months, and I decided that night to go to the Met. Listening to a production of *Otello*—arguably the greatest thing Verdi wrote—with Domingo and Renée Fleming, I was very *quickly* brought down to earth.

For me, writing is both the number-one nourishment for life as well as the number-one escape. When I was first starting out, writing was like diving into a cauldron full of terror and the unknown. It still feels like the unknown, and it still often terrifies me, especially at the very beginning of a piece. But now there's a comfort about going into it, because it helps me get away from the [professional] life I've built, which can sometimes be invasive and obtrusive.

Bernstein once told me that in the end, what a composer really does is share love. I've heard the same thing said in different ways, by people who are courageous enough to say it. By making music, a composer is sharing something ineffable—it's a natural process of putting it out and having it come back. I don't write music because I want to express myself. That is something that happens in spite of me. For me, more and more, writing is about listening and waiting. It's about receiving rather than willing something into being.

The moment I feel like I'm willing a piece, trying to carve it out in some grim and painful way, I stop, because it doesn't feel right to me.

Incidentally, there are all kinds of processes that musicologists and music hysterians [Danielpour's nickname for music historians] go through ad nauseam to analyze work that comes from a kind of unconscious consciousness. As in Mozart. He didn't have time to be conscious of all the amazing interconnections and cross-references in the *Jupiter* Symphony or *The Magic Flute* —he was moving too quickly.

So for me, putting myself into that place of listening is sometimes the hardest task of all, because there are so many distractions. I have so many things to do in the course of a week that have absolutely nothing to do with the writing of music but deal with all the peripheries of a career. Sometimes I take walks, sometimes I stay in the shower twice as long, sometimes I take the train instead of a plane, to help myself get to that listening place.

There is also time in between pieces that I need to honor. Sometimes I just have to allow the unconscious its own time, and that need usually expresses itself in the feeling that I'll do anything *but* write music for awhile. However, I don't always have the luxury of resting between works. One year, I finished a full-length ballet for the Pacific Northwest Ballet on the Fourth of July, and the next day had to start a new work for chorus and orchestra, to be premiered on the first of October. After the second piece was finished, I took an entire month off, because the next work was going to be a big one, and I needed to take a commensurate breath.

Music for me absolutely has to have an inherent sense of play, both in the writing and the making of it. I think I am one of a number in my generation who rebelled against the grim-faced, "suffering servant" notion of the composer who is pessimistic about his work, at best. Part of it has to do with the fact that the music those post-1945 composers wrote could only evoke the bitter side of things. They lost the vocabulary for joy, and for tenderness and playfulness. Composers like Copland and Barber never lost it, but the majority of serious composers, or those deemed serious when I was growing up (or who deemed *themselves* serious), did lose it. I saw myself, very consciously, as not being one of them. I learned an enormous amount from some of the composers who grew out of that aesthetic. But respect is not the same thing as love.

Nicholas Maw [the composer] says that a lot of the music written right after 1945 has no sense of internal memory—the music does not refer to itself at all. In much the same way, a lot of music of that time has no sense of *external* memory, meaning that it doesn't relate to music that came before it. It was as if a great deal of the new repertoire received shock therapy! For me, this was very odd, because I grew up at the piano playing Beethoven, which was rich with cross-references, and connected very strongly to Mozart and Haydn.

Bach and Mozart are at the apex of everything in terms of what we call the creative process, because they have in some sense gone beyond ego and self-involvement in their work. Some people have termed work of this sort transpersonal. It is music that is serious in every way but doesn't take *itself* too seriously.

The moment we take ourselves too seriously, we put ourselves in a prison in which we become, in André Gregory's words, both the warden and the prisoner. Stravinsky suffered, but his life, especially in his later years, was like a huge party because he treated it that way. It doesn't mean that he had no intellect, or that he failed to see the gravity of life. Of course he did. But he chose a perspective that kept him going and growing.

I say to my students all the time, "You're taking yourself way too seriously. You're thinking only about beautifully sculpted, perfect ideas. Why not look at the dorkiness inside, see the clumsiness, and realize that that may be where your real genius lies?" In awkwardness you can find tremendous grace. Just futzing around, sort of piddling with ideas—I mean, composers are in a constant state of improvisation, right? The lightning bolt everyone talks about is the result of incessant work, which should hopefully be informed by a sense of play. Every now and then you hear professional baseball players still talking about having fun. The fact is, for them baseball's a business, but it's good they can remember it's also a game. It's better to approach composing with "Let's see what happens if . . ." rather than "I've *got* to do this." Perfect things usually happen because we get out of the way, not because we make them so.

I'm often reminded—by forces outside myself—to lighten up. For example, there was the day in Rome [in 1990] when I'd laid out ideas for a new piece and I was feeling so pleased with myself that I decided to take a walk and buy a pair of shoes. But I couldn't seem to find the right pair, and after hours of frustration I became enraged because it seemed that in the short time that I'd been in Rome, the Italians had grown wise to American shoppers and taken away all the bargains! I was so beside myself, standing there in my scarf and trench coat in the November cold, thinking about what to do next, when all of a sudden a flock of pigeons let loose on me, covering my head and my shoulders. That was a message from above, you know!

There is a much-talked-about place that artists seek in their work, which some people refer to as "the zone." Once that state starts to make itself manifest, there comes with it a certain kind of high, which one starts to crave, more and more. It's when I'm in "the zone" that I feel by myself, the most vibrantly alone. When you can reach a place in which you feel radically alive, you want go back to it.

For awhile, one of the reasons I composed was that I felt I had something to prove. But you get to a certain place in your life where your accomplishments render that motivation obsolete, and you don't have to ask yourself over and over again, "Why am I doing this?" I remember hearing Stephen

Albert [the late composer] speak about the needs of people who are hungry for something other than spiritual junk food. He said he got a feeling that audiences want something meaningful, and of lasting value. I suppose a composer taps into that from time to time, but I have to honestly say that I don't think, while I'm writing, that I'm trying to heal the world. There may be a moment of that, but if I'm really honest about it, I have to say that I'm the gardener, I'm not the garden. I just attend to what comes.

I've had separate studios in New York over the years, and I've also worked at home. At this point in my life I'm happiest when I'm in a place where I know I'm not going to be interrupted—I like to separate church and state. Colonies like Yaddo and MacDowell have been very, very helpful to me, not just in terms of uninterrupted time. They have educated me about my working habits. They've shown me when I work best, and when to leave work alone in the course of the day.

The conscious mind seems to want visual or physical proof of what one has accomplished. But there have been times when I have gone to a colony and written the one little piece I'd come to do, but also completed three or four others that I didn't bother to write down at the time. It's because I go through long periods of thinking about pieces before I actually write anything. I eliminate certain possibilities, you know.

I sometimes feel like an opera composer in disguise. I've got to find my story and my plot before I can start writing the notes. So there's a period of thinking about a piece in a general way, thinking about the fact of the orchestra, thinking about what might work differently this time around. All of these things need time before I actually sit down and write.

Usually when I'm ready and I sit down to write, the piece comes. It's a question of knowing when I'm ready. I think people who have creative blocks have forgotten to notice the opportune time for beginning. They don't realize there are stages of gestation and production. A few people have referred to my gestation periods as creative blocks, but to me, they're just periods of waiting. I heard Stravinsky say, in a BBC documentary, "I have learned to wait like an insect!" That made quite an impression on me.

A good case in point is how my cello concerto came about, late in 1993. I had finished my second piano concerto in September and had taken a month to edit it. November came around and I thought, "OK, it's time to work on the cello concerto." Well, everything I did sounded stupid to me, just sounded not right, and I was thinking, "This is clearly not what you want to give to Yo-Yo Ma!" I started getting nervous. It was toward the end of November. The concerto was due in May. It was also the first semester in seven years that I'd taught, and the students—I love them all, but they were driving me bananas. There comes a point when you can be suffocated by obligations. I called the people at Yaddo and said, "Do you happen to have a period when I can come and work? Just give me two weeks." The only time they had was right away, from the first of December to the sixteenth. I said, "I'll take it."

The night before I started working there, I dreamed of an ancient ritual in which an oracle, a young man, came to speak to an assembly. His news wasn't good, and the assembly began to debate fiercely among themselves, questioning, interrogating. Finally the assembly asked the oracle to account for himself and the authority by which he brought the message. (Of course, this isn't the way things were done in ancient Rome or Greece, but it was, after all, my dream.) The oracle spoke in such a human, personal way that the assembly couldn't handle him anymore and sentenced him to death. At that point in the dream, I woke up and realized I had the dramatic scena for my cello concerto, and the cello was the oracle.

So with that idea in the back of my mind, swimming in the vague area between dreaming and wakefulness, I began working in a way that was anything but chronological. I had no idea where my ideas would actually occur in the piece. I ended up writing most of the last movement first, then went to the first movement, then the cadenza (an entire soliloquy movement). I did the second movement, which is the debate, last. When I was finished with this unorchestrated draft—a short score, but with some very detailed diagrams about who should be playing what—sixteen days had passed. I had a 640-measure piece.

Still, I had been thinking about the piece for months. I had been playing with the structure, eliminating what wouldn't work. I had known it would be a continuous one-movement work in several sections. There were specific effects I wanted in the cello part and in the orchestra. Even as I was writing the piano concerto I was beginning to think about these things. Making those awful sketches in November was my way of eliminating what I wouldn't use. Sometimes one has to get the bad work out before he can deal with the good music.

And of course at Yaddo I worked in a way that I rarely do, basically from morning until midnight. When I work at home, I normally go from about nine in the morning until lunchtime. Things can still come quickly at home —but not as quickly as at that time at Yaddo, because I worked there in long stretches. I also had a limited amount of time there, and I knew I had to come back home with something. A piece can come out as fast as the cello concerto did when you know you're not going to be interrupted, and when you know that the work is in you.

After that sixteen-day period at Yaddo I spent three and a half months on the orchestration. I worked with Yo-Yo during this time, too. He was not invasive, but he knew how to make suggestions. I sent him the cadenza, page by page, fax to fax. Each time he answered, "No problem, it can all be done." But when we got to the rehearsals, he suggested a few things that made the cello more resonant here, got the music to flow a little bit more over there. He played some passages in ways that I didn't think possible but that sounded so much better than the way I'd written them. Once, fifteen minutes before a concert, he said, "You know, in measure 475 I'd like to try this part an octave higher because I think it's going to project a little better." He was that flexible with a really tricky, fast-moving passage.

I made a lot of adjustments (e.g., adding dynamic markings or a fermata, cutting a beat) on the cello concerto after the first rehearsal—I always do, with an orchestral piece. It's a very important part of the creative process, and I think a lot of composers should do it more often.

Conductors should also learn to deal with a composer's revisions. It's a myth that once a piece is written out, it's finished and you can't touch it. I usually make a final edition right after the first performances of a piece. It's harder to go back into a piece a year after I've written it, because I'm not the same person anymore.

The experience of writing music is akin to a waking dream, and we composers seem to be involved in creating this dream as a means of coming into a deeper reality, as a way of approaching the deepest parts of ourselves. This experience of the waking dream is for me one of the great mysteries, both in music and life. If you write enough music, you begin to experience your life as being a waking dream. At that point, art is not just an imitation of life; it is a mirror.

Richard Danielpour, Selected Works

SMALL ENSEMBLE

The Enchanted Garden (Preludes, Book I) (1992)
piano solo

Sonnets to Orpheus, Book I (1992)
soprano and chamber ensemble
text: Rainer Maria Rilke

Sonnets to Orpheus, Book II (1994)
baritone and chamber ensemble
text: Rainer Maria Rilke

String Quartet no. 2, *Shadow Dances* (1993)

String Quartet no. 3, *Psalms of Sorrow* (1994)
baritone and string quartet

Urban Dances, Book II
(1993)
brass quintet

LARGE ENSEMBLE

Anima Mundi (1995)
orchestra

Concerto for Cello and Orchestra (1994)

Piano Concerto no. 2 (1993)

Symphony no. 2, *Visions* (1986)
soprano, tenor, orchestra
text: Dylan Thomas

Symphony no. 3, *Journey without Distance* (1990)
soprano, chamber chorus, orchestra
text: Helen Schucman

Richard Danielpour, Selected
Recordings

The Awakened Heart; *First Light;*
   Symphony no. 3, *Journey With-*
   out Distance: Faith Esham,
   soprano; Seattle Symphony
   Orchestra/Schwarz
Delos DE 3118

Concerto for Cello and Orchestra
Yo-Yo Ma, cello; Philadelphia
   Orchestra/Zinman
Sony Classical SK 66299

The Enchanted Garden; *Psalms for*
   Piano; Quintet for Piano and
   Strings
Christopher O'Riley, piano;

Chamber Music Society of
   Lincoln Center
Koch International Classics
   3-7100-2H1

Metamorphosis (Piano Concerto
   no. 1)
Michael Boriskin, piano; Utah
   Symphony Orchestra/
   Silverstein
Harmonia Mundi 907124

Sonata for Piano
Michael Boriskin, piano
New World 80426-2

Urban Dances for brass quintet
Saturday Brass Quintet
Koch International Classics
   3-7100-2H1

DAVID LANG

$$(\text{B. } 1957)$$

avid Lang was born in Los Angeles and received his education at Stanford University, the University of Iowa, and the Yale School of Music. He studied composition with Jacob Druckman, Hans Werner Henze, and Martin Bresnick. Lang's musical life thrives in "downtown" New York, where he is cofounder and coartistic director of Bang on a Can, an organization dedicated to adventurous new music (best known for its annual new music marathon). He has been a visiting professor of composition at Yale and composer-in-residence at the American Conservatory Theater in San Francisco.

Lang's compositions are often inspired by provocative titles, among them *Eating Living Monkeys* (a piece for the Cleveland Orchestra), *International Business Machine* (for the Boston Symphony), and *Hell* (for the Netherlands Wind Ensemble). His opera *Modern Painters*, based on the life of the Victorian art critic John Ruskin, was commissioned by the Santa Fe Opera, and with poet Mac Wellman he has recently completed a fully staged opera for the Kronos Quartet based on Ambrose Bierce's "The Difficulty of Crossing a Field."

David Lang lives in New York City with his wife and children. This interview took place in New York in October 1995.

*   *   *

One day when I was nine years old, it was raining at Bellagio Road Elementary School, in Los Angeles, so we couldn't play in the mud. We had to spend our lunchtime indoors, in the big assembly hall, and the teachers thought, well, let's keep the kids in and show them a movie. They showed us the most recent Leonard Bernstein Young Person's Concert movie. I'd never seen this before; I'd never given any thought to classical music. I didn't know who Leonard Bernstein was. I didn't know anything. But there was this movie, and it was Bernstein and the New York Philharmonic playing music by Shostakovich, and Bernstein was talking about Shostakovich as a young composer.

This was the first time anyone had told me that someone had done anything worthwhile when they were young. This was the first time that youth seemed like a good thing. I remembered very vividly that Bernstein said Shostakovich wrote his first symphony when he was nineteen and became world famous overnight. And I remember thinking, I'm nine years old. I have ten years. I can do that.

That's really what started me—a tremendous amount of naïveté and a tremendous amount of incredible arrogance. After that, I decided, OK, I'm going to learn my music, I'm going to try to play some instruments. I borrowed instruments from friends of mine, and parents of friends of mine, and eventually I got into my little elementary school band. I wanted to play the trumpet, and they didn't have a trumpet, so I played the trombone. I started buying records and listening to music. Before I left elementary school, I wrote my very first piece, which was a trombone accompaniment to a record of a Beethoven violin sonata, played by David Oistrakh and Sviatoslav Richter.

I didn't know how to write anything down. I sort of wrote note heads, and no ledger lines. It was really stupid. But that's the way it happened—I started writing pieces for myself, and by the time I got to high school I had boxes of orchestra pieces, and my high school orchestra played them, and I was totally involved in music. I had private lessons in composing with Henri Lazarof at UCLA. I studied with him two days a week.

My father was a doctor, and my mother had a degree in English and was a librarian. They didn't stop me from doing music, but they expected me to go to medical school. They started giving me records by Berlioz and Borodin, because Berlioz went to medical school and Borodin was a chemist. They were trying to give me information and divert me at the same time.

I also played in rock bands and jazz bands as a kid. I was interested in both classical music and pop music. For some reason, I chose to go the classical route, and I ended up getting my doctorate at Yale, so I have this messy combination of influences. I think that's one of the reasons why I'm so interested in trying to figure out new ways to organize pieces. I am not just a classical musician. I know what sort of thinking goes on in that world, and I also know what sort of talent you need in order to be a good orchestrator, or a good melody writer, and I am aware that I don't have that. It's the same with pop music. I know how difficult it is to make really great rock and roll, and how limiting it is to work with the commercial world. I don't want to be part of that. I love different types of music. It wouldn't surprise me if someone wrote a beautiful minimal country-and-western opera. Putting things together that don't belong together—hybridization—is very interesting to me.

I like to think about ways ideas are organized in the world, and I think about political issues and social issues, and how social systems work—how people get along with each other, how people change their functions in groups.

You can't really experiment with that in public. I suppose if you wanted to get yourself a little country and become a dictator and push people around, you could make some of these experiments happen. Or if you were in the CIA, in the '50s, giving people drugs, you could try to figure out how to do things against people's wills. But one place you can actually experiment like that is in music. You can find out how people get along, or how ideas move, by creating pieces that are big models of these social functions.

One thing I've been interested in forever is how the orchestra is a model of the perfect early-eighteenth-century society. It was a kind of a utopian idea. There was a benevolent dictator, looking over these different little groups, which have their function, which collaborate with each other, through the stern but all-knowing intervention of the dictator. I think that a lot of my pieces show how our current society models our musical institutions, or our musical ideas. So I don't worry whether my melodies are more beautiful than Rachmaninoff's, or if I orchestrate as well as Ravel. The answers to both of those questions are no. Trying to equal or surpass something that's gone before is suspect to me. I know that plenty of good music is being written that way, but I don't understand why anyone should do that. My ideas about social models give me a reason why music still has value. They make it possible for me to think about pieces in ways that I think are somewhat adventurous. I don't want to think I am going over ground which has been gone over before, by me or by anyone else. I don't want to do the same thing twice.

A frequent complaint that people make about my music is that every piece seems to be different. Every piece seems to attempt to do something different, or has a different structure or a different story, and some pieces are incredibly loud and raucous and rhythmic. I wrote a piece two years ago in which nothing happens. Just a piece called *Slow Movement*. It's half an hour long, for a bunch of instruments that are out of tune and amplified. Basically, a chord changes very, very slowly, and that's the entire piece. In a way I feel like that's my best piece.

I want to figure out a way to write so that the world is fresh with every piece. In this pop-oriented world, people are encouraged to turn style into a marketing device, and I'm not interested in that. You could get into a situation such as Philip Glass, or other composers who have developed recognizable styles. After awhile the world won't let you change, even if you want to. I think Philip Glass is a great composer, but if he wanted to write a piece that didn't have his trademark signatures, I'm not sure the world would know what to do with it. It would be confusing. Maybe that's a good enough reason to do it!

When I was twenty-one, I wrote a piece for violin and piano called *Illumination Rounds*. It was a very difficult piece, and it became very successful. People started playing it, and I got asked by a lot of other hotshot soloists [on other instruments] to write a really flashy, obnoxious piece just like that for them. I realized I'd stumbled on something that was a career. I saw that if you write a piece that shows people off, they will play it, and you won't need any more ideas in order to live the rest of your life. It really scared me because I could imagine being eighty years old, still in that same place. I had a terrible over-reaction, thinking that music that pleases the player or is overtly flashy is dishonest, somehow. I started thinking in circles, wondering if a piece I just heard was beautiful because the composer wanted it to be beautiful, or because the composer knows the player enjoys playing it beautifully. I started realizing how you could lose your voice.

That's when I started making impossible tasks for myself. I started setting up ridiculous rules for pieces. The piece I wrote right after that was a trio for flute, oboe, and cello in which all the instruments played everything in unison. There was no note longer than a sixteenth note, and they were all played *fortissimo*. I felt that if I wrote long notes at *pianissimo*, the instrumentalists would try to blend with each other and try to make a beautiful sound. I wanted to make it *impossible* for the instruments to make a beautiful sound.

I figured the instrumental sound would be determined by which register the instruments were playing in. As this melody went up and down, depending on who was stronger in that particular register, the quality of the sound would change, and that would be the interest in the piece. I love that piece, a piece called *Frag*. I think it's a fantastic piece. But no one enjoys playing it because it's very difficult, and totally unwieldy and unsympathetic to the players, which, as a sadder and wiser person, I realize is a terribly important thing. It's very easy to write music that we all like. It's harder to write music that is fresh. But at some point, writing music that's fresh has diminishing returns.

Illumination Rounds was inspired by a particular kind of bullet that was invented to be fired during night fighting in Vietnam. Helicopter gunships couldn't adequately steer or aim machine guns at night, so someone figured out a way to make bullets light up and leave a phosphorescent trail. Those were called illumination rounds. If you're the gunner, the trail is more important than the bullet, because that's what you aim by—what you need to see is the trail. From that I got two parallel ideas. One is the idea itself of the bullet; the other is the trail it leaves. I thought this was an interesting way to model a piece: one player is the actual thing, and the other player is the kind of hazy thing that falls behind it. I thought the confusion between the image or idea and the place where the information is located could be illustrated by the violin and the piano.

I got in a great argument with [the composer] Frederic Rzewski, who heard a performance of this piece and thought it was one of the most frustratingly unpolitical political pieces he had ever heard. I don't like political pieces that come out and tell you that war is bad and peace is good, and hit you over the head. Sometimes it works, but it has to be very simplistic. I thought that by dealing dispassionately with the technology of war, I'd found a very sophisticated way of delivering a subtle political argument. Maybe it was too subtle.

That was the first piece in which I used a social model that deals with how people actually think about something in the world. Since then I've done it in every piece. I never wake up and say, I have to write a piece, so what does a cello do that sounds really good, and what are some nice chords in the piano? I just can't think like that.

I have a file on my computer called Possible Pieces. In it right now are about fifty titles. Each one has a little description next to it about the concept of a piece that might satisfy that title. So I'm thinking all the time about ways in which things that happen to people can influence a piece of music. The moment I get a commission I figure out which title is appropriate, or I think of a new title that's appropriate. When I know the philosophical structure behind a piece, I know how to proceed. Some of the pieces in my Possible Pieces file are not attached to orchestrations, and some of them are. If somebody said, "I want this kind of piece," I might look in the file and say, "Oh yeah, I have an orchestra piece like that I want to write."

Right now I'm working on a commission from the San Francisco Symphony, a big piece called *Grind to a Halt*. I've had this idea for years, to write a piece called *Grind to a Halt*—one big, long scrape. The point of it is that there are millions of things going on in the orchestra at once, each one in the process of slowing down. Some events repeat exactly the same way but get farther apart. Some events actually slow down. The whole idea is a complicated scraping of gears. It's very full and beautiful and fantastic and grating, and there's so much going on that you don't know what you're supposed to listen to.

Having written an opera, the kind of piece where you tell people what to feel every moment, I now like working on a piece where so much goes on that your musical gaze wanders from place to place. The composer hasn't prechewed it for you. The coherence comes from the fact that these millions of objects are all ultimately moving in the same direction.

I'm not sure the San Francisco Symphony is aware of how big a risk it is to commission me. There are so many different kinds of pieces they might get. But why should people get the piece that they expect? People should be surprised. There should be some awe and wonder in the world.

My preferred way of working, which I haven't been able to do for the past few years, is this: I sit in a café with a pen and a notebook and drink a lot of coffee. I write down everything I can think of that relates to my idea and make little charts and graphs, trying to figure out structures. I also try to figure out the different things instruments can do. I don't just say, "Oh, I need a happy sound, so I'll choose the piccolo for a little chirp, or a little tweet."

I like the sense that musicians have personalities and roles, that they relate as people across time. So trying to convert the *Grind to a Halt* idea with the people idea is what I've been working on most, lately. What are these people, and what do they do, and why are those noises being made at all?

I don't usually get as much time as I want. I end up having to map out a piece at the same time that I'm searching for the musical material. Once I know the roles of the instruments, once I've made some big decisions about how the orchestration works in each section—how the laws that I've made actually work—then the last thing I do is fill in the notes. For me the notes are the least important part, or the least interesting part.

You know, composers are able to push pieces along by force of will. The late Beethoven string quartets never sound the way you expect them to sound, yet they work because there's an incredibly huge will behind them. You can sense the will on the large architectural level, while on the note level, you can get lost.

I really do believe that the notes aren't that important. I think we're coming out of a period where the notes were the most important part of music. Composers wanted to invent these complicated pitch systems to control the notes, but that's not really where the music happens. If music happens, it's for other reasons. There's no technical difference between a dry, academic serialist and Luigi Dallapiccola or late Stravinsky. Yet Dallapiccola and Stravinsky have individual voices, and their music really works.

Music happens in the will, the level at which a listener can detect the composer's intention. It's possible to convey that intention on a level that is not very interesting. You can say, "Well, I'm going to play around with these frozen pitch levels and pitch sets." But as a listener you go, "So what?"

I compose on my computer. I just write the notes on my screen. I don't even input them on the keyboard. I use this quick and dirty program that I really like, and I'll say what it is and probably get sued. The program is called Encore —it's simpler than Finale. It's very much like sitting at your desk with a pencil. It's not time-consuming. You just have a little mouse and you click on the notes and that's it.

I try to do things in my pieces that keep my intuition off-balance. I don't want to be reminded of anybody else's music when I write, and I don't want to be reminded of music I've already written. I make up all these rules about how instruments relate, or how registers work, or how tunes work. I take scraps of music I come up with intuitively and subject them to really strange rhythmic processes that pull them apart. If outside ideas come in, if I sing a melody to myself, it's probably something that I'm not allowed to do by my structure. Or if I am allowed to do it, I force myself to sing another melody I haven't sung before.

Why anyone should *be* a composer is a really interesting question. I tell my students that all the good melodies have been written, and all the good ideas for pieces have been taken, and all the good harmonies have been figured out, and the great orchestrations already exist. I do believe this. I'm not sure that the point is to wake up every morning and say, "Well, I'm just going to sing a pure song this morning, and it will be something the world really needs to hear."

I have no doubt that I could sit here and write a really nice melody off the top of my head. I have no doubt that I could harmonize it with a pencil and make it sound really great. I feel that those rules are easily understood. Maybe I can't make a *great* melody, or *great* harmony, or *great* orchestration—those are talents. But I know how to make passable ones. I could have a passable career as a happy tunesmith, and there's nothing wrong with that. Many people have that as a goal—it's good for them and the world needs happy tunes. But for me, the interesting ideas are where those happy tunes *aren't*. The interesting things are in the dark places, or in the ugliness, or in the noise or the grit.

It's difficult to write a really ugly piece. If you listen to all the revolutionary pieces written at the same time as *Pierrot Lunaire—Rite of Spring*, for example — they are easy to listen to, now. But *Pierrot Lunaire* is still hideous. And that is a talent—I mean, how did Schoenberg do that? We're never going to get used to that. It's always going to be creepy. We will never have the experience of hearing *Rite of Spring* the way the people did when they first heard it. Never. But a hundred years from now, *Pierrot Lunaire* is going to give people pretty much the same experience that the original audience had.

Once I was asked to write an antiwar piece, and I thought, "Everybody's going to go, we hate war, give me a flower." And then I thought, "Oh come on, I don't want to do that. Why should I do that?" So I wrote a piece called *By Fire*. I took one text by a CIA bomb observer who was really bored during the early H-bomb tests in the South Pacific. He saw all the tropical birds, and then he watched the bomb go off and noticed that all the beautiful birds burst into flames. He was a cold, callous observer, and he simply wrote, "I never saw anything like that." He leads up to that moment where you expect him to have a moral response, and he has none.

The other text I used is from *The Art of War* by Sun-Tzu, an ancient Chinese war theoretician. It's the chapter on how to use fire in war. He says you've got to use fire, you've got to use bombardment! He sounds really cold. Then at the end he tells you the reason you have to know these things is because a war that goes on one day too long is immoral. You should be very careful, because once someone's dead, they're not coming back, and once your state has been obliterated, it's not coming back.

I thought, here is one text that seems to be leading up to an antiwar moment and it doesn't achieve it, and here is one text that's only about war, which turns out to be very moral.

There are two solo singers in the piece, and a chorus. The entire chorus amplifies the CIA observer at the beginning, and then gradually, group by group, they defect. By the end the CIA observer is isolated and everyone is singing with Sun-Tzu. There's not a single note in that piece that's longer than a sixteenth note, and everything is *forte*. Choruses don't have time to tune those notes up. That way, I kept from writing the kind of music you expect from a chorus, the beautiful tuned chords.

This reminds me of a childhood memory. When I was in high school, I was a really snotty kid and I had written a lot of music and I thought I knew a lot about music. A string orchestra in Los Angeles was playing a piece by Carl Ruggles. I'd never heard of Carl Ruggles before—I was fourteen years old—and I thought, "I'm going to go see that concert, 'cause there's a piece I've never heard before, and he is a twentieth-century composer." The piece was called *Lilacs*, and I had an idea of what a string orchestra piece called *Lilacs* would be. It would be really beautiful and sweet. It was going to be like flowers. And when I heard it, it was the most ugly, crunchy piece. And I had this revelation. I got tricked. And because I got tricked, I had a fresh experience. I heard the depth of that ugliness for the very first time, and I loved it.

David Lang, Selected Works

SMALL ENSEMBLE

Cheating, Lying, Stealing
  (1993/1995)
bass clarinet, cello, piano, electric
  guitar, electric bass guitar

Face So Pale (1992)
six pianos

Illumination Rounds (1981)
violin and piano

My Evil Twin (1992/1996)
three clarinets, two horns, harp,
  electric organ, electric bass
  guitar, two violas, two cellos

Orpheus Over and Under
  (1989)
piano duo

Slow Movement (1993)
amplified ensemble: two flutes,
  alto sax, tenor sax, baritone
  sax, electric bass guitar, two
  synthesizers, accordion,
  percussion, violin, cello

LARGE ENSEMBLE

Are You Experienced?
  (1988–89)
chamber orchestra

Bonehead (1990)
orchestra

Grind to a Halt (1996)
orchestra

Hell (1997)
wind ensemble

STAGE

Modern Painters (1995)
opera in two acts
libretto: Manuela Hoelterhoff

Publisher: Red Poppy, distributed
    by G. Schirmer, 257 Park Avenue
    South, 20th floor, New York, NY
    10010. Tel. 212-254-2100; fax 212-
    254-2013.

David Lang, Selected
Recordings

The Anvil Chorus
Steven Schick, percussion
Sony Classical SK 66483

Are You Experienced?
Netherlands Wind Ensemble
Chandos CHAN 9363

By Fire
New York Virtuoso Singers
CRI 615

Cheating, Lying, Stealing
Bang on a Can All-Stars
Sony Classical SK 62254

Face So Pale
Piano Circus
Argo 440 294-2

Illumination Rounds
Rolf Schulte; Ursula Oppens
CRI 625

Orpheus Over and Under
Double Edge
CRI 625

Slow Movement
Icebreaker
Argo 443 214-2

Spud
Le Nouvel Ensemble Moderne
CRI 625

Under Orpheus
Netherlands Wind Ensemble
Chandos CHAN 9363

While Nailing at Random
Kathleen Supove, piano
CRI 653

SEBASTIAN CURRIER

(B. 1959)

ebastian Currier grew up in Rhode Island in a musical family and studied the violin, which he later forsook for the guitar. He wrote his first compositions for a rock band he and his brother Nathan played in as teenagers, but he continued to study classical music. "A lot of instrumentalists aren't free to improvise because they're taught to play only what's written, and that forms a certain mind frame," he says. "I'm happy I had the experience of playing rock music, because it opened me up." Currier attended the Manhattan School of Music and earned a doctorate in composition at the Juilliard School.

Currier enjoys writing music from many different psychological points of view. In *Vocalissimus* (for soprano and chamber ensemble), he set the same short poem of Wallace Stevens eighteen different ways, as interpreted by a formalist, a mystic, a recluse, a satirist, an introvert, and other temperaments. *Theo's Sketchbook*, for solo piano, is an anthology of the life's work of an imaginary composer, from juvenilia to old age. One of Currier's most-played compositions is *Aftersong* (for violin and piano), which has been performed worldwide by the violinist Anne-Sophie Mutter.

Sebastian Currier is on the composition faculty of Columbia University and composer-in-residence at the Bowdoin Summer Music Festival. He lives in New York City. This interview took place in New York in October 1995.

·   ·   ·

Music has always spoken to me, and it has always been a part of my life. My mother and brother are both composers, and my father is a violinist and teacher. Both my brother and I were given violin lessons by our father at a very young age, but it never really caught on with either of us, and after that, our parents left us to explore music on our own. We both ended up playing in a rock band, and I guess that was my first experience composing, since we made up most of our songs. My brother played keyboards and I played the guitar, which led us back naturally to the classical world.

During high school I studied classical guitar and started to compose, more and more. Growing up within a family of musicians brought me opportunities I might not have had otherwise. I remember one time—I was probably in my midteens—when my father had a group of friends over to read string quartets. After they had read through some Haydn and Mozart, I came downstairs with the score and parts to a quartet I had written, and my father asked if they would mind reading it for me. They graciously attempted it. I don't remember what the piece was like—it probably wasn't much—but I do remember that I was not happy with the way they performed it!

More important than these occasional readings, though, were all the recordings my parents had around the house. I used to listen to them for hours on end. I remember how, still engrossed in rock music, I started to listen to this other music: Beethoven piano sonatas, Bach's *Goldberg Variations*, Bartók's *Music for Strings, Percussion, and Celesta*. A whole universe opened up in front of me. As much as I loved rock music, it was entirely pale by comparison. The range of expression was so vast, the way one idea followed another was so intricate and compelling. There seemed to be nothing one could not express.

Most of this music is still very much with me and is probably at the heart of everything I write. It's true that some of the pieces I listened to then have not survived the test of time for me as well as others. Shostakovich's Fifth Symphony, which I loved, seems less to me now than it did then. But Beethoven's Piano Sonata, opus 109, which I have known for some twenty years now, is still for me a piece of such awesome beauty that it never fails to take me into another world. There is something very reassuring in that. Sometimes I fear that its magic might wear off at some point, but it doesn't seem to.

I love to compose. Even though I work slowly and find it often very difficult and at times frustrating, the process of composing is ultimately very satisfying to me. I like to work whenever I can—morning, afternoon, evening. I like the regularity, I like always to be working, and tend to feel badly during periods when for some reason or another I'm unable to write. When I'm working on a piece, I have the urge to shut out the rest of the world until I'm finished, and when I finally do finish, I start the next piece right away, often the following day. In the process of writing a piece I usually make several drafts—

first, I sketch through most or all of the piece, then go back and rework what I've written. I usually do further reworking when I make the final copy.

To a certain extent, the way I work depends on the piece itself. Sometimes I start by searching in the dark for some musical fragment—a few notes, a harmony, a tune—without any preconceived idea about what the piece might be as a whole, while at other times I first form a definite idea about the piece in its entirety and then proceed to work on the details. The former is, I guess, working from the bottom up, the latter from the top down. Each creates its own set of problems. The problems, though, are complementary. In each the difficulty is to reconcile the large-scale structure with the smaller-scale details, the whole with the parts, the global with the local, the general with the specific.

When I begin with a musical fragment, I almost always find myself facing a brick wall shortly after coming up with the initial idea. What do I do now? Where does this idea lead? What will be consistent? What will change? For me, this point in the compositional process—just *after* the beginning—is often the most challenging. I think this is because it is here that I must start to figure out how the part relates to the whole, how my little musical kernel will become a larger structure—a movement, a section, or a piece. I don't think I fully solve this problem before I proceed, but I do limit the number of possibilities or alternatives before me. It's like being in a maze and marking off the pathways you've quickly found to be fruitless, so you may devote your attention to a few of the most promising routes. As I continue, the form of the whole becomes more and more fixed in my mind, and there is less and less tension between the small and the large.

When I begin with an idea about the whole, I am usually confronted by a different problem. I have some broad idea about the piece, but this idea is only an abstraction until I come up with musical material that represents it— it's very much the problem of how to get from the general to the specific, the large to the small, the abstract to the concrete. And the devil is in the details! I think anyone involved with the creative process knows firsthand how difficult—or impossible—it is to get from an abstract idea to a concrete manifestation in some medium or another. When I proceed to work on a local level—measure by measure—there are always a thousand little concerns that seem to have little or nothing to do with the broader conception I wish to flesh out. Every moment, these little concerns threaten to send the piece off in some direction opposite from the one I intend. I find this process frustrating and at the same time very interesting. I've actually written a piece that is in a sense about this, called *Entanglement*.

The idea of *Entanglement* is this: imagine that by some strange fluke, two composers have in their mind's eye, in abstract form, the identical sonata. These composers are like night and day—one rational with a sense of humor, the other disillusioned and cynical. They both start with the same conception, but when they turn the abstract into the concrete, their outlooks and temperaments come into play, and the resulting two sonatas, though fashioned out of the same idea, turn out to be dramatically different. *Entanglement* weaves these two opposing sonatas together. In a way, the piece is about the compositional process and mirrors the difficulties I experience when I try to bridge the gap between a general idea and a specific realization.

Entanglement is one of several pieces I have written (which include *Vocalissimus, Theo's Sketchbook*, and *Quartetset*) where the concept clearly precedes the moment-by-moment working out of the musical material. These four pieces form a set defined by a process. In a way, they are all about the process of writing music. I think there's a tacit assumption that when we listen to music we hear the composer's voice—it's in the first person. By contrast, most fiction is either in third person or, if it is in first person, the voice itself is fictional. The writer, either way, is one step removed. She expresses herself through a complex intertwining of different, often competing characters. I have found it liberating to do something similar in musical terms.

Vocalissimus is a song cycle that sets the same short Wallace Stevens poem ["To the Roaring Wind"] eighteen times, each from a different perspective or viewpoint. It is based on the idea that when a composer sets a text, he can't help but interpret it, and in doing so shows us as much about himself as about the text. Thus, in *Vocalissimus* it is almost as if eighteen different composers were at work! They are abstracted composers, though, and each is identified by a character type—recluse, formalist, optimist, pessimist, et cetera.

Theo's Sketchbook examines the creative process as it changes, as time goes by. It's a collection of pieces by an imaginary composer, which span his entire lifetime—from a composition he wrote in childhood to a lullaby he wrote for his granddaughter.

Quartetset is a little harder to pin down. The two voices here are based on broader stylistic differences. I think probably every composer today is self-conscious about style—it's certainly something I think about a lot. *Quartetset* is built upon a seamless but constant juxtaposition of past and present music. While writing the piece I thought about my relationship to the past and came to the conclusion that such composers as Beethoven, Schubert, or Bach are not, for me, composers of the past, but of the present! I am drawn to their music, surrounded by it; it is a part of my everyday life. I listen to works of Schubert with much greater frequency than I do works of Carter. I respond much more directly to Beethoven than to Boulez. I feel I have infinitely more to learn from Bach than from Cage. Cage *already* seems dated, Bach *still* seems forward-looking. It is in this spirit of the contemporaneousness of the past that I wrote *Quartetset*. Yet that is, of course, only half the picture. There is much in the work of my contemporaries and those of the more recent past that I hold dear and respond to very directly. *Quartetset* attempts to reconcile these two worlds.

Working with musicians is something a composer has to learn to do, because there is always some give-and-take. Who I am writing for generally does not affect what I write, but when I know a performer's playing very well, I have it in my ear. I have written most of my piano music for Emma Tahmizian, and I think I always have the sound of her playing in my mind, even when I'm not writing for her. I remember one occasion when I wrote a piece that involved another pianist who I think is an extraordinary musician. There was one passage he had difficulty executing as I wished, and after working on it for awhile, he suggested that I must have been thinking of Emma's playing when I wrote the passage. He was right!

In general, I have had very good experiences working with performers, but there is always a delicate balance between insisting on exactly how you want a performer to interpret your piece and giving them the freedom they need to understand it in their own way. I have found through experience that trying to exert too much control can be counterproductive. I worked with Anne-Sophie Mutter before her performances of *Aftersong*, and she felt I was a little too detailed in terms of subtle shifts in dynamics, articulation, and tempo in the second movement. She wanted more freedom to offer the general idea and not to have to do exactly what I had written. I went along with her and was very pleased with the final result. For example, she played some passages nonvibrato, which I hadn't specified, and I'm not sure now that I'd want them any other way.

I find that in my everyday life, my emotional side and my rational side are often—too often—at odds. Making music is one of the only places in my life where this conflict finds resolution. For me, one of the most important aspects of art is that it requires and creates balance and harmony between thought and feeling.

It seems to me that we place too much emphasis on the idea of progress in the arts. I have a little thought experiment that can serve as a litmus test. Imagine for a moment that Beethoven had not written his C-sharp minor quartet, opus 131. You attend a new music concert and hear a piece by some composer or another that is note-for-note opus 131. Is it still the masterpiece you thought? As a new piece, it would seem obviously outmoded and anachronistic. It would also seem derivative, sounding very much like a late quartet of Beethoven. You might want to dismiss it as a fake, a forgery. Yet there it is, note-for-note, opus 131, which—let us say for the sake of argument—you love above almost all others. If your estimation of it is now diminished, then you believe progress occurs in the arts in a way analogous to the sciences. Writing opus 131 today would be like reinventing the steam engine. What was difficult and worthy of great admiration in the 1820s has become easy or at least much easier in the 1990s. It's a very external and objective view. If you believe, on the other hand, that the piece you are hearing premiered in 1997 is still as meaningful as opus 131 because it *is* opus 131, then I think you are seeing an essential point. It is a much more subjective, internal viewpoint and is based on the fact that you recognize the uniqueness of opus 131 and feel that it is an end in itself. The fact that it gives you great pleasure, that you admire its dramatic architecture, respond to its sharp juxtapositions, carry its themes in your mind all seem to outweigh the simple fact of *when* it was written.

Sebastian Currier, Selected Works

SOLO/SMALL ENSEMBLE

Aftersong (1993)
violin and piano

Brainstorm (1994)
piano solo

Broken Consort (1996)
flute, oboe, violin, cello, two guitars

Entanglement (1992)
violin and piano

Frames (1998)
cello and piano

Quartetset (1995)
string quartet

Theo's Sketchbook (1992)
piano solo

Verge (1997)
violin, clarinet, piano

Vocalissimus (1991)
soprano, flute, clarinet, violin,
    cello, piano, percussion

Whispers (1996)
flute, cello, piano, percussion

LARGE ENSEMBLE

Chamber Concerto (1996)
violin and string orchestra

Microsymph (1997)
orchestra

Publisher: Carl Fischer,
    62 Cooper Square, New York,
    NY 10003. Tel. 212-777-0900;
    fax 212-477-4129.

Sebastian Currier, Selected Recordings

Vocalissimus: Susan Narucki, soprano; ZiZi Mueller, flute; Hyako Oshimo, clarinet; Rolf Schulte, violin; Fred Sherry, cello; Emma Tahmizian, piano; Daniel Druckman, percussion; *Theo's Sketchbook:* Emma Tahmizian, piano; *Whispers:* ZiZi Mueller, flute; Fred Sherry, cello; Emma Tahmizian, piano; Daniel Druckman, percussion
New World NW 80527-2

AARON JAY KERNIS

(B. 1960)

*A*aron Jay Kernis grew up in Philadelphia. He studied the violin as a child, began teaching himself the piano at age twelve, and went on to receive his formal training at the San Francisco Conservatory of Music, the Manhattan School of Music, and the Yale School of Music, working with composers as diverse as John Adams, Charles Wuorinen, and Jacob Druckman. Kernis first gained national attention when his *Dream of the Morning Sky* was premiered by the New York Philharmonic at the 1983 Horizons Festival. In 1998, he was awarded the Pulitzer Prize in music for his String Quartet no. 2, *musica instrumentalis*, written for the Lark Quartet.

Kernis's output includes orchestral, chamber, and keyboard music, as well as choral settings and more than a dozen works for voice and instruments. Among his recent compositions are *Still Movement with Hymn*, a piano quartet commissioned by American Public Radio, and Double Concerto for Violin, Guitar, and Orchestra, commissioned by the St. Paul Chamber Orchestra, the Aspen Music Festival, and the Los Angeles Chamber Orchestra for Nadja Salerno-Sonnenberg and Sharon Isbin.

Aaron Kernis lives in New York City with his wife, pianist Evelyne Luest. This interview took place in New York in May 1998.

•   •   •

When you compose every day, it becomes so natural that you stop thinking about why you're doing it. When I was in my early teens, it was an outlet for emotions or for things that I couldn't say to my parents or my peers. Composing became a process of transforming what I felt inside into music. But not long afterward, I began to feel like I was compelled to compose by reasons somewhat out of my control. I rarely talk or think about destiny or fate, as my mother often does, but I can't imagine being anything other than a composer.

There was a significant period of time in my life when studying music and working with composition teachers caused a more intellectual, rigorous way of thinking about the process of composing. In recent years I've been trying to let go of much of what was imposed upon me, while retaining the things that I took from school that turned into a natural part of working, the tools I use.

It's like learning a foreign language and getting to the point where you no longer have to think about grammatical constructions. The unconscious and conscious use of the tools join together and become completely enmeshed. I'm sure I'll always have a long way to go with that process. In fact, I think composing is going to be an endless process of leaving things behind and picking new things up. I do want to see it as a self-evolutionary process, but it's also compelling never to know the end, never to know what the long-term results over a lifetime will be. It's always a discovery, always a mystery. I think it's necessary for it to remain that way. If it became too utterly conscious and intellectualized, it wouldn't be as much fun or as compelling.

Although the process of composing continues to be mysterious, there are three or four different ways that it tends to proceed. The first process I'm going to describe has to do mostly with pieces without text.

I have a number of pieces about war and grief and loss, and other pieces about artistic experiences that have inspired me—seeing the mosaics in Ravenna, for example. All of them started with an emotional response to something, or a visual response to an emotional experience. So in a way I take experiences, or empathize with experiences that others have had, and use them as metaphors to build a work. I'll develop a piece around an experience, working out a series of emotional states as a structure.

The best example I can give of this is *Colored Field*, a concerto for English horn and orchestra (1993). A few years before I wrote it, I went to Poland for a series of TV interviews with composers. Before I left, I was encouraged to do whatever I could to visit Auschwitz and Birkenau. So I hired a taxi from Katowice and went there. In Auschwitz I was utterly numb. I had no idea what or how to feel. It's such a cold, orderly, and clinical place. There are large areas where behind plastic or glass, there are thousands of shoes or glasses or pieces of luggage that no one claims or inhabits. There is the shock of an enormous absence.

When I went over the train tracks to Birkenau I happened to meet a family from Brooklyn, and I looked after their two boys while the parents went off on their own. Birkenau is the opposite of Auschwitz because it's set in very lush fields—there are long houses where the healthier prisoners lived in the middle of the fields. And while I was looking after the kids, they sat down on the ground and started eating blades of grass. Suddenly I had a hallucination and saw the fields rise up above me like a tidal wave, awash in a sea of blood and bones and bodies, because in the eating of this grass, the children were internalizing the horror of this place without knowing it. This grass had continued to grow where all these horrible, unspeakable things had occurred, where so many innocent people had died—all brothers and sisters of mine, in a way. This hallucination just happened spontaneously. It showed that I wasn't completely numb, that I was taking the experience of these camps in and processing them internally. But I didn't know what to do with the vision.

A few years later, when I'd already written a few pieces that were related to war, I began to draw parallels between the ethnic cleansing in Bosnia and the Holocaust. There was another important reason I was particularly affected at that time—I had a very severe breakup with a girlfriend, just after the Persian Gulf War happened. The breakup wasn't like a war, exactly, but it was very, very difficult. So there was a certain amount of personal suffering that I was experiencing then, combined with watching the Persian Gulf War on TV, reading about Bosnia and the Holocaust, and having experienced that hallucination at Birkenau.

Around that time I was asked to write an English horn concerto [for Julie Giacobassi and the San Francisco Symphony], and I didn't know what I was going to do, but soon I made a connection between the English horn and the human voice. And then, with all this stuff related to war in my mind, I began to think of the individual against the machine: the English horn as a human voice against the machine of the orchestra. Then the image from Birkenau came back. It wasn't just the hallucination, but the ironic fact that although unspeakable things had occurred there, nature had continued to go about its business. In other words, the world just doesn't stop for us or our individual lives. So in *Colored Field* I decided to surround the English horn with two string orchestras, one on either side. Then I would pass chords back and forth from one group to the other in a circular pattern, to musically touch the wind of time, the wind of nature. In the first movement of *Colored Field* I made a musical analog to the hallucination as, starting with chords passed back and forth in very lyrical music, we descend into a darker and grittier, black, ugly, mucky sound, that is a metaphorical representation of what I imagined was beneath the surface of the ground.

At the very end of the work, when you suddenly reach this very beautiful, lush F major section, the pure tonal chords that surround the English horn gradually get sucked into greater and greater dissonance and become corrupted from simplicity and clarity to a massive, thickly dissonant orchestral texture. That is an example of how I was able to develop the opposition between the benign forgetfulness of the pastoral to the darkness of what lies just beneath the reach of memory and recent experience. That gives a little taste of how I used one experience as the basis for the largest structural elements of an entire work.

In *Colored Field* I worked with specific images that elicited particular physical and emotional responses, but sometimes it happens that when I'm first asked to write a piece, entirely different kinds of images will spring to mind. It could be the orchestra or the performers that the piece is to be written for. Maybe they're far away, in the act of performing, but I don't hear what they're playing. Other times I'll just see colors or textures. Whatever it is leads me ahead with the piece because the image can help me to build a structure and imagine a sound to begin with.

There are also pieces that have virtually no images. A good example is my double concerto for violin and guitar (commissioned for Nadja Salerno-Sonnenberg and Sharon Isbin). It was really hell to write, and I had to build it purely out of musical material. I had no visual starting place, but I had to get in there and get to work. Gradually a structure began to appear. Only at the end of the process (and I wrote the first movement last) did I have an idea of what the whole piece would be like. When I was a teenager, I'd seen Nadja Salerno-Sonnenberg perform on the *Tonight Show*, and I thought, what if, instead of playing Wienawski, she was jamming with the *Tonight Show* jazz band? That gave me a way into the sound and musical material of the first movement.

My new string quartet [String Quartet no. 2: *music instrumentalis*] started off because I wanted to deal with baroque dance forms and medieval dance rhythms. There wasn't an image—it developed from these purely musical ideas. This was a case where the piece turned out to be formally very different from what I first expected. I thought it would be five movements, but I started cannibalizing one movement into another and wound up with three. The first movement is like a dance medley, with a first big A section and a closing A section that is a development of the opening medley. Stuck in the middle of these two A's is a minuet and trio that originally was an entirely separate movement. While working on the first movement, I decided that the relaxation that I needed between those A sections was one of the smaller movements I'd already conceived. So I took one and squashed it in. That's one way that a piece can become significantly transformed during the act of composition.

The initial working out of a piece for me depends a great deal on improvisation at the piano, through finding basic ideas that I like and developing them. Sometimes I chart a piece in advance; other times I begin to write and allow the structure to suggest itself gradually. When I first started composing as a young kid, I didn't have a clue about structure, I just wrote from here to there to there to there, seeing how it all came out along with the listener—more like telling a story without quite knowing where it's going. For awhile I use big wedge structures, big crescendos and decrescendos, always moving in a straight line toward a goal. A really important development of my work from 1979 to 1983 involved highly structured mathematical process pieces. I didn't know what algorithms were then, so I would use mathematical processes with a very simple additive/subtractive approach and then find some specific arrival point in time. I don't think I even knew then about the Golden Mean.

Working with a rigorous mathematical structure having to do with time and notes or chords and texture enabled me— after I dropped that approach in 1983—to hold onto the essential nature and importance of those structures and to develop an approach to structuring time. But I also had to learn very painfully, very slowly, how to work with structure in a nonrigorous way, to be more intuitive, flexible, and open while still retaining a deep structural sense one could feel clearly.

I do a lot of planning in my head. I'll start at the beginning or maybe I'll come up with something that I know is the end of the piece, and work toward it. Sometimes—I haven't done this in awhile—I'll take a yellow legal pad and write down words that tell me where I'll start harmonically, and where I'm leading to, what textures I imagine, what instruments are playing when. That's often really helpful. I don't write in sentences, or in a narrative. With the more visual pieces, I may touch on the progression of images that got the piece going, but usually the words are an outline of texture and some of the harmony. Sometimes I'll know where I'm starting with the harmony and where I want to go to at the end, but I won't know any of the stuff in the middle. But of course in the midst of writing, the place where I'm going often changes.

These verbal outlines amount to a kind of architectural blueprint. Sometimes I include some little motive or idea that I found improvising at the piano. Oftentimes the outline occurs just when I'm developing the initial ideas for a work.

The first couple of weeks with any piece are the hardest, because I usually hate everything I come up with. I have to give the musical ideas time to settle before I can look at them more objectively. Usually by the time I can look at them more objectively, they're pretty definite. I don't throw a lot away, but I do transform a lot of my initial ideas. If I like an idea enough to write it down, it's usually going to be used for something. But it takes a while for me to go from the improvisation phase to allowing myself to commit the ideas to paper.

At the beginning I may spend only ten or fifteen minutes a day working, because at that point the real work is mostly conscious. As time goes on, a large part of the process moves from the conscious to the unconscious. And then when the work gets going really fast, it's bypassing the conscious almost completely. While I am very aware of what's going on, oftentimes the music is being written faster in my head than I can get it down on paper. Usually when the process gets to that point, the music has found its way. When I'm in the middle of a piece, in the so-called throes of inspiration, when the difficulty and the initial agony and the unpleasantness disappear, the work just moves on without my even thinking about it. It's almost as if all the thought processes that were begun have culminated. But I almost never finish riding that wave of inspiration all the way to the end of a piece. Something will stop me just before the end, and I'll agonize terribly. I'll lose that momentum I began with and not want to let go, because being fully integrated into the work is such a pleasure, such a remarkable high, that I want to prolong it, and it turns again to agony.

I don't make drafts. When I've truly finished a section, I've done all the polishing that section needs. I make changes as I go forward, and will not, unless there's a bit that's nagging at me, go back. When a piece is truly finished it will go to my copyist. But just before that, it's still too fragile for me to let it out. I rarely show a work in progress to anyone, although a couple of times I've shown something to Evelyne. There was one awful point recently when I had finished the second movement of my string quartet and was ready to throw it all out, because there was one place near the end that I could not make work harmonically to my satisfaction. I became so obsessed with it and so uncomfortable that I felt I would have to throw the whole thing away. At that point I said, "Evelyne, I've just got to play this for you." It was as if I needed to know whether I was still sane. I played it for her and she said, "This is the most beautiful thing you've ever written." That was enormously helpful! That meant that I could say to myself, "Well, maybe this isn't *so* bad."

Other than visual images, a lot of my work comes out of singing. I sing a lot when I'm improvising. My primary instrument is piano, but I sang in chorus throughout high school. Most of my instrumental lines are much longer than the human voice can sustain, but they're very vocal. Working with text for a vocal piece often gives me an initial structure to work with. In a way it's a lot simpler than making instrumental pieces.

But finding the right texts to set is incredibly difficult. I search for poetry all the time. I'm very lucky if I can find five poems in the space of a few years that I could imagine setting. There is great poetry that sings by itself—it doesn't need to be set because it already sings. The trick for me is to find poetry that can accept and benefit from vocal treatment. I generally look at poetry by living writers. With the exception of *Goblin Market* by Christina Rossetti, which is virtually unknown in the United States, many of the texts that I choose are by little-known writers.

Once a poem or a series of poems catalyzes a thought process, then I start drawing other poems in and try to make a universe of texts that work together. The rhythm of the texts and its images will help to get the musical ideas going.

I always worry about overmarking the music, overarticulating what I want. I used to really overdo it, so I've been trying to be more concise about my dynamics, my accents and articulations. But that doesn't necessarily produce the most satisfying results. Actually, I think I should be putting in more and more markings to get exactly what I want.

The last thing I put into a work are the dynamic markings. Dynamics are so specific to the situation. Are you going to be in a concert hall where *pianissimo* trombones will be perfectly balanced? If you write a harp *fortissimo*, will it come out sounding *mezzo-piano*, or will it actually sound *fortissimo* in the concert hall?

I had a big problem with the first movement of my second string quartet. It's a web of counterpoint almost from beginning to end, and in the first performance, the primary melody at any given point was very difficult for the listener to discern as the principal line. This meant there wasn't enough differentiation and balancing of voices. And so I started changing the dynamics significantly, telling the performers when to play out. Now, as I'm getting the score ready to print, I'm adding primary and secondary voice indications so that no matter what dynamics I use, it's clear to the performer what has to be heard on top.

Environment is important in the composing process. This room [in his Manhattan apartment] has a lot of light, and it's great that we're up so high—you can see a lot of sky. It would be great if there were no traffic or extraneous noise. The sound of kids playing doesn't bother me—birds, great. We have many doors separating my workspace from Evelyne's, and an air filter to use if necessary to help blot out Evelyne's practicing even further. Of course I would like a little cabin in the country, too, eventually.

I used to go to artists' colonies quite a lot, but since I've gotten married I haven't gone back. I miss the communal aspect, getting to know different artists whom I would only meet in that setting. Yet there's never been a time at a colony when I could start working well within a few days. It took at least one or two weeks, and sometimes I'd never work well. When I go into a new situation, into a new space, it takes awhile for me to adjust to the physical surroundings. Sometimes I even sense the last people who've been there. In those instances I feel like the space is inhabited by other creative spirits, and it takes times to assert my own.

When I accepted the composer-in-residence position in St. Paul, it took me a while to settle in creatively after I moved to Minnesota. There's no way I would have known to take into account the psychic time I'd need to get used to the new environment, the new position. So I lost some time, fell behind with a number of pieces, and it's been very hard to pick up and get back on track. The more outside responsibilities I have, the more composing seems like an obstacle course and all too often gets right down to the wire. Deadlines are useful, but sometimes a work simply needs more time to find its way toward completion.

A large part of my compositional process used to be sleeping. I would work for ten minutes at the beginning of a piece and get so frustrated and upset that I would lie down on my couch to think and then fall asleep. After that I might try again to work. I've learned that this is all part of the subconscious development of the work. And it's been hard for Evelyne and, before that, for my parents, who think in terms of results. People close to me see that I'm not "doing" anything and it's hard to explain that the process is under the surface and needs to be given time to become something concrete. A lot of people don't understand that. We're taught to have results at certain points, results that need to be seen and counted. Then work turns into yards to be measured: how many pages, how much does it weigh?

There's a social part of the process, too. I've always been the sort to go out to a lot of concerts, and I've been very happy not to have to teach full-time. That doesn't mean it hasn't been rough financially. But in all these years, it has been less important for me to have a lot of comfort than to have just enough, as long as I have the space and time to write as much as possible. Anyway, a big part of being a composer is in meeting performers, hearing performers, being inspired by artists and orchestras and halls, and not being a hermit. One of the things that I always tell students is, don't think that if you just sit at home and write you will necessarily have a full life as a composer. People are not waiting to discover you. You must give people the opportunity to know who you are and what you do.

There are a couple of myths about composers worth dispelling. One is that the only "real" ones are dead. I think a lot of performers and conductors would rather not have to deal with a living creator, would rather make decisions by themselves. They'd like to be creators themselves. It's seems a lot easier all the way around.

The other myth is the whole "starving artist in a garret" thing. We creative artists suffer without having to put up with silly Romantic notions, though I will say, definitely, that suffering has helped my work. That's a pretentious statement, but it's not meant in that way. It's meant in the sense that honing down to the essentials to reach the most crucial elements of music and expression is hard and requires a great deal of painful self-examination.

Let me see if I can explain that in a circuitous way. The initial stages of writing, if not the whole process, are like staring into a mirror with a supercritical eye. First you just notice the blemishes and the scars. Then over time, you get to know the person you're staring at. After awhile you give that person a little slack and learn that there's someone with depth in there. It's like getting to know a person from an initial stage of loathing, through a metamorphosis, to the point where the person is your deepest friend.

Being married to this wonderful woman really helps me because that process of self-examination is so difficult. You've got that lump of clay in front of you, and you're trying to bring the face or figure or shape out of it, and you don't know what it is—it could be *anything*. Having some peace and time to think, and creative space and a supportive partner, all help to ease the process along.

Aaron Jay Kernis, Selected Works

SOLO, SMALL ENSEMBLE

Before Sleep and Dreams (1990)
piano solo

Goblin Market (1995)
narrator and ensemble
text: Christina Rosetti

Hymn (1993)
for accordion

Invisible Mosaic II (1988)
Sixteen players

One Hundred Greatest Dance Hits (1993)
guitar and string quartet

Simple Songs (1991)
soprano or tenor and ensemble
text: from "The Enlightened Heart" (ed. Stephen Mitchell); Bible

Songs of Innocents, Book II (1991)
soprano and piano
texts: Charles Henry Ross, John Keats, May Swenson, Anonymous

LARGE ENSEMBLE

New Era Dance (1992)
orchestra

Praise Ye the Lord (1984)
mixed voices a cappella
text: Bible

Second Symphony (1991)
orchestra

Symphony in Waves (1989)
chamber orchestra

Publisher: Associated Music Publishers, 257 Park Avenue South, 20th floor, New York, NY 10010. Tel. 212 254-2100; fax 212-254-2013.

Aaron Jay Kernis, Selected Recordings

America(n) (Day)dreams for mezzo-soprano and ensemble; *Mozart en Route* (Or, A Little Traveling Music) for strings; *Nocturne* for soprano, trumpet, two glockenspiels, and two pianos; *One Hundred Greatest Dance Hits* for guitar and string

quartet; *Superstar Etude no. 1*
for piano; various artists
New Albion NAR 083

Colored Field for English horn and
orchestra
Julie Ann Giacobassi, English horn;
San Francisco Symphony/Neale
Still Movement with Hymn
Pamela Frank, violin; Paul Neu-
bauer, viola; Carter Brey, cello;
Christopher O'Riley, piano
Argo 448174-2

Invisible Mosaic II; Symphony no. 2
City of Birmingham Symphony
Orchestra/Wolff
Argo 448900-2

Quartet for Strings: *Musica Celestis*
Lark String Quartet
Symphony in Waves
New York Chamber Symphony/
Schwarz
Argo 436287-2

Song Cycles
Brilliant Sky, Infinite Sky, for
baritone, violin, percussion,
piano;

Love Scenes for soprano and
cello; *Morningsongs* for bass-
baritone and chamber
ensemble; various artists
CRI 635

INDEX

Cultural Revolution (1966–76). *See*
    Chinese Cultural Revolution
CUNY (City University of New York),
    33, 203
Currier, Nathan, 229, 230
Currier, Sebastian, 229–34
    background and training, 229–30
    compositional process, 230–31
    compositional sources, 229, 232
    dynamic marking, 233
    instrument, 229, 230
    performer relationship, 233
    teaching post, 229
    texts, 229, 232
    on timelessness in music, 232–33
    work habits, 230–31
    youthful influences, 230
    works:
        Aftersong, 229, 233
        Entanglement, 231–32
        Quartetset, 232
        Theo's Sketchbook, 229, 232
        Vocalissimus, 229, 232
        list of selected titles and record-
            ings, 234

Da Capo Chamber Players, 55, 56, 60,
    97, 120
Dallapiccola, Luigi, 51, 224
Dallas Symphony, 87
Dallas Wind Symphony, 87
Damasio, Antonio, 194
Danielpour, Richard, 211–18
    background and training, 211
    commissions, 211
    compositional philosophy, 213–14
    compositional process, 213, 215–17
    compositional sources, 211, 213
    instrument, 211, 212, 214
    on musical cross-references, 213–14
    on performer relationship, 215,
        216–17
    on post-1945 musical grimness,
        213
    reasons for composing, 212–13,
        214–15
    teaching post, 211
    work habits and environment, 215,
        216

works:
    Concerto for Cello and Orches-
        tra, 215–17
    Piano Concerto no. 2, 215
    String Quartet no. 3, *Psalms of
        Sorrow,* 211
    list of selected titles and record-
        ings, 217–18
Danse Generale (Ravel), 93
Daphnis and Chlöe (Ravel), 93
Daugherty, Michael, 173–80
    background and training, 173, 174
    on clichés, 178–79
    commissions, 173
    compositional process, 175–77, 178
    compositional sources, 174–75, 176,
        177
    influences, 173, 174–75
    teaching post, 173
    work habits, 175, 176, 177
    works:
        "Candleabra Rumba," 178
        Dead Elvis, 177
        Desi, 176
        Elvis Everywhere, 173, 176, 177
        "How Do I Love Thee," 178
        Jackie O, 173
        Metropolis Symphony, 173, 178
        "Rhinestone Quick-Step," 178
        Snap!, 175–76
        Le Tombeau de Liberace, 176, 178
        list of selected pieces and record-
            ings, 179–80
Davidovsky, Mario, 97, 203
Davies, Peter Maxwell, 49, 68
Davies, Robertson, 129
Davis, Miles, 12, 174
deadlines
    Adolphe on, 199
    Baker on, 78
    Bolcom on, 28
    Godfrey on, 100, 103–4
    Harbison on, 46
    Kernis on, 242
    Larsen on, 145
    Ran on, 119
    Reich on, 17–18
    Rouse on, 126
    Stokes on, 6